A Journey of Days Continues

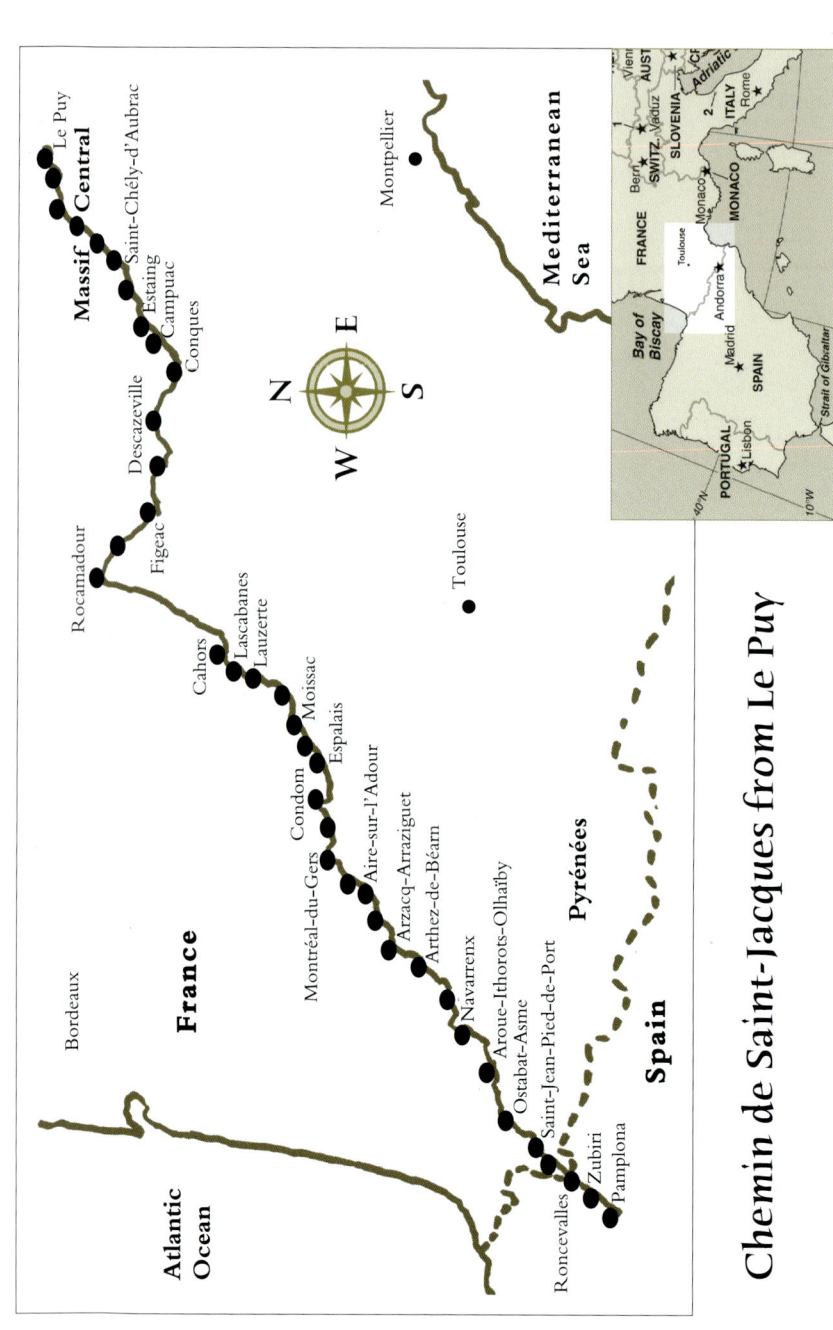

Chemin de Saint-Jacques from Le Puy

A Journey of Days Continues

Mud, Mountains,
and Mindfulness
on the Camino
de Saint-Jacques

Guy Thatcher

Guy Thatcher

Enjoy your journey

GENERAL STORE PUBLISHING HOUSE INC.
499 O'Brien Road, Renfrew, Ontario, Canada K7V 3Z3
Telephone 1.613.432.7697 or 1.800.465.6072

http://www.gsph.com

ISBN 978-1-77123-037-7

Copyright © Guy Thatcher 2013

Cover art, design: Magdalene Carson

Printed by Image Digital Printing Ltd.
dba The IDP Group, Renfrew, Ontario
Printed and bound in Canada

No part of this book may be reproduced, stored in a retrieval system,
or transmitted in any form or by any means without
the prior written permission of the publisher or,
in case of photocopying or other reprographic copying, a licence from
Access Copyright (Canadian Copyright Licensing Agency),
1 Yonge Street, Suite 1900, Toronto, Ontario, M5E 1E5.

Cataloguing data available at Library and Archives Canada

To my beloved wife, Carroll, with whom all this seems very meaningful. You know what you mean to me.

FOREWORD

Capacity to wonder? What drives man? Is it curiosity or is it a need we feel to fill up some vague void that sends back echoes of partial emptiness that lie within us? Truth may be that it is different for each of us. Guy Thatcher takes us with him again on his walking quest, though he, like many seekers, is not completely aware of what his quest is. The good news for us is that he is still seeking that undefined goal.

I am fortunate in that through my wife's friendship with the author and his wife I have had the opportunity to meet the author and encounter his gift of questing and enjoy some of the wonder that he seeks and feels in his travels and his wonderings about life. We are able to experience the three-dimensionality of his observations as he walks his journey. We discover his perceptions and consequent reactions to his daily experience and thereby walk with him as he seeks why he is there.

We have the opportunity to share his insightful journey in his second book and come away again, enriched by his thoughtfully described experiences. This is a small and fascinating book about the pilgrimage walk he took on the Chemin de Saint-Jacques, which is an extension of the pilgrimage path from the rest of Europe to Santiago in Spain, where it is known as el Camino de Santiago. Santiago is reputedly the last resting place of the disciple James, and has become internationally popular for people of all ages and backgrounds who walk that long walk for all imaginable reasons of their own.

I ask that you approach this book slowly, using a relaxed approach to its reading so that you can get the respectful and very relaxed approach of Guy's experience to this long walk. This will enable you to understand his reactions to the whole experience and thus you will get to know Guy. To me, it has proven to be a wonderful experience.

His approach is indicative of the very thoughtful outlook he has about the whole experience of his journey and what makes his description of his journey consequently so interesting. The journey gave him many days for reflection, which he shares with us. To my way of thinking this is one of the primary benefits of being alive: the opportunity to follow the tracery of our own thoughts, our own lives, and the mysterious wonder of it all as we try to figure it all out.

The best results are that we not only come to know much of the ancient history of the land but come to know much new about ourselves. It is a dual gift Guy gives us, and a wonderful shared experience.

Richard Kays

ACKNOWLEDGEMENTS

I wish to acknowledge the *hospitalières* and *hospitaliers* along the way, whose remarkable dedication, hard work, and love of others provided me and other pilgrims with shelter, food, drink, good beds, warmth, trust, and the feeling of being part of a loving family each day. They do this from their extraordinary sense of responsibility to the people who walk these routes now and have for thousands of years. Many—perhaps most—of the hosts are also pilgrims as well. You will meet some of them in this book.

I wish to acknowledge the many people with whom I walked, some of whom had walked hundreds or thousands of kilometres from their homes in France, Germany, Switzerland, Belgium, or Holland. Others had travelled thousands of kilometres from their homes in North or South America or Japan. They were always willing to share, to care, to help if need was apparent, to listen, and to simply walk quietly beside me. You will meet some of them in this book as well. Most of the names are real. A few have been changed to allow individuals their privacy in their grief.

I wish to acknowledge the unsung volunteers who maintain and mark the routes over which I walked. When I went astray, which I did a couple of times, it was not for lack of direction, it was for lack of my paying attention. As a group, they maintain over 60,000 kilometres of trail in France alone.

I wish to acknowledge the team from General Store Publishing House: my publisher, Tim Gordon, who believes in my writing and whose enthusiasm is contagious; my editor, Jane Karchmar, whose sensitivity to the thin skin of an author is matched by her excellent advice; to Magdalene Carson, my book designer, whose creativity continues to amaze me; and to my publicist, Andrea McCormick, for her efforts to get the book in front of a wider audience.

And I wish to acknowledge my family, particularly my wife, Carroll, whose encouragement to continue my journey made it possible for me to go back to France and finish what I had started. Her constant love, challenging me to do even better, enthusiasm for the ideas developed in the book, and practical advice (don't forget your Tilley hat!) make my life the joy that it is. Carroll provides me the space to have the private time that I need.

PROLOGUE

13 April 2011—in Ottawa

Ten a.m.—I have only a few hours now until I leave Ottawa for my walk across France from Le Puy-en-Velay to Pamplona in Spain on the Chemin de Saint-Jacques. This is the French term for what the Spanish call the Camino de Santiago. Yesterday, I had the last opportunity for grandchild therapy for the next ten weeks. My son Christian brought our lovely grandchildren, Cian, four, and Bella, two, from Brooklin near Toronto to Ottawa for the weekend so that I could spend time with them. I am prepared to go, feeling calm and wondering what in hell I was thinking when I decided to do this. I have done a lot of training for this walk.

What am I doing here? Five years ago, I went off to Spain to walk the Camino de Santiago. I had intended then to walk from Saint-Jean-Pied-de-Port in southern France to Santiago in northwestern Spain. It did not go as planned. I ended up waiting five days in Pamplona for a backpack that never arrived, then started from there and walked to Santiago. I always had a sense of unfinished business about not walking over the Pyrénées. Eventually I decided that I had to walk the pilgrim path from Saint-Jean-Pied-de-Port to Pamplona over the Pyrénées. But it seemed silly to fly all that way to walk for four or five days in Europe, so I decided to make a longer pilgrimage, this time all the way from Le Puy-en-Velay to Pamplona, something over 800 kilometres. So I'm heading to Le Puy.

I plan to use the cruddy used suitcase I bought for ten dollars at Value Village to disguise the backpack when it travels without me. This is my plan for having my pack take the same planes that I will be on tomorrow. I will let you know how this works. I will be wearing my boots, carrying my rain jacket and all electronics that are going with me. Also my guidebook, the Miam-Miam-Dodo

French-language guidebook[1] detailing the route from Le Puy-en-Velay to Saint-Jean-Pied-de-Port.

It's just after six p.m., and I am once again sitting in the departure lounge at Ottawa International Airport. I am heading out for Paris via Frankfurt; once again I have given my precious backpack to Air Canada to get safely to the airport in Paris. (They didn't manage this four years ago. I gave them my backpack to go to Madrid and never saw it again.) I ask to see the baggage tag and it is indeed to CDG, Charles de Gaulle in Paris. My plan was to put the backpack inside an old black suitcase. The plan failed because when I tested the suitcase at Value Village, the zipper that I tested was, unbeknownst to me, for the expansion section of the suitcase. The main zipper was non-functional and I didn't realize that until a few hours ago. Happily, Carroll had mentioned something about a nylon carrying bag for backpacks and I picked one up at Mountain Equipment Co-op. It works fine, so the package on the luggage belt is a nondescript black nylon duffel bag. Shouldn't tempt anyone.

I almost came without my trusty Tilley hat, onto which Carroll has sewn a lovely, pink scallop shell from the West Coast of Canada, a happy gift from Mary Virtue[2] in Victoria. I had my hat on when I got into the car to go to the airport, then stuffed it down between the driver's seat and the centre console and promptly forgot that I had done that. When I got out at the airport, I picked up my backpack and my carry-on bag, then realized that my hat wasn't there. I was prepared to leave without it. Apparently I was a little stressed. Carroll got into the driver's seat, and jumped out triumphantly with the hat in her hand. What a relief . . . and not an auspicious start to the trip. I must not leave things behind!

The weather here is grey, cool, a little rainy, very low ceiling. It would be good walking weather. I have no idea what to expect when I get to Le Puy. I hope that it is at least clear because I want to get some photos of the town's major features.

---

1   The name Miam-Miam-Dodo sounds like some adolescent attempt at humour, but that would be wrong. It is an abbreviation, repeated, of the Latin *MInister AMat DOminum*, which translates to *"The servant loves his Lord,"* referring to the relationship between Christians and their God.

2   Mary Virtue was a teacher on the Hospitalero course Carroll and I attended in Toronto. It provides training on how to work as a voluntary staff person at a pilgrim hostel in Spain or France. She has previously been a pilgrim on both the Camino Frances—the classic Camino de Santiago—and the Camino del Norte in Spain.

14–15 April—Ottawa to Paris and Bordeaux

It is 10:30 a.m. on 14 April, and I am now sitting in another lounge, this time in Frankfurt. I am between flights, waiting for the plane to Paris. It's sunny and warm, here. The flight was uneventful, as all flights should be. Because I have lots of Aeroplan points, I flew business class. That meant that I had a little pod all to myself—a seat that reclined into a bed—and excellent food and service, so I slept and ate well. Seems a little bizarre, flying in luxury at 600 kilometres an hour to start an 800-kilometre walk, but hey, it's my *camino*.

Twelve-thirty in Paris. I am here, and there is my backpack on the luggage carousel. What a relief! That is one big concern out of the way.

Less than one hour to fly from Frankfurt to Paris, then about two hours to get out of the airport. Then I need to get a SIM card for my phone, exchange some money for Euros, and find a bus that goes to or near Gare Montparnasse, from which I will be leaving tomorrow morning. I discover that my very modest, inexpensive hotel is on rue du Maine, not avenue du Maine. This takes a while.

It is already four p.m., which is when I am supposed to meet my cousin Roger and his wife, Jackie, who have come from the north of London to see me today and are staying about five kilometres (about three miles) from here. I haven't seen them in years, so it is a real pleasure and compliment for them to come all the way from Whipsnade to see me here. Whipsnade is famous for its zoo. Roger and Jackie live so close to it that they can hear the lions roar at night. Scary. I've stayed there with them and was very glad to have fences, the walls, and a roof between me and the lions. Their roaring with the underlying rumble that I could feel made the hair on the back of my neck stand up.

I find a cab driven by Marc-Étienne Monet, fifties, fleshy face and body, no English, and who is very excited when he finds that I have come to France to walk the Chemin de Saint-Jacques. His wife walked it some years ago.

At their hotel, I meet Roger and Jackie, as well as Will Inrig, the grandson of old friends. Will is studying here in Paris. I thought he was studying film, which he was, but now he is studying Fine Arts and will start at the Sorbonne this fall. We walk down the street to a small brasserie on the bank of the Seine and have drinks and a light dinner. It's wonderful! Jackie asks me probing and thoughtful questions about why I am doing this, and I answer truthfully, "I still don't know why." She cautions me, very sensibly, about trying to recreate the experience. I think about this and wonder why I am walking the *camino* again. I do have some reasons, although I don't think this is an exhaustive list; there is something deeper underneath that I don't yet understand.

- ✦ It will be a physical challenge and I believe that I can do it

- ✦ It will be a psychological challenge to be alone and walk for a long time in a strange country with a language not my own first language

- ✦ I want to rekindle and strengthen my sense of wonder

- ✦ I want to experience the countryside and the people

- ✦ I want to examine my spiritual side

- ✦ I want to regain the feeling of simplicity that I had while walking the *camino* in Spain

- ✦ I may be able to offer fellow pilgrims some assistance

- ✦ I will learn something new

- ✦ I will teach someone

- ✦ I will relearn old lessons

- ✦ I will be able to give and accept gifts readily and with love

- ✦ I want to feel really alive, a part of humanity, and part of all life on the planet

After dinner, I say goodbye to Roger and Jackie, promising to meet again soon, and Will takes me off to Montmartre to see the lights of Paris at night. Then he generously gets me back to the door of my hotel. I use the European plug adapter that I brought from Canada for my cell phone to charge it overnight. This will have fateful consequences.

In the morning, I catch the TGV (Train Grande Vitesse) fast train to Bordeaux. The time passes quickly, and I alight in Bordeaux to find Ian McLeod sipping on a beer in the garden of the station restaurant. I spend a delightful afternoon and evening with Ian and with his wife, Sylvia, ex-pats from Toronto whom we have known for about thirty years and who have lived here—about an hour outside Bordeaux in Saint-Pierre-de-Bat—for over twenty years.

16 April—Bordeaux to Le Puy-en-Velay

In the morning, Ian delivers me back to the Bordeaux station in what we both think will be lots of time. Fate intervenes. At the ticket wicket, I present my papers with proof of purchase. The agent looks at the paper, looks at the computer screen, looks again at the paper and, after some moments, says (in French), "The tickets were printed yesterday."

I say, "Not by me."

It's an opportunity for a bureaucratic meeting. He then enlists the assistance of several other agents, who all examine the screen and my papers with great interest but little illumination. By now, it's fifteen minutes to train departure. I ask if I have to pay again. "*Oh, non, monsieur.*" More time passes. More scratching of heads. Ten minutes to train time. Finally a supervisor is called in. She looks at the screen, looks at the tickets, and says that everything is fine, all seats are reserved, but I must pay after all. So out with the trusty credit card and pay—again—for my set of tickets that will take me from Bordeaux all around France on four trains for ten hours to get to Le Puy-en-Velay. I get my ticket, find Track 6, find Car 12, find Seat 66 and am on board with five minutes to spare. What if I'd had no money?

From here to Le Puy is not far as the crow flies, but I am not travelling by crow. There is no train service east to west in central France. The trip by train is long and circular. I am heading for a town in the Massif Central, which is a huge elevated region of mountains and plateaus in south-central France, covering about 15 percent of the country. It averages about 1,200 metres (4,000 feet) high. It is almost empty of population. The Massif was a major barrier to communication until a major north-south highway, the A75 autoroute, was finally completed in 2010. Bordeaux is east, Le Puy is west, so the train goes from Bordeaux in flat agricultural (vineyards) country south to Montpellier—where I see the Mediterranean, an unexpected and brief pleasure—change trains for Lyon, heading northeast, change trains in Lyon for Saint-Étienne, heading west, and change trains again in Saint-Étienne for the last train to Le Puy.

I almost blow it in Lyon. I think that I have a two-hour layover, but the train is behind schedule (unheard of in Europe), and I have about ten minutes. I get to the right track and am about to get on the train when I read the routing on the side of the train. No mention of Saint-Étienne. I ask a redcap: "*Est-ce que c'est le train pour Saint-Étienne?*"

"*Non.*" It's not my train. It pulls out in a few minutes, another pulls in—this is my train. I would have gone off in the wrong direction. I haven't done that in almost fifty years, when I once went in the wrong direction in Belgium. I am Canadian. We are not used to trains actually operating exactly on time.

On the last train from Saint-Étienne to Le Puy, the entertainment is provided by two young, clean-cut, seemingly competent young men across the aisle who pull out a parcel, two large sheets of brown wrapping paper, and Scotch tape and proceed to "wrap" the parcel. It takes a very long time, especially given the result. Charlie Brown and Linus could have done it better. When they are done, I am sorely tempted to ask to take a picture of the finished work, but I suspect they might be insulted. Across from me sit two other males—teenaged, pimply, callow youths, big grins on their faces as they tell me that they don't speak or understand a word of English. Apparently, this is a matter of pride for many young French today. It's a shame. Why wouldn't you want to speak more than one language?

This last train ride is like being in Norway or the mountainous parts of Western Canada: many tunnels, running on mountainsides beside a fast river, either the Haute-Loire or one of its tributaries. It is a three-car train and makes a very familiar and satisfying clickety-clack as it runs over the track. The area here is called Rhône-Alpes, describing it quite accurately. It has been sunny and warm all day. I am finally starting to feel excited about this journey.

An observation today: I have seen literally thousands of people today at the various train stations and on the train. Not a single one—not one—was obese. Very few were even chubby. It seems to me that this is a terrible indictment of our North American lifestyle and of our whole lethal food industry. We are killing ourselves by demanding fast poor foods and they are killing us by feeding us what we demand: sugar, salt, and fats, for profit.

In Le Puy-en-Velay, a city of about 29,000, the only flat parts are the river valleys; the Loire and the Borne merge here. The old city is very hilly, very steep. At the train station, a local woman suggests that I take a taxi up to my lodging. It is very, very good advice. It's steep, and the roads are irregular stone cobble, much of it volcanic rock. My *gite d'étape* (hostel) is next to the cathedral in the old town, at the very top of the hill. It is directly under the famous, but ugly, statue of Our Lady of France, situated on top of one of the *"puys."*

I check in to the *gite*, run by Franciscan nuns. I am greeted by two young nuns—which I find most unusual (not the greeting, their lack of age)—and given my room. Unexpectedly and very pleasantly, it is a single room with a bed and wardrobe, spotlessly clean, toilet and showers nearby, and a French door directly onto the street. I expected to be in a dormitory, a *"dortoir."* When Karsten arrives tomorrow, he will have a room next to mine. Four years ago, I walked in Spain for two weeks with Karsten, a thirty-one-year-old schoolteacher from Berlin. We have agreed to walk together for a week or so this year. I am looking forward to seeing him.

The huge statue of Our Lady of France, erected on a *puy* directly above my *gite*, has an interesting history. It was created in 1860 from 233 melted-down cannon taken by the French from the Russians in the Crimean War.[3] There is a British and Canadian connection as well. The British also took Russian cannon, melted them down, and formed the medals of the Victoria Cross from them. So every combat veteran from Great Britain and the Commonwealth countries, including Australia, South Africa, New Zealand, India, Sri Lanka, and Canada who won a Victoria Cross in any war from then on—and lived to tell about it—has a little piece of old, repurposed Russian cannon on his chest.

---

3   The Crimean War was fought from October 1853 to February 1856 between the Russian Empire and an alliance of the empires of Britain, France, and the Ottoman Empire. The prize was the spoils of the decaying Ottoman Empire. It is famous in the west for the Charge of the Light Brigade and for Florence Nightingale's attempts to bring nursing compassion and care to wounded British soldiers. It ended in an unsatisfactory negotiated peace, but the Russians lost the cannons that the French and British had captured.

17 April—in Le Puy-en-Velay

Why am I here in Le Puy-en-Velay rather than somewhere else to start this walk? There are four accepted pilgrimage routes in France that lead toward Spain and the Camino de Santiago. Clockwise from Paris, they are from Paris, Vézelay, Le Puy-en-Velay, and Arles. From Paris, the *chemin* runs almost south through Bordeaux, from Vézelay southwest, from Le Puy west-southwest, and from Arles almost due west. I chose the Le Puy route because it is said to have the best infrastructure for walkers and because the bishop of Le Puy made the pilgrimage to Santiago in 950. If it was good enough for the bishop, it's good enough for me, although I still have no clear idea about why I am doing this walk.

Continental France is divided into twenty-two regions, analogous to provinces in Canada or states in the United States. The regions are further divided into departments, analogous to counties. I will be walking through three regions from south central to southwest: the Auvergne, Midi-Pyrénées, and Aquitaine. I am starting in the Auvergne on the Massif Central. What becomes apparent as I walk is that the people still refer to their regions in terms of the pre-revolutionary provinces, not the modern regions or departments. Two hundred and twenty years—folks here have long memories.

The *puys* here are volcanic cones, created when a volcano forms underwater. This was not understood until Surtsey erupted off Iceland in the 1960s. This must have been a very exciting place twenty million years ago. There are hundreds of these remnants of extinct volcanoes over about 400 square miles on the Massif Central, which has the highest concentration of extinct volcanoes in the world—over 450. One hopes that they are actually extinct. There has been no volcanic activity in about 10,000 years.

Few are as dramatic as the three in Le Puy. One lower *puy* is completely covered by the cathedral. The other *puy* (not the one surmounted by the statue, but the one from which the city got its name) is surmounted by a church reached only by 284 steps. It was built in 961 by the local bishop, Gotschalk, in celebration of his pilgrimage to Santiago in 950–51. He was the first documented French notable to make the pilgrimage to Santiago. The church is memorable partly because every bit of construction material was carted up those 284 steps. That must have been some project management task!

I had planned to make the trek up the steps, but by the time I have walked up from the lower town to the cathedral three times, I decide to let well enough alone. The third time, I am sucking for air and have to stop a couple of times to catch my breath. Carroll will be relieved. What I don't know is that I have a bigger problem than the altitude here that will catch me unawares over the next week.

If I had been wandering around Le Puy in the summer of 1865, I might have run into a friendly and gregarious young Englishman who was having a

Chapel on the puy *in Le Puy-en-Velay.*

bedroll of oiled canvas made here so that he could start a walk from Le Monastier, a town about twenty kilometres south of here. He bought a donkey to carry his gear, not realizing that donkeys walk more slowly than people and have a mind of their own. He walked for twelve days—as far as Saint-Jean-du-Gard, 201 kilometres (125 miles)—and wrote a small book about his adventures called, appropriately, *Travels with a Donkey*. This was his second book. It made him more famous. He went on to write many more books, all bestsellers with the English-speaking audience, including *Treasure Island*. His name, of course, is Robert Louis Stevenson. When he died, too young, in Java, he was one of the best-known and best-beloved writers in the English language.[4]

A century or so even earlier, I might also have met a local boy who grew up to be Maréchal Lafayette, hero of the American Revolution of 1776. When the French were supporting the Americans in the Revolutionary War, they weren't doing it because they were special friends with the Americans, but because they were deadly enemies of the British . . . and the Americans were fighting the British, thus taking some pressure off the French in Europe. There is a street in the upper town named after him. I take a photo of the street sign.

---

4   The trail that he walked is now the GR 70, known as the Stevenson Trail.

A century later, in the 1880s, the French people—not the government—also donated that powerful symbol of America's dreams, the Statue of Liberty. It was intended as a centennial gift in 1876 but that plan derailed when neither the French nor the American government could get their people to ante up the cash needed to build the base, which the Americans were responsible for building—so it arrived ten years late, in 1886. It was quite an embarrassment for both countries.

I have discovered, back at the *gite*, that I have evidently left my power adapter carefully plugged in, in Paris. The power source here has a different configuration from that in North America, needs an adapter plug, and I can't plug anything in. This is a crisis. Both my computer and my cell phone depend on regular recharging, and I can't do that. Both batteries are exhausted.

It is mid-afternoon and I am sitting on the terrace of the Restaurant La Grande Ourse ("The Great Bear") in the town below the cathedral having only a beer because it is not the hour for food (it's not my rule, it is the restaurant's). And I discover that this restriction is very common across France. It is very pleasant out; sunny, late spring to early summer. I ask about possible Internet access. There are two Internet cafés in town, but both are closed because it is Sunday. I was cautioned about the French issue with hours of business and days off. Their quality of life is just fine, but for those of us visiting, it may be not as fine. Sundays and Mondays are problematic, as are Holy Days—and there are lots of them.

While I sit here, the entertainment—there is always entertainment—is water pouring down the half-dozen steps from a public washroom across the very small square. The fire department is on the scene, but the water continues to pour down the steps. I don't want to know what is in the flow of water.

Karsten is due at 5:15 on the train, so I go to the station to welcome him. I haven't seen him in four years, since we walked together for two weeks on the Camino de Santiago and then met a month later in Berlin. The train arrives and disgorges its passengers. Some locals, several pilgrims, but no Karsten. I am disappointed and a little concerned, but it turns out I needn't be. I walk back up to the *gite*, where he arrives at about eight p.m. His flight from Berlin to Lyon was delayed four hours, so he caught a later train. I am very pleased to see him. We will be off in the morning.

The Journey Starts — on the Aubrac Plateau

I am on the Massif Central, the huge plateau that covers south-central France. It is remote from the rest of France: later springs, earlier autumns, and harsher, longer winters. The part of the Massif that I will be walking over is called the Aubrac Plateau. It's high, mostly over 4,000 feet; not as high as the Alps, but a lot higher than Ottawa, where I live and trained, so it is daunting nevertheless. I will need to be aware of the altitude, especially for the first few days. I am in the Auvergne region, renowned as one of the most rugged, remote, and least-populated regions in Europe, let alone France. It is about half the size of Nova Scotia, roughly the same size as Vermont or Massachusetts. I am in the Haute-Loire (upper Loire) department, the only one of four in this region in which I will be walking. The Loire River, only sixteen kilometres from its source, runs across this department, thus the "Haute" in Haute-Loire.

18 April — Le Puy-en-Velay to Montbonnet

*"We shall not cease from exploration and the
end of all our exploring will be to arrive where we
started — and know the place for the first time."*
—T.S. Eliot, "Little Gidding"

The Chemin de Saint-Jacques is the French name for the Camino de Santiago, both meaning "the Way of St. James." It is an ancient pilgrimage route ending in Santiago in northwest Spain. We are off to a slow start today, but it's okay because we have booked our place for this evening. It has been strongly recommended that we do this each day to be sure of a bed in the evening.

I have to get a memory card for my camera and I have to see if I can find a power adapter. We take a cab to a shopping centre, where there is a Wal-Mart equivalent. They have power adapters, but a plastic edge has to be cut off to accept my plug-in; the manager kindly arranges this for me. At about ten-thirty, we are finally ready to go. It is a long, hard, paved climb out of Le Puy, then rugged, wild countryside, a narrow trail along a cliff edge . . . I did not know that Karsten is afraid of heights, making this a bit of a challenge for him.

I am finding the climbs unexpectedly challenging, the heavy breathing and busy heart rate a little uncomfortable. Finally we come out into rolling hill country to Montbonnet, a tiny town with just over 200 inhabitants. We stay in a lovely new *gite*, La Grange; exceptional food and comfortable beds. There is a glass wall facing east, where I can see many low mounds, which are old collapsed volcanic cones, all covered in forest. The prices here are about 50 percent higher than they were in Spain four years ago, but the tradeoff is that the food is excellent and the *gites* are more comfortable—no bunk beds, usually only a few beds to a room. It looks as if I will be spending about thirty Euros per day on food and lodging. That's about forty dollars. Not bad. About nineteen kilometres today; difficult but not outrageous terrain. This is about to change. The weather remains fine, with cool, sunny, strong winds.

19 April—Montbonnet to Monistrol-d'Allier

Only fourteen kilometres today, but a very difficult trail. With Karsten, I am heading for Monistrol-d'Allier. Over the distance, it descends about 400 metres, but most of that, near the end of the day in the last kilometre, is a precipitous and extremely dangerous descent—about thirty degrees—down into the gorge of the Allier River. It is a rock-strewn dirt trail in a forest, bare tree roots, lots of opportunity to turn an ankle or break a bone. This is worse than any portage I was ever on in Algonquin Park and worse than anything that I walked on the Appalachian Trail. The weather is sunny and warm, which is a good thing, because this descent would be extremely dangerous if it were wet and slippery.

This *cannot* be the old pilgrim trail. In earlier times, some pilgrims rode horses, and no one ever rode a horse down this. I think that the intention is to keep the pilgrims off the winding road down, but whoever made the decision is doing the pilgrims a grave disservice. My shoulders and back hurt a lot from using my poles to control the descent, and my quad muscles are shaking with fatigue. For the last part of the way down, I am concerned that the big thigh muscles will give way. I am so concerned that I neglect to take a single photo of this portion of the *chemin*. It never occurs to me to just descend more slowly. Karsten is somewhere behind me. I realize that neither one of us could help the other if we were to encounter a problem here.

When I get to Monistrol, another tiny town straddling the Allier River in a deep gorge, I am absolutely exhausted, almost weepy with fatigue. I just want to stop where I am, not move another step. I am beginning to understand how someone, exhausted, could just sit down and die right there. Karsten helps a lot when he points out the *gite*, La Tsabone, just a little bit ahead and above us. I can see it and I think that I can get there. In the *gite*, I shower and sleep for two hours. I feel like a new man, except that my back and thigh muscles are very sore. I do not realize that this bodes very ill for the next days.

There are only three of us in this *gite*, Karsten, me, and a Frenchman named Regisse who is planning to walk the whole distance to Santiago — about 1,500 kilometres. The delightful and friendly young hosts here are Nicolas and Coralie. They have wireless in the *gite*, quite a surprise down here in the bottom of the gorge, and Coralie gives me her user name and password so that I can use it. The food is excellent, which I am finding is the norm on the French part of "*le chemin.*" I had wondered about how well Karsten would manage in French. It turns out that French is one of the subjects that he teaches at a grade school in Berlin. His French is better than mine. The young couple visits with us for an hour in the *gite*. The conversation is in French, of which I get only bits. One of the bits that I get is that she is pregnant with their first child, which gives me an opportunity to show off pictures of my grandchildren — I never miss a chance.

20 April — Monistrol to Saugues

Today's plan is to walk twenty-two kilometres from Monistrol to Le Falzet, but I am not going to get that far. In the first ninety minutes, I climb out of the Allier Gorge on a path up a cliff side over 300 metres at a 20 percent grade. The cliffs are on my left, the gorge to my right. The views are spectacular, but I am more concerned about keeping my footing. A slip here could really hurt! After we reach the top and Karsten catches up, he tells me that he is afraid of heights and this bit scares him. I am not surprised. It scares me. I have to stop often to catch my breath; my heart is beating too fast . . . and my legs hurt.

On the flat above the gorge, Karsten and I meet Jocelyn, a slight, fifty-something-year-old from Paris, with bright, shiny eyes. She tells us that her husband and her adult daughter are opposed to her walking the path alone. She told them that she will not be alone, she will be walking with Saint Jacques. She also tells me that she is happy to join up with us. She is gregarious, openly religious, but not trying to convert anyone; a happy person.

After seven or eight kilometres, another 100-metre climb. It gives me a lot of difficulty. We stop in a small village, Vernet, for a drink. After resting for fifteen minutes, I am still breathing heavily, my heart is still beating much, much faster than I like, and I realize that I have not recovered from yesterday's descent and today's ascent from the gorge. It occurs to me that I am pressing perilously close to the edge of my physical envelope and that I don't actually know where that edge is.

I am barely rational and feeling a little panicky because of the high heart rate and the very heavy breathing. It is not quite, but close to, an out-of-body experience. I can picture myself here, sitting on the bench, head down on the table, just trying to catch up. It occurs to me that, if I keep on now, I could easily drive my heart beyond its limits, and I don't know what the effect would be, although my imagination runs riot. I can picture a little tasteful monument somewhere farther on saying, "*A Canadian pilgrim perished here on 20 April 2011*," and that is *not* part of my plan. I do not want to be an example to others, at least not like this. So I ask the owner of this little bar, who is in a wheelchair—a farm accident—if I can get a ride into Saugues (pronounced sew-g, with a hard "g"). He offers to drive me, and I sag into his car with my gear. He doesn't want to take any money, but I insist. I do not think that I can do this on my own.

He drops me at the *gite*, and I sleep for four hours. I am up for ninety minutes to have a brief visit to the town, sleep another two hours, up for dinner, and sleep from nine p.m. to seven a.m. undisturbed. That's a total of sixteen hours. One would think that would do the trick. Karsten and Jocelyn arrive before dinner, and we share a room. So now we are three.

The dinner includes an excellent beet, tomato, and lettuce salad. This is a recipe that I will have to try when I get home. We have local cheese after dinner. Later we are advised that the local cheeses, while absolutely delicious, are also generally not pasteurized, so we should be cautious. How can we tell?

There is a local legend from a couple of centuries back. Local children were found dead, having been dreadfully mauled. It was decided that this was the work of wolves, and so a bounty was placed on them. Finally, a huge wolf was killed . . . and the killings stopped. There is a huge wolf monument overlooking the town. It commemorates the Beast of Gevaudan. There are still wolves in the area, although I don't see or hear any.

I have thoughts of failure. I had not intended to be carried any portion of this journey. This was not part of my plan, but it appears as if my plan will need to be modified. I am disappointed because I thought that my training was adequate, and it would have been for the Spanish *camino*, but not this part out of Le Puy. Tomorrow should be better. I think that I am through the worst. Someone points out that we are walking at over 4,000 feet altitude and I am not accustomed to the height. So perhaps that is the problem.

Here in Saugues, in the church, there is a Canadian connection. Did you ever wonder where all those Jesuit priests came from who came to early Canada to convert the heathens? One of them came from here. There is an altar in the thirteenth-century church dedicated to Noel Chabanel, born here on 2 February, 1613, trained as a Jesuit, sent to Canada, and martyred by the Iroquois on 8 December, 1649. He was thirty-six.

I think that the Iroquois perhaps overreacted to the missionary effort, torturing and burning the Jesuits, but I do have some sympathy for the Indians. I have always found the concept of sending missionaries to proselytize others both arrogant and condescending. What makes anyone believe that the people they are coming to "save" need saving? Saving from what? What makes them think that the heathens are so burdened in what looks to me like happy lives that putting on European clothes and praying to a foreign god will magically transform them? How would we like it if animist missionaries from Africa or Shinto missionaries from Japan came to Europe or North America to bring us the good news?

Given that the culture we have imposed on North America includes the destruction of the environment and the wanton overuse of the available resources, I am not at all sure that the Indians were wrong. They would have been better off if they had had a more restrictive immigration program in place.

Enough grumping for one evening. Off to bed and hope for better things tomorrow.

21 April — Saugues to Le Sauvage

Today, I am planning to walk about twenty kilometres to Le Sauvage. I only get about halfway when I am wiped out again, and at Le Falzet I stop for a break, sitting at a picnic table outside a little bar. This time it's heavy breathing, continuing high heart rate, and a strange visual phenomenon. My eyes will not adjust to the bright light. I sit here with my head down and my eyes take in so much light that almost everything is blindingly white. It takes about ten minutes for my normal vision to come back. I don't like this turn of events and I find a ride to take me to Le Sauvage. Karsten and Jocelyn, both very concerned about me, continue walking.

Le Sauvage is a remote farm domain that stretches back to Templar days; it is about 1,000 years old. It is one huge building complex in the middle of a 5,000-hectare preserve, completely isolated. The driveway from the nearest road is almost three kilometres. My oldest son, Francis, is having a birthday today, and I cannot contact him. There is no Internet, no cell phone coverage, and no WiFi. I hope that his day is a good one; better than mine so far.

In the twenty-first century, we can scarcely imagine the world in which people lived a thousand years ago. It is so remote here, even now. I wonder what life was like for the people who lived and walked in France 700 or 1,000 years ago. I am going to take you back to that time in Western Europe, recognizing that the picture I paint will be sketchy, imperfect, incomplete, and, while not totally wrong, not totally right, either. I'll start by pointing out that, for most people, the world was the *only* world, around which the sun purportedly revolved. Life had not changed much in the past five hundred years and would not much for another five hundred. If you were born a peasant, you died a peasant. If you were born into nobility, you died a noble.

Most of Europe was still covered by dense forest, with open fields near larger cities, and smaller fields next to the villages. But cities were not cities such as we know them now. Paris, for example, had 20,000 inhabitants in the year 1000 and 250,000 three hundred years later. Compare that with 2008, when the city of Paris had 2.25 million and over twelve million in metropolitan Paris — forty-eight times the numbers of 700 years earlier and 600 times the number from 1,000 years earlier. Roads connected cities but were considered very dangerous, because they were. Travelling alone was a fool's game, so travellers banded together to gain safety in numbers and often brought along their own guards.

Imagine, if you can, a time when 20 percent of newborns died at birth (often with their mothers) or within a week or two of birth; 30 percent of children died before the age of five; half the people born died by the age of thirty (for women it was twenty-four). Imagine a time when marriages lasted on average fifteen years, typically ended not by divorce like today, but by the death of one or the other spouse from disease, famine, or warfare. A girl could get married, legally, parental consent or no, at the age of twelve. Young women died, typically, in their early twenties. For women, this death was most likely in childbirth. If you lasted to forty-five or fifty, you would look like an octogenarian of today.

Because of the high mortality, people who were powerful were often very young, capable of making all the mistakes that immaturity and inexperience can cause. Kings and generals were often in their early twenties, sometimes in their teens. Bishops and cardinals were appointed, even sometimes from the clergy but more usually from politically powerful and ambitious families. An example was Cesar Borgia, Bishop of Pamplona at sixteen, a cardinal at eighteen. His father was the pope.

Imagine a time when most people were almost always hungry, malnutrition was the "normal" state, when there was a famine on average every five years,[5] when the vast majority of the population, the rural peasantry, was only a few days away from starvation. The youngest babies had the most difficult time of it. Because the childhood mortality rate was so appallingly high, older children who survived were considered blessed by God and fed before the infants, who were less likely to survive anyway. Peasants were sometimes so desperate that they sold the clothes they had and went naked in order to have food for a few more days.

And it was not just the poor rural peasants whose brief and difficult lives ruled the mortality statistics. The same toll was taken in the nobility. "Noble families became extinct, victims of high mortality and low fertility or casualties of war. The best available statistical evidence suggests that more than half of all noble families died out in the male line every century."[6]

---

5 As an example, famines of the fourteenth century in France occurred in the following years: 1304, 1305, 1310, 1315–17, 1330–33, 1349–51, 1358–60, 1371, 1374–75, and 1390–91. Source: ***http://www.medievality.com/famine.html***

6 Jonathan Sumption, *The Hundred Years War I* (Philadelphia, PA: University of Pennsylvania Press, 1991), 30.

Medieval health was terrible. Health care, as we understand it, did not exist. The church taught that health depended on your devotion to God. It followed that getting ill was a punishment directly from God. Prayer and penitence was the way to gain God's forgiveness and so return to health. Accessing a doctor didn't usually help. "Real" doctors, those who treated royalty and the aristocrats, were rare and very expensive. Even they were limited by lack of knowledge in what they could do.[7] For the rest of us, the doctors were well-meaning monks or quacks. Mostly, medicine was a matter of "suck-it-and-see." They didn't charge much but they usually didn't accomplish much, either. Many of the pilgrims were desperately ill people, or with family members desperately ill, looking to gain relief or a miraculous cure by embarking on the path to a recognized shrine.

But never mind the normal vicissitudes of health. Sometimes, really bad diseases struck. The Black Plague, which ravaged most of Europe in the mid-1300s, may have killed about one out of every three of the entire European population, although the impact was lower here in the southern interior of France, because the plague followed the major trading routes. Perhaps the worst pandemic of all time, it may have killed over 100 million people in Europe, and who knows how many elsewhere. And it came at what was already a terrible time. Climate change resulting in cooler and wetter weather created lower crop yields even as the population was increasing. The lethal combination of less food and more mouths to feed created great and recurring famines. Add to this the predation caused by roving bands of mercenaries, idle, unpaid, and unfed from the armies of the incessant wars, and you begin to get the impression that the Middle Ages were not a great time to be alive and a peasant in France (or anywhere else, for that matter).

It's very cold here. Today's high is fifteen degrees Celsius (about sixty Fahrenheit), with a strong headwind and sunny in the afternoon. We are very high, and outside it looks like the very beginning of spring. The buds are just starting to show on the trees here. We are told that

---

7   Speaking about the quality of medical care at the time, here is the opinion from the medical community in Paris in 1348 about how to avoid the plague. In their professional opinion, the plague had been caused by a really bad conjunction of Saturn, Jupiter, and Mars in the sign of Aquarius a few years earlier: "No poultry should be eaten, no waterfowl, no pig, no old beef, altogether no fat meat. . . . It is injurious to sleep during the daytime. . . . Fish should not be eaten, too much exercise may be injurious . . . and nothing should be cooked in rainwater. Olive oil with food is deadly. . . . Bathing is dangerous. . . ."

most years there is still snow at this point, but this year is an exception. So we're lucky.

The *gite* is good, clean, and well-equipped, but they do not serve meals and there is *nowhere* else to eat. Mme Chausse, the manager, tells me that produce is available to make one's own meal. I just go to bed and sleep. After Karsten and Jocelyn arrive, several other pilgrims, including Felicia, Sophie, and Francine arrive, and they organize a meal for everyone. This helps me a lot, and I perk up.

Felicia, twenty-seven, from Paris, is a pretty, blonde clown, solidly built with a round, expressive face that she uses to good effect. Sophie, thirty-nine, also from Paris, is a small, elfin woman with short, dark hair and sparkling, dark eyes, a huge, toothy smile, a dancer's body. Francine, forty-six, is tall, blonde, Aryan-looking, with long legs and a lithe body. She is sharp-faced and in repose looks melancholy, but when she smiles, she smiles with her whole face and eyes. They are all only on the *chemin* for a short time and all started in Le Puy. They will join us tomorrow, so now we are six walking together. I am still hoping for better days.

22 April—Le Sauvage to Aumont-Aubrac

Today is my granddaughter Bella's second birthday. She had a very tough start but is now just a little determined, auburn-haired delight. I will be with her in spirit as she celebrates with her father, Christian, her two-year-older brother, Cian (born during my previous walk across Spain in 2007), my daughter, who is her Aunt Meredith, and Carroll, her grandmother and my beloved wife.

We plan to walk about 28.5 kilometres today to Aumont-Aubrac. It's a long way, but today is Good Friday, and there will be some kind of religious processional there, which I would like to see. I am off by myself at 8:45 and walk all day alone. We are still high, but the terrain is more forgiving. It is sunny and windy, and after thirty minutes, I take off my fleece and add it to my pack. The season has changed again. It is warmer, and the trees are well into bud here. At noon, I stop for a break in a small town, have a great omelet with *cepes* (local mushrooms), then see my "family" outside and call them in to the place where I am eating. They all stop for lunch as well. The restaurant owner is so pleased that he tells me he wants to hire me to bring in customers and gives me a small bottle of good red wine as a thank-you. It's Cote du Vivarais, 2006. Of course, I have to add this weight to my pack. But I expect to drink it later.

I decide since it is still a long way—another fifteen kilometres—and I am doing well, to send my backpack on to Aumont-Aubrac. It's expensive. If I had sent it from yesterday's *gite* first thing this morning, it would have cost eight Euros, but now it will cost twenty Euros to send it half the distance. The lower price is a daily service and this price is for a cab.

Between here and Aumont-Aubrac, I get a warning that perhaps I am not quite as fit and well as I thought. I am walking up a shallow grade on a country road that is in a low cut between two fields. I have my head down and apparently am not at all alert. As I am walking, I become aware that directly beside me is the fender of a car. It's faded blue and the car is stopped on the road facing me. I did not see it coming toward me as I was walking. It's a good thing that one of us is alert. It is the taxi that carried my pack to the next town. The driver has sought me out because he wants to tell me that the *gite* that I sent the pack to has no reservation for me. That's okay because the reservation was made by either Felicia or Sophie in her name. I am apparently almost unconscious as I walk, certainly not paying attention to my surroundings. Clearly, this could be dangerous walking on these country roads.

Just before I get to the road to Aumont-Aubrac (I can see the sign for the town), I have an experience for which I have had absolutely no training. The whole incident takes much less time than it takes to tell it. The question is: "*What do you do if you encounter a wild boar fifty metres from you on a trail?*" I am less than 700 metres from the road into Aubrac when there is a commotion in the brush just ahead of me to the right. Two wild boars burst out of the brush. One is partially obscured in the ditch, the other stands facing me on the trail. *Now* I am alert. Extremely alert.

When I was flying helicopters in the Canadian military doing NATO service in Germany, we were told repeatedly that wild boars in Europe can be very dangerous and to avoid them at all costs. I do not appear to have an option at the moment. I am now paying extremely close attention to my surroundings. Later on, I will think about that tasteful monument to the Canadian pilgrim gored and trampled here today by a wild boar, but this is not my thought at the moment. He appears to be about seventy-five centimetres (thirty inches) high and about the same across, perhaps 100 kilograms (220 pounds) of angry (I am assuming) wild black pig. He has yellow tusks and is looking directly at me. We are both surprised. But this is his territory, not mine.

My instinctive and immediate reaction is to yell and to bang my aluminum walking poles together with a loud clatter up high in front of me. He takes this surprisingly well and, after a few seconds, charges back into the underbrush on the side of the trail. I am delighted by his choice, since I don't have a plan B—I am too tired to run, and, in any case, there is no place to run to. It is just brush on both sides, nothing to climb. I have no time to be scared . . . now. That comes later. For the rest of the trail, less than ten minutes, I keep checking over my shoulder to see if he has changed his mind, but there is no sign of him. I am relieved and very happy when I reach the paved road and turn right toward Aumont-Aubrac.

I walk on in to Aumont-Aubrac, find our *gite*—Le Calypso—where my backpack is waiting for me. I take a bed in the *dortoir*, but when the rest of my "family" arrives, I find that we have a room to ourselves. The place is good: clean, four to a room, sheets, blankets, towels, our own shower. I share with Karsten, Jocelyn, and Sophie. The other three are in the *dortoir*. Sophie gives a foot massage to Karsten, Karsten does the same for her, then she does my feet. It is a bit of heaven. I ask if I can adopt her.

We have been told that we must eat at the restaurant La Ferme du Barry. It has a great reputation. Sophie organizes this for all of us. There are ten of us at the table, all pilgrims, and there is plenty of red wine. The owner and chef, Vincent Boussage, makes a local specialty called *aligot*. It is a combination of mashed potatoes and local cheese (the *aligot* part) that is pureed into a rich substance that stretches for several feet. It is almost like taffy and is heavy on the

Vincent with aligot.

carbs, which is just fine for walkers. Felicia watches in awe as Vincent lifts the *aligot*. This is followed by a salad and the best fish ever. This hotel, *gite*, and restaurant has a wonderful and well-deserved reputation. We would have stayed here, had there been room.

En route back to our *gite*, I walk back holding hands with Sophie. We pass a group of people with candles waiting to enter the church. This is the Easter processional that I had wanted to observe, but I am too tired to join them. Back to our own *gite*, where I spend a warm and restless night. Today was a long walk.

23 April — Aumont-Aubrac to Nasbinal

Today's plan is to walk to Nasbinal. It's about twenty-six kilometres. The day is dark, rainy, and cold. The forecast is rainy with the possibility of thunderstorms the next three days. Here in Aumont-Aubrac we encounter a tall, well-set-up young German, Max, who speaks good English but almost no French. He joins the little family that we have created, and we walk together. He is a friendly, open, delightful young man in his early twenties, about eighteen months from finishing a degree in psychology, after which he wants to travel in the Far East. I wear my rain jacket and put the rain cover on my pack. It is very cold, but not raining much. I walk half the distance, past fields with huge boulders—"erratics," leftovers from the retreating glaciers of the ice age—then stop at a wide spot in the road called Les Quatre Chemins. It is a crossroads (four roads, of course) with a burned-out *gite* and a temporary trailer set up with a little counter and some tables to serve snacks and drinks. Nothing else here—no village, no stores.

My stamina has abandoned me . . . again . . . and I decide to get a cab to today's destination. I learn that it will be a two-hour wait for a cab—discouraging, but I decide to wait. I am hoping that someone will want to stay with me, but I do not want to ask. Karsten and the others decide to walk on. Max asks me if I would like him to stay. Francine says that he is a good person, to which he replies that he is just lazy. I say that it is perfectly reasonable and okay to be both good and lazy.

When the cab finally arrives, it is driven by an attractive young woman in tight jeans. Very tight—I can see that she has dimples. She is very pleasant and deposits us right at the *gite* Nada in Nasbinal. Interesting name, since *nada* means "nothing" in Spanish. I sleep for a couple of hours, until the rest of the group arrives. I really feel the need for a day of recuperation and tell them of my plan to stay here and rest for a day.

Several people suggest that perhaps tomorrow I just get a ride directly from here to our next destination, so that I can have my day off and we can still stay together. I agree with this, and we go off to have dinner together at a nearby restaurant. I am barely present. I am feeling strange—not really well and not really here. We return to the *gite* and go to bed. At eleven p.m., my pulse is still racing along at 120 beats per minute, and I make a reluctant decision to pack it up. This is just not working. I expect to have a sense of loss but instead get an immediate and enormous sense of relief. Clearly something is physically wrong with me; it is more than just altitude or exertion, and I am guessing that it's my cardiovascular system. Not a good thing out here in this remote area. Even a minor cardiac "event" here could turn into a major event pretty quickly.

I have learned some really important lessons on this walk already. One is that the strong sense of family that Karsten, Marina, Paula, and I had four years ago was not a one-off event. Being here with like-minded people in a remote wilderness environment promotes a rapid sense of interdependence. I have heard this referred to by my daughter-in-law Laura (TJ) as "trail magic" and am beginning to understand it a little better.

Another lesson specific to this journey is how to deal with the loss of a dream when the plan simply does not work. I shall have lots of time to contemplate this in the days and weeks to come. For the moment, it is enough that the decision, when it is finally made, is a relief, not a burden. My stamina appears to be diminishing, not increasing.

While I believe that I could probably complete this journey as planned, it no longer feels necessary, and I do not want to discover on the trail that my problem is a real physical one. I think that the issue is likely the combination of no acclimatization for altitude, plus the unusual exertion required in the first few days.

Tomorrow is a short walk, only fifteen kilometres, so I decide to walk with my pack as far as Saint-Chély-d'Aubrac. At that point (135 kilometres from Le Puy-en-Velay), I shall finish. It also happens to be where Sophie will finish and return from there to Paris. With luck, I shall go with her. I am not very comfortable with my comprehension of French, so having her nearby is great.

24 April — Nasbinal to Saint-Chély-d'Aubrac

Today's walk will be a short one, about fifteen kilometres to Saint-Chély-d'Aubrac. The reason behind the wide disparity in the distances day to day is that the villages here in the Auvergne are not as evenly distributed as those on the *camino* in Spain. We are still on the high Aubrac plateau, but we will leave it — and the Auvergne region — today. There is a descent later today of about 600 metres (2,000 feet) from the plateau into the region of Midi-Pyrénées. (It is a long way from the Pyrénées here.) It will be interesting to see what effect the lower altitude has on the weather and on the season — and just possibly on my physical state.

It is Easter Sunday today, so almost everything is closed. As soon as possible, I need to get Internet access to book my flight from Paris to Ottawa. It is cool and looks like rain, but it doesn't actually rain, which makes it very good weather for walking. My fleece is off after about fifteen minutes.

There are many, many walkers on the path today. Most of them are carrying day packs or no packs, so they are probably just out for a day's stroll . . . cross-country. The path today is a first — it is actually cross-country, not between fields but over them. Much of it is green fields, with gates, and a recently worn dirt path across the field. I never saw this in Spain or here, before today.

GR marking: go this way.

GR marking: don't go this way.

I do not think that I have mentioned the way-finding. In Spain, it was the ubiquitous yellow arrow that led us across Spain. Here, it is a small, distinctive marking: a white rectangle above and a red one below. This is the marking of a "Grande Randonée," or GR, a designated walking path in France. There are 60,000 kilometres of GRs in France, maintained by 5,000 volunteers. Every day as I walk, I thank these anonymous volunteers for the work they do.

There are two differences between the marking in Spain and in France. In Spain, the yellow arrows mark one unique path and they are one-way, toward Santiago. In France, GRs are all marked with the white and red, and they are two-way and sometimes cross each other. At one point in a village today, I am ready to head off on a marked route when Francine points out that this is GR 6, not GR 65, the one we want. It is easy to tell the difference, but you have to look and be able to see.

Francine chooses to walk with me today. I am being carefully looked after by my little "family." She confides that she is non-religious and does not know why she is here. She says that she is from a small city, Besançon, about 220,000 inhabitants, in eastern France near the Swiss border. She is forty-six, recently separated from her partner of twelve years. He is about my age, a generation older than her, with five grown children and long separated from his wife. He has recently retired and feels terribly guilty about abandoning his family.

I do not know how long ago this happened, or whether Francine was involved in the separation, but from what little I know of her, it seems unlikely. In any event, he assuages his guilt by spending what little money he has on his wife and children. Francine seems to be the victim of another person's poor choices and now she is paying the price. As well, her mother died six months ago. Her mother had left the family home when Francine was ten, and she did not see her again until she was thirty. They reconciled before her mother died.

The melancholy seems deep inside her. We spend a lot of time talking, and I tell her that she is a loving and lovable person, which is absolutely true. I am very happy that I am here at this point and time in her life, when she really needs someone to tell her that she is a good person. I also tell her that I find her beautiful, which I do. She is not pretty in the conventional sense and has probably never been told that she was pretty. I tell her that pretty is pleasant but passes with time, while beauty is deep within and lasts forever. I see her as beautiful. When she smiles, her eyes smile, too . . . she is a lovely lady and I am very glad that we are together today. Perhaps our time together today is why I needed to be here on this journey. It certainly feels right for me.

Eventually, we start to descend a long, shallow, dry watercourse, lots of loose rock, slow walking, and potentially treacherous, but not dangerous if you walk slowly and pay attention where you place each foot. Partway down, we come to a clearing where we stop for a rest.

I take off my pack and put my head down on the grass between the rocks, covering my face with my hat. Francine does the same, a few feet from me, except that she takes off her boots and socks as well. Francine comments that this is paradise. There are a few spring flowers in the clearing, purple and yellow, tiny. As I doze, I hear people walking past us. One group includes a woman who talks from the time she is within earshot until she disappears around a corner far below. It seems that she is not happy with the silence all around us. But she is soon gone.

After perhaps half an hour, we get up, put our gear back on, and continue down the trail. Soon we arrive in Saint-Chély-d'Aubrac, where Sophie, who was walking ahead of us, has found all of us a place to stay. I was concerned all day since we had not been able to confirm anything in the morning . . . and there are a lot of people out here. When we enter the village, Francine suggests that I stay with our packs at the first open bar — yes! — and have a beer while she goes to find Sophie. The weather has turned superb and it is late spring here in this deep valley. Two days ago, it was almost winter. I am on my second beer, feeling very relaxed, when Francine returns with a big golden retriever — the house dog.

We have a wonderful room at the very top of a fifteenth-century tower. The very long circular stone staircase is worn from 600 years of people walking up and down it. This is the Tour des Chapelains, built to house the many priests who served this entire area, fifty-one of them. Now it is a welcoming place run with wonderful panache by Jean-Claude Brunier, who serves all his guests an aperitif at 6:45 and tells us the history of the building. Afterwards, we go out together for dinner. As usual here, the food is excellent.

This is my last night with the group, and I am feeling very loving toward them all. I will miss them but I feel right about my decision to leave. The lesson is that you can't always achieve the dream but if you don't achieve it, it doesn't need to be failure. Failure is the unwillingness to try to achieve the dream because you *might* fail. At least I know that I made the effort and, in trying, I think that I may have made a real difference in the lives of some of the people with whom I have travelled. Feels like success to me.

INTERRUPTION

25 April 2011—Retracing My Steps

It's time to say farewell to my erstwhile family of fellow pilgrims: Karsten, Felicia, Jocelyn, Francine, and Max. Sophie will be travelling with me today, so it's not quite farewell for her. We have a wonderful breakfast with our host, Jean-Claude, then have a little movie session in which Francine asks questions and Felicia takes a movie with her camera, then they pack up to leave. It takes a little while, because Karsten isn't ready. In the half-light of dawn, someone has taken his boots and left another pair, same brand, a half size larger. The other person is going to have a long day with too-small boots. Note: Karsten did get his own boots back at the end of that day.

Finally, they leave, and Sophie and I slowly make our way to the same bar where I had the beer yesterday and where the transport vehicle will pick us up around eleven a.m. to take us back to Aumont-Aubrac. There, Sophie will catch the bus to take her onwards, while I will stay overnight and catch the bus tomorrow (today's train to Paris is full—it's the last day of Easter vacation). Sophie will help me find a place to stay in Aumont-Aubrac. We will have several hours there. It's warm, peaceful, birds singing, sunny, just a lovely day in this remote valley.

My "family": Karsten, Max, Felicia, Sophie, Jocelyn, and Francine.

Yesterday evening, I was able to get Internet access and book my flight home for Thursday, two days from today. Not Air Canada at around $4,500 (that's one-way from Paris to Ottawa, economy class), but the Polish airline LOT at $1,674, about one-third the price—and I get to visit Warsaw, another unexpected treat.

In Aumont-Aubrac, after a fifty-five-kilometre drive, we find me a room at the Sentiers Fleuris, a lovely, welcoming place, with dinner, bed, and breakfast for thirty-eight Euros. Sophie and I go out for a bite before she leaves. She tells me that she has thought about her father a lot during the past few days. He is in his late sixties, has what sounds like terminal cancer, widespread in his abdominal cavity and lungs. He wants to walk a piece of this trail with her so she plans to come back this fall with him. She tells me that she had a very strict upbringing, left home, made some bad decisions (it would have been great fun making bad decisions with Sophie), and after five years was lost and searching. She met a young priest to whom she told everything. He said that it could all be fixed. She is now a devout Catholic, very happy, thirty-nine years old. It turns out that her birthday is 14 July, same as Carroll's, and that she loves the fireworks (she lives in Paris, where they celebrate Bastille Day every July 14th). Every year, she figures that they are especially for her.

After our lunch, she goes to the church for a visit, I go back to have a little sleep. At 3:30, she comes back to my place, and we walk together to the station. The bus comes, we embrace and say farewell, and she is gone. I walk back to the hotel in a rain shower with the sun shining through. The hotel has WiFi, so I compose and send several days of my blog, then have dinner with another wonderful, welcoming host, André, who does the *aligot* thing again, to the amazement of the assembled crowd. I sit for dinner with two Italians and three Germans, a small family from Munich, all of whom speak good English.

Overnight, I think about staying on one more day here instead of spending two overnights in Paris (Will Inrig has found me a place to stay in Montmartre) but I decide that I would rather be near where my plane will be on Thursday, so I will go to Paris in the morning.

About reassurance and religion.

In my past writings, I have often come across as somewhat hostile to religion. During this walk across France, I have come to the realization that my hostility may be misplaced. I have been walking with a couple of people—Jocelyn and Sophie—for whom their religion is a strong reassurance that they are on the right path. I am not opposed to religion; I am opposed to how some people abuse it.

I'll give an example that took place a very long time ago, not far from where I am walking in France. One of the really unattractive events of thirteenth-century France was the destruction of the Cathars, which spelled the end of the Albigensian heresy (after Albi, a town south of my intended route). The Cathars were a peaceful and popular large group of Christians residing in southern France whose beliefs did not coincide with those of the Roman Catholic Church, which was dominant at the time. The Church ordered a crusade in France to crush the Albigensian heresy in southern France. This crusade came about because the Albigensians, also known as Cathars, did not accept the decisions made about Christianity by men—it was always men—in Rome.

The Cathars believed in individual access to the Gospels and did not believe in the need for intervention by other people—priests and bishops—between them and God. They translated the New Testament into the local language and taught it in schools. The Cathars were merchants and bankers and were nonviolent.

The Church believed that it was their duty to interpret the content of the Gospels for the people. They believed, of course, in the full patriarchal hierarchy of the Church. They distrusted trade and merchants, and forbade loans for interest. For a long time, the Church tolerated the Cathars, and their beliefs grew to be very popular in southern France.

In 1209, the pope, Innocent III, called for a crusade against these heretics. It was a crusade not against the Muslim occupiers of the Holy Land, but the first crusade ever against co-religionists—fellow Christians. The nobles and knights of northern France rallied to the cause. Could it have been because they were promised the lands of any Cathars whom they defeated? It was never a fair fight. The Cathars, like modern Quakers, were anti-war and anti-killing. Their opponents did not follow similar rules. The war was particularly savage.

When the fortified town of Beziers, the home of both Catholics and Cathars, was taken, the commander of the northern forces, an abbot, was asked how to deal with the townspeople, since the crusaders could not tell the difference. His response? "Kill them all,

God will know his own." And so 20,000 people, many of them devout Catholics, were massacred by a Catholic army bent on saving them from heresy.

The Crusade was a Holy War—a *jihad*, if you will. And if you died fighting in the Crusade, you went directly to Heaven, with a plenary indulgence. All sins, no matter how sordid, were instantly expunged. Many people of the time were troubled by the fact that the crusaders against their own co-religionists were given the same forgiveness that they earned when fighting against the Muslims in the Holy Land. The Troubadours made a lot of this. The radical and fundamentalist Muslims of this day whom we call terrorists are offered the same attractive deal when they become suicide bombers or die in *jihad*.

The Cathars not killed in the forty years of war were then slowly and systematically exterminated through a seventy-year-long and, of course, nasty Inquisition. The last Cathar was burned at the stake in 1321. The Cathars were exterminated by a combination of religious intolerance and greed by the knights and nobles of northern France.

So, my issue is not against religion per se, but against its frequent abuse by the people who claim to be the ones who show the way.

The ones who really scare me, from every religious group, are the fundamentalists, who know God's mind better than the rest of us and demand that we conform to their beliefs and customs . . . or die. Islamic Wahhabism, sometimes known as "petro-Islam," for example, is noted for compelling people within its control to follow its very strict ninth-century interpretation of Islam and it considers all other Islamic sects as apostate.

I won't even get started on the abuse of innocent children by lonely and desperate Catholic priests and the subsequent attempts at cover-up by the bishops.

26 April — Saint-Chély-d'Aubrac to Paris

I have a restless night, since I need to be at the station for the bus at 8:04. After a breakfast with hot chocolate made just for me, I pack my pack, pay my bill, and am on my way, walking the few hundred metres to the station. As I approach, I see a couple of familiar figures standing there. It's Jocelyn and Max! They have finished their journey and are also on their way to Paris. I had not expected to see them again, ever, and here they are. They took a taxi from where they stayed overnight. Although we buy our tickets together and we tell the agent that we are together, we do not end up in the same carriage. The train is quite full. I sit in a first-class carriage with too little legroom, so a total stranger (at least she is young and attractive) and I play kneesies all the way for the five hours to Paris. We never speak. Apparently I am neither young nor attractive enough for her.

In Paris, we three meet again on the platform, where Jocelyn busily organizes us to the Metro station, then finds out where I have to go. Max meets a friend here, and so we say farewell yet again. Jocelyn and I get on the same Metro car. She makes sure that I know where I am going (I have a Metro route map), then embraces me and gets off after three stops. She says that Saint Jacques meant for us to be together all this way. Who am I to disagree? I have two more stops to go, then a change of train and another few stops to the base of the funicular at Montmartre. Up the funicular, I inquire about rue la Marck. No one knows, because it is actually rue Lamarck. It is the street on the immediate back side of the cathedral and only a couple of minutes' walk to number 24.

I push the bell, and after a few moments, the door opens to a welcome from Maggie, the tiny, elderly, elfin woman whose home this is. I am shown to my room, lovely, with a garden view. I will be here for a day and a bit, then off to Canada via Warsaw. In the early evening, I walk through the square in Montmartre, which is a beehive of activity—tourists of every size, age, and nationality, and the local French selling them food, drink, paintings, almost instant portraits, silhouettes of themselves. It is as far as one can imagine from the quiet and solitude of the past ten days. It's not wrong, it's different and fascinating and it is another way the world works. We are also warned here about pickpockets. I can imagine that this place would be full of them, so my passport and wallet are safely stored away.

I am now looking forward to going home again. Carroll is always fascinated, as I am, by this particular piece of Paris. One more day . . .

27–28 April—Paris to Ottawa

My last day in Paris is a lazy one. Will Inrig is in school all day and into the evening, so I won't be seeing him. Sophie, who is somewhere here in Paris, and who had said that she wanted to meet me in Montmartre—"*J'adore* Montmartre," she had said—has a friend returning from Vietnam, so she will not be able to meet me. So I am as alone in this enormous city as I ever was on the trail . . . and here, it feels bizarre. I have had, so far, no recurrence of the physical problems that brought me here.

I spend my time getting the blog up to date and wandering around the square just on the other side of the cathedral, watching the tourists and the buskers, the painters, silhouettists with their scissors and quick hands, the waiters in their uniform of braces and trousers. Early in the afternoon, I have *moules-frites*, mussels, and French fries. As the sun goes down and the temperature drops with it, I say goodbye to the City of Lights, most of which you can see from the heights of Montmartre—it is the highest point in Paris, at 130 metres—go back to my room, and sleep through a restless night.

In the morning, I get breakfast served on a tray in my room and do the final pack of my backpack. It is travelling again as unaccompanied baggage, so I have put all the really dirty clothing on top, in the hopes that the smell will discourage anyone from investigating what else might be in the bag. There is no contraband, but I would like the pack to get home. I leave at nine and walk over to the taxi stand at Montmartre, where yesterday there was always a taxi. Not this morning.

At 9:25, just when I am into serious panic, a taxi heaves into sight, and I flag him down and get in. Yesterday when I asked, I was told that the price to get to Charles de Gaulle airport was forty Euros and that it would take only twenty minutes. Again, not this morning. The traffic is dreadful. The driver keeps assuring me that any moment it will clear up, but as we turn each corner, there is the same sea of red tail lights.

My flight to Warsaw leaves at noon, and I am supposed to check in by ten a.m. Ten o'clock comes and goes, and we are still on the road to the airport. But by 10:20, we are there. I go through the whole check-in process and say goodbye to my backpack once again. I do hope that I will see it in Ottawa. Today is going to be a long day in the air. My LOT flight to Warsaw is two hours, followed by a three-hour wait in Warsaw, followed by a nine-and-one-half-hour flight to Toronto, two hours to get through Immigration and Security, and a short flight to Ottawa. While the day is very long, the LOT aircraft and onboard service are both excellent—as good as or better than Air Canada and at one-third the price. The downside is the four extra hours of flying—Paris to Warsaw and back. The upside is that I get to go to Warsaw—big pastel apartment buildings, where, amazingly, even the little kids speak Polish!

We land in Ottawa shortly after midnight, and I am met by Carroll. I am just delighted to see her and to be home. As a bonus, my backpack shows up on the luggage belt. It's about a thirty-minute drive to our home, and I fall into bed at one a.m., which is seven a.m. on my body clock. I am home.

Over the next days and weeks, I will need to assimilate what exactly has happened to me over the past two weeks. Perhaps at some future time I will regret the decision that I made about a week ago, but at the moment it feels exactly right to me. When Carroll asks me why I didn't use the return ticket that I already had with Air Canada, I realized how disoriented I had been the last few days. I never even thought about the ticket, which I had with me. It is another symptom of my physical problem.

Looking Back

Looking back at my unsuccessful attempt to walk the Chemin de Saint-Jacques from Le Puy, I can now see clearly that I made three big mistakes.

The first was in Le Puy. I walked up to the cathedral area from the lower town three times on the day that I was there waiting for Karsten. The second and third times, I had real problems with my breathing. I had to rest a couple of times on the way up. I did not twig to the obvious fact that the altitude was a lot higher than that of Ottawa and that my breathing problem was a matter of less air density and therefore less oxygen in the air. Had I realized that, I could have stayed in Le Puy for a couple more days and acclimatized; or I could have made my first few days on the *chemin* really short hauls, ten or twelve kilometres only. Either solution might have reduced my later problems.

The second mistake was that I allowed myself to be diverted from my aim which was, as you will recall, to walk across France from Le Puy-en-Velay over the Pyrénées to Pamplona. Instead, I got diverted by the lovely group of people with whom I was walking after the second day and I accepted their decision of where we would aim for each day. This required me to walk farther than I wanted to each day, thus contributing to my fatigue and general sense of not feeling well. My option would have been to simply say goodbye to them all, including Karsten, and to have stopped each day when I had had enough.

Actually, my aim was not simply to walk across France. It was to walk across France and to see what experiences unfolded and what lessons could be learned. So in that sense, I did not betray myself. The lesson that I learned about how to deal with not being able to do something that I had planned for so long was a powerful one, so perhaps I achieved my aim after all. I could not have done both, it turns out.

And I learned more about relationships. We formed an uncommon level of trust in the group within a day or two. A couple of people in the little group were having some difficulties with their sense of personal worth, and I think that I helped them by a little talking, some gentle suggestions, and a lot of listening.

The third was that I didn't take the advice of my fellow walkers to see a doctor in the Auvergne or even after I got to Paris. I reasoned that they were unlikely to find anything during the cursory examination that I expected I would get there. I learn some six months later that I have diabetes. It is possible, though unlikely, that a local doctor would have spotted the diabetes much earlier.

When I arrive back in Ottawa, I make an appointment to visit my GP. When I tell him the symptoms that I experienced in France, he is quite concerned and orders a battery of tests: lung function, X-rays, blood work, cardiac investigation. After several months I am given a clean bill of health. I had the last test yesterday—a nuclear perfusion cardiac stress test—and the doctors have now checked out my lungs, my blood, and my heart. As far as they can tell, I am in very good health for a person of my age. The cardiologist says, "Whatever you've been doing, keep doing it." I tell him what I have been doing and he says that there should be no issue about continuing.

That seems to mean that my difficulty in the Auvergne in France on the Massif Central was a combination of altitude and physical stress, perhaps nothing more. I am wrong, as are the doctors, but I won't know this for several months. To say I am pleased would be a serious understatement. I am extremely grateful for the messages of concern about my physical and psychological health from so many of my friends, and also for the state of health care in Canada that has allowed me to get so thoroughly checked out at no direct cost to me. If this is socialized medicine, I am all for it!

Early in the New Year, my doctor orders another round of blood tests. When I meet with him after the tests, he reads something on his computer screen and tells me that my blood glucose level is 7.2. I tell him that I have absolutely no idea what that means. He says, matter-of-factly, "It means you have diabetes." This is a bolt from the blue. Normal is 5.0 to 6.0. We use a different measurement scale in Canada from the one used in the United States.[8] When I get an opportunity later that day, I look up the symptoms of diabetes on the Internet—and when I read them, I realize that I was probably suffering from the effects of undiagnosed and untreated diabetes last spring in France. The good news is that my type 2 diabetes, at the level it's at, can be managed with medication, something called Metformin. I also need to test my blood glucose level daily.

The doctor tells me that I might have a few gut issues with this drug. What he doesn't tell me is that slightly more than half of all patients starting on Metformin get diarrhea. I discover this in the most unpleasant way possible. I have started training for the upcoming walk in France. I am out on a long—eighteen-kilometre—training walk with my pack on a cold, blustery day when I feel a little twinge in my gut. And it happens again and again. It feels like gas, but when I relax the sphincter to pass it, it's not gas. Alarm! Over the next hour it keeps happening and it is not comfortable or pleasant. Carroll is not at home so I can't call for a ride. I am way in the country, few houses around . . . and would you let someone in who is smelling foul and wants to use your toilet? So I have to keep walking, which gets progressively more difficult. When I finally arrive home, I have to strip off everything, shower, and wash practically everything I have on. And it causes a nasty rash. You don't want to know. Do you remember the song "Ring of Fire"? Carroll isn't here when I arrive and clean up, for which I am grateful.

I have not had an incident like this since I was six and in Grade 2 and was tied onto a chair for running around the classroom. I think I had knocked a plant on the floor. My mother had words with the teacher afterwards. When I tell my doctor about my recent unfortunate experience, he apologizes. There is an alternate version of this drug, slower release, which has fewer unfortunate side effects. I start

---

8   The normal fasting range is five to seven mmol/L (millimoles/litre). The USA uses a different measurement standard, mg/dl (milligrams/decilitre) for measuring blood glucose. Multiply the Canadian measure by 18 to see the equivalent US measure (90–126).

on it and have no problems. Good thing. A loose gut would make walking across France problematic. I expect that it will be enough of a challenge without an added complication. I have high blood pressure, high cholesterol, and diabetes, the classic North American combination of lifestyle diseases. All are managed — not fixed — with medication. We shall see what unfolds.

It's mid-April, just about two days — forty-eight hours — until I leave here for Europe to begin my *next* attempt at walking across France and into Spain on the Chemin de Saint-Jacques, better known in Spanish as the Camino de Santiago. It is almost a year since I started this journey last April. I am, as you might imagine, a little trepidatious. This always happens the last few days before I leave for a long walk or do anything else that has an element of risk associated with it. It is especially strong this time because of last year's difficulties.

I get the unmistakeable message from the part of my brain that wants to protect me: "What are you *thinking*? You could just stay at home, enjoy the lovely and friendly warmth of your family, play golf, and eat fries whenever you want." But I persevere, not least because I have told everyone that I am going. It's just too embarrassing to tell everyone that I have changed my mind, especially since I have enlisted people to contribute to a hospice as I walk. There is an annual fundraiser, Hike for Hospice, which is a five-kilometre walk, and people are encouraged to enlist sponsors. I won't be in Ottawa for this, but I am going off to France for a walk of something over 700 kilometres and it occurs to me that I could get sponsors for *this* walk.

The response to my "hike for hospice" is very encouraging. We have raised over $1,300 already for the Hospice at May Court in Ottawa, and I have had messages from Toronto, Victoria, Atlanta, Houston, and Wellington, New Zealand, that people are also donating to their local hospices. I am just delighted by all this.

And speaking of delighted, last Friday, I had a "doesn't get any better than this" moment. Carroll and I were invited to my daughter Meredith's house for Fabulous Food Friday. Typically it's us plus a small group of close friends, perhaps a half-dozen of us. Since we had a TGIF for our community at five, we asked Meredith if it would be okay if we arrived later, at seven. No problem. At the TGIF, many people say goodbye and good trip to me. So at seven, off we go — it's a five-minute walk — to Meredith's.

When we get in the door, there are a lot more people than normal . . . and it turns out that it's a farewell and bon voyage party . . . for me! I am completely surprised and that has happened seldom in my life. It gets even better when most of the people at the TGIF show up at the door within a few minutes of my arriving, wearing big smiles.

I find out that everyone has known about this for weeks—and no one, not even the usual suspects, has blurted it out to me. The party is wonderful, and I feel thoroughly loved.

Meredith has had a tough time making this happen. Her fridge failed about ten days ago, and the company was able to get her a replacement only on Friday afternoon. My daughter is resourceful and very determined. I think that she gets this from her mother.

Now it's Monday afternoon. I have the travel itinerary done, the packing checklist printed, and everything that I need (not want) on a single surface to be packed into the backpack and into my carry-on. For those of you who recall the disaster five years ago, Air Canada took my backpack and poles as unaccompanied baggage, and I never saw it or them again. This time, to reduce the risk of loss, the backpack and my poles will travel as unaccompanied baggage inside a nondescript black duffel bag.

As the grandchildren, almost five and almost three, say, "Only two sleeps, Granddad."

18 April—Over the Atlantic

This is a first for me, using an iPad for the blog. It's shortly after eight p.m., and we have left Montreal for Paris. I am sitting comfortably in the cabin of an aircraft at 35,000 feet, entering data into my iPad. I have it on aircraft mode, of course, so that the wireless capability is off. The theory is that my wireless transmission could fool the aircraft's sophisticated navigation system and autopilot into doing something wrong. Of course, Air Canada doesn't need my help to screw up. Last year, CBC *News* reported that an Air Canada pilot woke up from his approved nap over the Atlantic on a night flight much like this one, saw Venus, thought it was the light of a nearby aircraft, and took emergency avoidance action, which put sixteen people into hospital on arrival. It was reported as severe turbulence (which it was) but implied that it was caused by weather (which it wasn't). I wonder when or whether companies will ever learn to tell the truth to their clients when something bad happens.

I had a similar experience in a car many years ago. We, a group of Royal Canadian Air Force (RCAF) pilot trainees, were driving at night from the RCAF station in Claresholm, Alberta, to Calgary at night on a long, straight highway. I was asleep sitting beside the driver. I woke up and realized (I saw) that there a vehicle head-on to us and closing fast. I grabbed the steering wheel to pull it to the right. Fortunately, the driver was awake and alert and held onto the wheel. He was not happy with me. The car I saw was miles away. We now know what happens in these situations. There is a part of the brain, the amygdala, part of the limbic system, which gets the message about threats faster than the conscious part of the brain. (It is part of the ancient mammalian survival system—you don't have to know exactly what it is if it appears to be a threat.) I would guess that the Air Canada pilot's reaction was the same as mine—an immediate response, even before thinking about it, to an apparent threat.

I am travelling on Aeroplan points and, since I have quite a few of them, I am in business class. That means that I am sitting in a comfortable little pod, just big enough for one but with every comfort known to man. One of the comforts is that the seat reclines fully into a bed, so I will get a few hours of good sleep before we arrive in Paris in the morning. We lose five hours on the flight, so it won't be a full eight hours of sleep, but enough to allow me to get quickly over the inevitable jet lag.

The pod has a potential downside, in that each passenger is effectively isolated from every other passenger. Since my plan is to sleep, that is not a problem for this flight, but since I often like to chat with interesting people, it could be a problem under different conditions.

The food in business class is excellent. It starts with an appetizer, then a salad, then four choices for a main course: grilled AAA beef tenderloin, roasted chicken, grilled sea bass, or Porcini mushroom and ricotta ravioli. Each is accompanied by wonderful options. The sea bass, which I have, is offered with fingerling potatoes, grilled vegetables, and cherry tomatoes. I pass on dessert: an apple, blueberry, strawberry, and rhubarb streusel tart, not because I don't want it but because I am tired and want to sleep. I can't imagine and don't want to know what they had in steerage.

19 April—in Paris

We have arrived at Charles de Gaulle airport in Paris after a mostly smooth flight, and after a few anxious minutes, I see, on the baggage carousel, my backpack in its nondescript black bag with a rainbow baggage strap. That is one concern put to rest.

Then I pick up SIM cards for my phone and my iPad. Here's something new: When you buy a SIM card now in France, you have to register it using photo ID within fifteen days or it is deactivated. Probably it's something to do with counterterrorism.

The next move is to go outside and find a taxi. Last year when I was here, I found a bus, but finding it and taking it into the city took about three hours. The taxi from the airport is a little pricey, seventy Euros, but it is worth it for the Le Mans ride the driver gives me. On the major roads, motorcycles drive not just within the traffic lanes but also on the markings between lanes, so they weave in and out of traffic, with inches to spare, at a very high rate of speed. And we drive along beside the Seine and past the Eiffel Tower. It's huge as you get close to it. I always forget how big it is.

There are a lot of construction cranes everywhere, and barges full of sand and gravel on the Seine, so I don't think the economy is quite as bad here as it is reported to be by the North American papers.

The hotel is directly across the road from the Tour Montparnasse, a black high-rise office tower of perhaps sixty storeys that is completely out of character with the neighbourhood, and very close to the Montparnasse train station, not the Bercy station that I thought I was booking near. Right city, wrong train station. This is the second time in less than a month that I have booked the wrong location online. The other one was potentially much worse.

I was trying to book a small Canadian resort, the Salzberger Hof Resort in Batchawana Bay on the eastern shore of Lake Superior for a couple of days in August. It's run by an Austrian family, and I've stayed there before. From their website I was taken to another, booking.com, where I entered data into the right fields, wondering idly why the price was in Euros and was finally rewarded with my confirmed reservation for the Salzberger Hof, only this one *was* in Austria. It took me several emails to Austria and to booking.com to get that sorted out; and the Austrian place informed me that I should know that Austria is not in Canada.

I expect to spend a quiet day here in Paris. The weather is cool, partly cloudy, but not raining, so that's a plus. I will be off tomorrow morning by train for points south. I am anxious to get on the road. I sleep for a few hours, then go out to find something to eat.

At seven p.m., I am sitting in a little bistro, the Odessa, facing out to watch the fascinating people as they walk by. It's cool and raining lightly, but turns sunny as the evening progresses. Fashion sense is still good here. Most people are in pants, jeans, etc., but every once in a while a *fashionista* walks by. There is one, an older woman, head held regally high and wearing a stunning patterned yellow jacket and skirt. She could be on a fashion show runway anywhere. People are smoking, walking dogs, carrying baguettes—so it is not just an old myth. There are very, very few overweight; none obese. North American agribusiness has not penetrated here . . . yet. I see only one identifiable Muslim in the passersby, although the pleasant and helpful hotel clerk is named Mohammad, which is a clue.

This is not a good place to jaywalk. Cars and motorcycles are fast, and the roads narrow.

I am absorbing the sounds, smells, feel of Paris as I sit here. An old couple goes by, arm in arm, laughing. They remind me of Carroll and me. We are so lucky. Almost fifty-four years married, and still lovers and best friends.

Off to bed. We will see what tomorrow brings. All being well, I will be at La Ferme du Barry in Aumont-Aubrac in time for dinner, for which Vincent, the owner, is justly famous (I ate there last year, but could not get accommodation).

20 April—Paris to Aumont-Aubrac

I get up early and have a leisurely breakfast at a tiny place on a side street near the hotel. Of course, I have two croissants and a *grande crème* (that's the new term I have learned for *café au lait*, or a latte). It's cool and overcast; the forecast is for rain, but there is none while I am in Paris. I get a taxi from here to the Bercy train station, and there confirm my ticket to Clermont-Ferrand and finally, finally, get a ticket for the bus from Clermont to Aumont-Aubrac. Neither I nor my travel agent could purchase this ticket online, even though the bus is run by the railway company.

The train leaves sharp at 1:00 p.m. Of course, we're in Europe, where trains always run on time. I sleep most of the way, although I do note that the land is flat as we travel south for the first two hours. The next ninety minutes, the land starts to roll. About forty minutes before Clermont,[9] we stop briefly at Vichy. Vichy is famous for its water and infamous for being the capital of the puppet government of the southern half of France during World War II. I will tell you more about Vichy, later.

At Clermont, I have twelve minutes to find and get on the bus, which, like all buses in Europe, is spotlessly clean. As we continue to roll south, the country gets seriously hilly and the weather gets seriously wet and cold—about five degrees by the time we arrive in Aumont-Aubrac. As I am travelling south, I note that the countryside is much like parts of my home province, Ontario, except that the houses are all stucco, grey to beige to yellow, and all the roofs are red tile . . . and there is the occasional chateau on the hilltops. As we get closer to Aumont-Aubrac, the roof tile colours change from red to dark grey or black.

I debus, get my backpack, and walk a few minutes to La Ferme du Barry, where I am welcomed by the owner, Vincent, and his wife. He does not remember me, but I remember him. He is a big, friendly bear of a man, who cooks the meals here, including his famous *aligot*, a mix of mashed potatoes and cheese that strings out like pasta. And dinner will be soon.

I have a bed in a room with four others, all men. Along with five women, we eat at a communal table; good, filling food and red wine; water for those who want it. My iPad is a big hit, since everyone wants to see either tomorrow's route on Google Earth (for them—I am taking transport to Saint-Chély-d'Aubrac—two days' walking for them) or their hometown. They are mostly French, with one Swiss woman, Fanny, and one Canadienne, Joimie. Also the images of my grandchildren Cian and Bella, which are my screen savers, are very popular.

I am glad to have today behind me, since it was one of the more tedious days, and I wasn't sure until about noon that I could get here today on the bus. So, all's well that ends well—and today is ending very well, indeed.

---

9 Clermont is where, on 27 November 1095, Pope Urban II called for the First Crusade to retake Jerusalem, which had not been under Christian control for almost 500 years.

A Little History—Vichy, France

At the beginning of World War II, after the unprovoked German attack on Poland in the autumn of 1939, both the French and the British declared war on Germany, put their forces into place in France, then waited . . . and waited . . . and waited. It was known as the "phony war." Hitler realized that the Allies were not going to attack Germany, so in 1940, he launched the blitzkrieg (lightning war), driving tanks and infantry, supported by close air support, through the supposedly impassable Ardennes Forest in Belgium.

The Allies were stunned by this flanking manoeuvre and quickly lost ground. These ancient enemies, France and England, did not trust each other, and the lack of trust created an ongoing communication crisis. The French decided that they could not withstand the onslaught and sued for peace. The British, feeling betrayed, evacuated the remnants of their army through Dunkirk, declaring a victory by getting most of their men out, but leaving virtually all of their heavy weaponry. The evacuation at Dunkirk is a story in itself, with thousands of private British boats assisting the navy to evacuate survivors.

A lot of people over the years have accused the French of simply rolling over when the Germans attacked. What I did not know was that, in the first month of the attack on France, the French sustained over 100,000 killed in action. That was the result of the German blitzkrieg . . . infantry, tanks, and artillery supported by air power . . . shock and awe in action. That is not rolling over. It is approximately twice the number of American fatalities during all the years of the Vietnam War. I think that the French believed, with some accuracy, that they were going to lose a second generation of young men to another war in twenty years and decided that that was too high a price to pay.

The Germans occupied the northern half of France and installed a puppet government under Marshal Pétain in the southern half, with the government in Vichy. One of the unhappy parts of the history of Vichy France is their treatment of the Jews. There were many, many Jewish refugees from the rest of Europe who had fled to apparent safety in France prior to 1939. As the Germans executed their "final solution," the deliberate extermination of the Jews, Vichy France was only too eager to assist. While many Jewish French citizens were helped by their gentile neighbours, the Jewish refugees, most in refugee camps, had no one to help them. The rules concerning who was a Jew in

Vichy were more draconian than those in occupied France or in Germany itself. They were rounded up by French police and transported to the camps in their tens of thousands. Most did not survive.

There was, of course, an active resistance movement both in occupied France and in Vichy, but, as a wise and cynical Frenchwoman said much later, there were a lot more resistance fighters after the war than during the war. For many years after the war, the French government simply denied its complicity in the roundup of the Jews, but this denial has since been rescinded.

Sometime later during this pilgrimage, I spent some time with someone from Switzerland who talked about the difficulties that the French people had during the war. The German occupation of France was quite ruthless. If any member of a family was caught assisting the resistance, he or she was executed along with all the members of the immediate family. The Swiss woman asked rhetorically whether anyone with a family could in conscience assist the resistance when everyone knew the price. I have never been in a country under occupation, so although I know what I would want to do, what I hope that I would do, I have no idea what I would actually do in the event of this level of repression. Would I be prepared to sacrifice my children, my wife, my own life? I am again grateful that I was brought to Canada as a young child and never had to face the agonies that so many people did during the war.

21 April—Aumont to Saint-Chély-d'Aubrac

I spend a restless night in the *gîte*. The bed is comfortable, but the room is warm and close and extremely dark. I have clearly not finished with jet lag yet, since I am wide awake at two a.m., but cannot turn on a light, since there are three other people sleeping here. So I lie here, thinking about all kinds of things. I get up a couple of times, walk into a wall in the dark, and use the convenient bathroom. I must remember to get out my tiny headlamp and have it available at night. Lots of little etiquette things to remember when walking with a pack and sleeping with others. I doze on and off, and eventually, it is seven a.m. and there are stirrings in the other beds. I get up, test my blood glucose—it's fine—and head downstairs for breakfast.

Breakfast is coffee with hot milk (separately), oranges sliced into sections, and baguettes with butter and a homemade jam made from blackberries. People are very quiet; not the bonhomie of last night but a mental preparation for the day. I tell them that I may see them in a few days, since I will be one day ahead of them, but plan to stop for a rest day after four days' walking.

Vincent calls a cab for me, and it arrives at 8:30. I pay my bill here — it's thirty-three Euros ($43) for dinner (with red wine), accommodation, and breakfast, a bargain, in my view. Since I have the technology with me, I am tracking my expenses for this trip. People often ask me what it cost for my walk on the *camino* in Spain, and I can't tell them. This time I am better prepared.

I wish those remaining "*Bon chemin*," and off we go, just the driver and I; he tells me in almost accent-less English: "I don't speak English." It is one of the baggage transport taxis, and the driver evidently knows the route, which is very curvy, extremely well. The weather is low overcast, and so misty the driver has to use the wipers. It is also cold. He drives it competently, about thirty kilometres per hour faster than I would, right on the edge of control.

As we approach and then leave Nasbinal, the countryside is littered with boulders, some as large as trucks. All the fields are lined with stone walls. It looks like the result of decades of hard work, clearing the fields of stones, and every spring, new ones start to emerge from the ground. It is probably the residue from an old glacier as the ice receded, about 10,000 years ago.

We start to see snow in the trees, then more and more as we climb toward the pass, the Col d'Aubrac, until the roads are edged with banks of snow and the surface is slushy and quite slippery. My driver gets very cautious here. We have climbed into the cloud cover, so visibility is about 100 metres and it is COLD. The fields are completely snow-covered, and the pilgrims we pass are bundled up against the cold and the wind. They, perhaps fifty in total over many kilometres, are all walking on the road, since the hiking path is impassable with snow. It looks like Napoleon's retreat from Moscow. Frankly, I am happy to bypass this section, which I walked last year. Last year it was much warmer here with no snow. I am told that snow cover is normal here for this time of year. We pass the Col d'Aubrac (Aubrac Pass) at 1,372 metres (4,500 feet) and start down the 600-metre drop into Saint-Chély-d'Aubrac. It is a steep and windy descent, almost a switchback. When I walked this section last year with Francine from Besançon, it was warm enough that we were able to lie down and sleep just beside the path. Not this year.

On arrival in Saint-Chély-d'Aubrac (I have to use the full name because there is another Saint-Chély-d'Apcher just north of Aumont-Aubrac), I find that the *gite* here does not open until 3:00 p.m. It's just after nine a.m., so I have six hours to kill. I leave my backpack—I am assured that it is safe—and walk in the cold rain into the village, find an open restaurant, order a *grande crème* and a croissant, plug in my iPad, and start writing.

I frequently read and hear about acts of humanity (think of Mother Teresa) and of inhumanity (think of Darfur in the Sudan) and I wonder about the use of those terms. The *Oxford Universal Dictionary* defines them in terms that are generous toward our species, but I think that we have them all wrong. I speculate that the reason we humans are the dominant primate on the planet—for the moment—is because of our "humanity," and by that I don't mean the classic definition of "kind, benevolent, civil, courteous, or obliging."[10] I rather think that it is our *lack* of those traits as a species that makes us dominant.

What brings me to this conclusion is a recent article that I read about mountain gorillas. An experienced observer of a mountain gorilla tribe was recently surprised to see a small bush baby—a small nocturnal primate—resting quietly in the middle of the family area. The comment was that this was not unusual for mountain gorillas, but if this had been a gathering of chimpanzees, the smaller animal would have been torn limb from limb. Mountain gorillas, which can weigh up to 600 pounds and stand over six feet tall, are very peaceable. When threatened, they have a ritualized procedure that is intended to avoid fighting at almost any cost. They are non-territorial, unlike us, and the silverback male, the leader of the family, defends the group rather than the territory.

These gorillas will, however, fight to the death to protect their infants. My immediate thought was that we humans are much more closely related by DNA to chimpanzees than to mountain gorillas. My next thought was that gorillas and chimpanzees—indeed, all other primates—fear humans for a very valid reason. We are more violent and less restrained, more willing to use deadly force, than chimpanzees. We are the dominant primate precisely because of our willingness to use force and the threat of force to get our way.

---

10   Definitions from the *Oxford Universal Dictionary*, Third Edition (Oxford: Clarendon Press, 1955).

Look at our societies. The political leaders are powerful and extremely territorial, whether elected, appointed, inherited the position, or just seized the power. Many of Africa's evolving civilizations were overwhelmed by European expansion in the 1800s and early 1900s, and by the slave trade before that. Wars are fought regularly over borders and the quest for power. Hitler took Germany and the rest of Europe into ruin over his quest for *"lebensraum,"* living space for his expansionist empire. George W. Bush has taken the United States on a long and perilous journey into financial ruin with his misguided and never-ending war on Iraq. Scarce resources create tensions between nations. Even the longest undefended border in the world, that between the United States and Canada, has at times been regarded by U.S. politicians as negotiable, sometimes peacefully, more often by threats of trade sanctions, boycotts, or war. During the Second World War, the U.S. built a highway from northern Alberta to Alaska. It was not an option that the Canadian government could have refused. The Americans actually started building it *before* getting the Canadian government's rubber stamp approval. The U.S. needed it, therefore it happened.

Business leaders are ruthless, greedy, and generally uncaring of the people who are their clients or who work for them. I give you the mortgage bankers in the United States as an example. Executive compensations and the rate of increase in them are absolutely incredible. In 1965, the average CEO made twenty-four times as much as the average worker. By 2005, the average CEO made 262 times as much as the average worker. You don't need a calculator to figure out that the American dream has come true for the executives of the larger American firms. The average CEO of a company with at least $1 billion in annual revenue made about $400 more in one day in 2005 than the average worker made in a year.[11] These CEOs cannot possibly justify earning hundreds of times their production workers' pay. The argument appears to be that if they are not paid these stupendous sums, they will just leave and go work for someone else who *will* pay them. What has gone wrong with our society? Is there no morality left? Is it really all — ALL — about the bottom line?

What is it about wealth? For some people, no matter how much wealth they acquire, they continue to seek desperately for more. It

---

11 Source: The Economic Policy Institute, ***http://www.stateofworkingamerica.org/news/SWA06Facts-CEO_Pay.pdf***

seems to be something that never satisfies. Look at the recent "great recession" of 2008–2009, the effects of which continue today. It was caused by the incredible greed of a great many people. And even after governments around the world indebted themselves for generations to come in an effort, so far successful, to prevent the "big recession" from deteriorating into another great depression, the financial superpowers continued to display the same greed. Example: Goldman Sachs in early 2010 set aside $15 billion for bonuses![12]

Compare this, if you will, to the decision made by a retired couple from Lower Truro, Nova Scotia, who won over eleven million dollars in a lottery in July 2010. They gave it all—all—away to charities, family and friends, churches, and hospitals. As Violet Large, seventy-eight and suffering from cancer, explained; "We haven't bought one thing. That's because there is nothing we need." There are some real people out there. And here on the *chemin*.

Religious leaders, one would think, would be the welcome exceptions to this rule, but not the ones I'm familiar with. Television evangelists have been exposed as greedy, corrupt men (mostly men). The Catholic Church is an old, powerful, and very wealthy patriarchy, which is not interested in giving up any of its power to women. It grew out of early Christianity, but there is little that remains in the Church of what was originally taught.

There is a reason why so many people push so hard for the separation of church and state. When they are not clearly separated, they collude to keep the masses under control and obedient to the state. The Divine Right of Kings is the concept that the right to rule derives from God and that kings (political masters) are answerable for their actions to God alone. That makes rebellion the worst of political crimes. During George W. Bush's administration, there were very sophisticated attempts to blur the lines between church and state in the United States. It's a very worrisome trend.

Two small groups of pilgrims come into this little pub, have their coffee or hot chocolate, and depart for farther down the road. My plan is to walk about seventy kilometres over the next four days, then take a rest day in Conques. After that, 100 kilometres in five days to Rocamadour and another rest day. Rocamadour is off route, but I really

---

12   Source: ***http://www.theguardian.com/business/2010/jan/21/goldman-sachs-bonus-cut***

want to see this town built into a cliff over a river. The images I have seen of it have been stunning, and friends who have been there tell me it's worth the detour.

Today is the birthday of my oldest son, Francis. Happy birthday, Francis. He practises law in Thunder Bay with his wife, Mary Bird, and they live just outside Kakabeka Falls. Both Thunder Bay and Kakabeka Falls are a little too urban for their tastes. Carroll and I visited them about six weeks ago. They were in very good spirits, since he had just gotten very good news from the neurosurgeon who operated on him for a broken neck that had gone undetected for six months, until he started having mobility problems. He was being treated for concussion, which, while present, was not the main problem. He was able to take off the collar he had been wearing for three months and resume something like a normal life, including driving and being able to see down the front of his body.

Here in Saint-Chély-d'Aubrac, it is raining lightly, continues cold . . . and that is the forecast for the next few days. I see a lot of rain pants being worn, so I think I will try mine out tomorrow.

It is just after one. I am now in the *gite*. I am told by Sylvie, who operates this warm and very clean *gite d'étape*, that it has been raining here for two weeks steadily, with more to come. The rain is heavier now. The boots have to stay outside under a wide porch awning, and I note that someone has exactly the same boots as mine; so I am glad of my little boot identifiers.[13]

I am in a room with three beds. One is occupied by a man who has walked from Lyon and intends to walk to Santiago (or, as they call it in France, Saint-Jacques). He is reclusive. I don't even find out his name. There are many people here, but he speaks to no one, joins no conversation; reads books from the plentiful supply here. The other is a German named Guido, dark, lean, talkative. I have showered, washed all my clothes, and they are drying. I asked if there was a *sechoir* (dryer) and was told there was. It turns out to be a collapsible drying rack next to a ceramic heat source. Since there are a lot of clothes hanging here, they are going to take a long time to dry — hopefully by morning. We end up with two drying racks, because everyone has lots of wet clothes from the weather.

---

13 I have put little brass-coloured beads on the bottom row of lacing of my boots. These should keep people from taking my boots by mistake.

We do not have WiFi here, although we have free use of their computer, which is online. The downside is that it has—no surprise—a French keyboard with key locations different from those I am used to. I walk downhill into the village, where there is WiFi, and use Skype to talk to—and see—my daughter Meredith, granddaughter Bella, sister-in-law Maryan, her son Paul, and his son Craig. The technology is, for me, simply staggering. I am sitting in a remote village in France, they are in a car near Toronto, and we can speak to and see each other in real time.

People keep coming in here, all very wet, so we are now about eighteen people, from France, Germany, Austria, Switzerland, Holland, Poland, Australia, and Canada. There is an animated conversation in German at the table where we wait for dinner. I join it for a while, then lose track of the drift of the conversation. I am looking forward to dinner. If the smell is any indication, it's going to be good.

And it *is* good. A puréed pea soup, followed by rice with a really good pork curry, flavourful and so much that we cannot eat it all. A cheese plate follows, then dessert—a custard with pieces of meringue on top and what tastes like maple syrup at the bottom.

One of the arrivals, a Dutchman named Henk, tells me that he and three others walked on the *chemin* in the high country around Nasbinal, and it was deadly, very dangerous, snow up to their knees, and they could see nothing but snowfields in fog. When the path finally crossed a road, they took the road all the way to here.

He also told me that there was a pilgrim, a couple of days back, a ninety-two-year-old Frenchman, carrying a twelve-kilo backpack. I guess I will never get to be the oldest walker on the path!

JOURNEY RESUMED

22 April 2012
—Saint-Chély-d'Aubrac to Saint-Côme-d'Olt

This is to be my first day of walking and a major test to see if the combination of the training that I have done over the past two months—eighteen kilometres every third day, and the medication I am taking for diabetes—will do the trick.

I have breakfast at the *gite* in Saint-Chély-d'Aubrac: hot milk and coffee in a big bowl, a little orange juice, and bread with butter and some marmalade. I am on the road by eight-thirty, dressed in long johns, marino wool undershirt, shirt (courtesy of Ed Zenowski), pants, fleece, rain jacket, and hat. My pack has its rain jacket on as well. It is not raining as I leave, but starts within a few minutes, not heavy, but cold. I am expecting this section to be pretty easy, about nineteen kilometres and a drop of 600 metres, but I am quickly disabused of this expectation. The walk out of Saint-Chély-d'Aubrac is uphill, perhaps 200 metres of vertical, and then it switches between uphill and long downhills all the way to Saint-Côme-d'Olt. To add to the fun, it's been raining for the past two weeks, so the path has, as often as not, a fast stream running in the track.

There are a lot of people on the path, almost always someone in sight before or behind. Since the way-finding is very well marked, this

The "pilgrim's bridge" in Saint-Chély-d'Aubrac.

is just a little extra reassurance that I am going the right way. On one of the uphill sections, I am taking tiny steps, trying to keep out of the water (we can't keep out of the mud) and just sucking for air. This is one of the times when I don't look up to see how far it is to the top. It would just be discouraging. The track always turns to one side or the other at the top of each climb, so I don't get to see just how far I have still to go. This is a good thing.

Within an hour, I have my fleece off and stowed, and within another hour, I have the rain jacket off, since I am sweating with the effort of climbing and descending. The good news about last year's medical tests is that the heart is strong. Of course, eventually I have to put the rain jacket back on, since the rain returns.

At one low point on the trail, I cross a bridge over a fast, full, mountain stream. The bridge is about two metres wide, about ten metres above the water, and is just the trail with some grass on either side. Karsten (you will remember Karsten from Berlin, who walked with me in Spain in 2007 and again from Le Puy last year), who does not like heights, would not be impressed by this bridge.

Where the land opens up, the vistas are breathtaking, pastoral, rolling country, little villages each with its inevitable church spire. I can hear birds, rushing water (often under my feet), the wind, and the sound of my own footsteps (often the squelch of my own footsteps). What I cannot hear is the sound of traffic. When I am on a paved country road, there is no traffic. Except once: on one road, a four-wheel ATV followed by a motorcycle roar by, both the vehicles and their riders covered in mud. They are in the mud voluntarily!

At one point about halfway through the walk, I turn a corner by a small building to find a group of pilgrims standing there. The explanation is soon obvious. A local farmer and entrepreneur and supporter of pilgrims has built a shelter and put out a table of coffee and tea with powdered milk and a small box asking for one Euro donation for a cup. It's a donation we gladly make. It lifts my spirits, and, I am sure, those of my fellow pilgrims. Some of these pilgrims were my fellow guests in Saint-Chély-d'Aubrac last night.

On arrival in Saint-Côme-d'Olt, I cannot find the *gite* that I seek. I had had Sylvie, the host in Saint-Chély-d'Aubrac, call ahead and make a reservation for me. I see four young people, locals, and ask them where it is. But I start by saying, in French; "*J'ai un question. Je suis Canadien Anglais.*" One of the pert young things—and she is pert—responds with a huge grin: "*Et je suis Française Française!*" Big laugh all around, and I have the perfect retort, but while I am trying desperately to translate the past tense of "I have" as in "I had gathered that," the moment passes. My language skills fail me just when I need them most.

And I learn an important lesson. Well, important for me. I do not have to explain where I come from when I speak a foreign language. The audience will figure out soon enough that I am not local and, if they care, will ask where I come from. And I will then, only then, tell them that I am Canadian; and only if they really care, *Canadien Anglais*.

She is certain I understand the directions: walk back 500 metres, turn left, and there it is, a private home. But it is closed. It says "Open," but the door is locked. I sit in the garden under an overhang (since it has started to rain hard) for about an hour until the door opens, and I am welcomed in. This is not like any *gite* that I have ever been in. It is the second floor of a very nice private home. There are only five places . . . and I am the only guest. This gets me a double bed, a light over the bed, kitchen facilities, but no food.

I wash out my smalls and my detachable pant legs, which are mud to the knees, and then sleep for about ninety minutes. It feels great.

Today is election day in France. They are voting for president. It's an interesting and effective way to conduct this exercise. There are ten candidates from extreme left through the centre to extreme right. After today's results, the two with the highest counts will have runoff election in two weeks. This way, they guarantee a majority result. Sarkozy, right of centre, is expected to be one of the two. Hollande, left of centre, is another probability. Local opinion is for Hollande. We shall see what happens. (Hollande does eventually win.)

And since it is Sunday in France, I discover that the recommended restaurant is not open for business—but they do let me use their wireless connection, so I talk with Carroll and my daughter Meredith, who are in Brooklin (near Whitby, Ontario) celebrating our granddaughter Bella's third birthday and our nephew's daughter Kaitlyn's first communion, for which Carroll created the dress.

There are two other pilgrims sitting here as well, and one of them, Aurele, tall, blonde, legs that go on forever, about forty, from Paris, suggests that I ask where they are staying and see if I can have dinner there. I do and I can. I am just about to head there for dinner.

I eat dinner with just four other people, Aurele and her companion, Jean-Louis, Eileen from England, and her boyfriend, Nicolas, from France. Jean-Louis speaks little English, so we converse mostly in French. They are all walking the *chemin*, although Eileen has only two weeks of holidays, so she will walk as far as she can in that short period.

Dinner, cooked and served by Antoine, is excellent. Before I tell you about it, I learned some new French usage. Today is Bella's birthday, so I told him about this and that she was three today. I used the term *"jour de naissance"* and added that she is three today. He looked confused, then brightened and corrected me, since in French, *"un jour de naissance,"* is only the day that you are born. All other birthdays are *"anniversaire de naissance,"* which actually makes more sense, if you think about it.

So, to dinner. Five courses: carrot soup, a purée with tiny bits of carrot, a slice of pâté, a main course of sausage with tomatoes and onions mixed, plus green beans (green veggies at last!), a cheese plate, and crème brûlée. It is all excellent and all this for 15 €, plus 1.5€ for a quarter litre of red wine. What a bargain! After dinner, we discuss tomorrow.

Apparently the *chemin* from here to Estaing goes scenically up and over the hills, likely lots of mud, while the road goes directly and follows the river. The river road option is highly recommended. I will decide in the morning, although the river option is looking better by the moment.

It is raining as I walk back to my *gite*, so I get a little wet in my fleece and sandals. But they will be dry by morning. I have passed today's test. Let's see what tomorrow will bring.

23 April—Saint-Côme-d'Olt to Estaing

I sleep a long time in my grand suite and wake up with the light—not the sun—coming in through the window. Outside, it is grey and raining lightly. Oh, well. I have good rain gear, and it is getting a great test.

At eight a.m., there is a knock on the door, and M. Roue, my host, brings in a tray of breakfast. So not only do I have this whole floor to myself, I get room service, including two kinds of homemade jam and *gateau maison*, a sweet bread made by Mme. Roue. All this for 18 €.

By the time I leave at nine-fifteen, the clouds have broken up, and there is sun peeking through with lots of blue sky showing. It looks very promising for the day. I very soon have to take off my fleece. But it is a cruel trick. Within the hour, the skies have clouded over and then the eventual rain starts, lightly at first and then more steadily. I have decided to walk the highway option, just north of the River Lot, rather than the GR 65 option. I can see the hills immediately south of the river, and they look severe. They are heavily wooded and come right down to the water's edge. The river is about twenty metres across and is fast water, but it is not over the banks. Just wait until all that snow at Nasbinal melts!

Where I am, on the north side of the river, just above the floodplain in a narrow valley, it is flat, with sparse traffic; the sides of the highway are flat crushed stone, so walking is easy. When traffic does come along, I step as far as I can to the left, usually into the tall grass and sometimes just stop and wait for the vehicle to pass. Just to my right, across the highway, the hills climb in terraces to the summit. This south-facing slope is wine country, which is confirmed when I pass the Maison de la Vigne du Vin et des Paysages d'Estaing, which is a winery but is, unfortunately, closed.

I arrive by twelve-thirty; I made very good time: just over three hours for nineteen kilometres—much, much better than yesterday—five hours for 16.5 kilometres.

Estaing is officially one of the prettiest villages in France. Unofficially, at the moment it is one of the wettest and coldest—and most closed. This is a very photogenic town. There is a four-arch bridge over the River Lot, which is about thirty-five metres wide as it winds through the town. I stand on it and get some, I think, good shots of the very old skyline here, including the Chateau d'Estaing.

During the American Revolutionary War, the Count d'Estaing was an admiral in the French navy who assisted the American navy with a couple of unsuccessful naval sieges at Newport, Rhode Island, and at Savannah, Georgia. When he was guillotined during the Terror in the early 1790s, the line died with him. A former French president, Valery Giscard d'Estaing, purchased the Chateau in 2005 with his brother. You might think that they are related to the former family, but you would be wrong. The Giscard family bought the rights to the Estaing name in 1920 and became Giscard-Estaing instead of just plain old Giscard.

The chateau at Estaing.

The bridge is just wide enough for one vehicle, so when a truck goes over it, I have to stand in a small, triangular lay-by, obviously built for pedestrians caught as I am by a vehicle. Clearly, when it was built, the vehicles were horse- or man-drawn.

And, of course, since we are in France, practically everything is closed, either for lunch or for the day. One restaurant is open, where I meet the Aussies, as well as Henk and a couple of others from two days ago. Soon after I arrive, they all head for Golhinac and points west, so I likely will not meet them again.

I order a substantial meal for lunch, which is a good thing, since I discover that virtually everything will be closed this evening, including this restaurant. While I am eating, Aurele and Jean-Louis arrive and join me at my table. They are mud to the knees, which is funny, since it was Aurele who suggested the road as an alternative to the trail.

We go to a small *tabac*, where the lady signs us in for the communal *gite* and gives us keys, warning us to keep the door locked at all times. The *gite* is 300 metres up the road in an old church building. It is a single dormitory of twenty beds, but every two beds are in a small, separate cubicle with a curtain door, so there is the illusion of privacy—not auditory, but visual. We have to be out by nine a.m.

Eileen and Nicolas have arrived at the *gite* as well, so it is turning into old home week. Several of us walk back into town, in a non-rainy moment (which doesn't last), and the nice lady from the *tabac* has called one of her friends, who has opened up her food store so that we can purchase the makings for dinner and breakfast. I also get my credential stamped at the *tabac*.

Several other people have arrived at the *gite*, so we are about ten people. One of them is Sylvie Charette, probably in her thirties, from the south shore of Montreal. She started in Le Puy and is going to see how far she can get in forty-five days. There is a pair of young Germans, sisters: Patricia, dark, and Victoria, blonde, both small and pretty, whom I will not see again for about a month and then will see them almost daily.

I watch Aurele standing at a window in the *gite* and I see that she is very highly stressed. Something is eating her up. I wish that I could help, but that option is not open at the moment.

And here is a factoid that Marina will just love. Jean-Louis whistles the theme song from *The Wizard of Oz* when he is doing something. Takes me back to my walk in Spain on the *camino* to Santiago with my young Germans.

24 April—Estaing to Campuac

It is my plan today to walk to Golhinac, but today is a day full of surprises. There is no surprise that it is still cold and raining. It was cold and raining when I went to bed and I slept fitfully with two blankets. I was, however, alone in my little cubicle for two, so I could spread out my gear on the other bed. In the morning, I eat some yogurt and a banana that I bought yesterday and share some tea that Aurele and Jean-Louis have made.

I gear up, wearing my fleece, my rain jacket, and my rain pants—yes, it is raining that hard—and off I go across the River Lot on the huge four-arch bridge and start to follow the signage. There is an immediate hard left turn followed by the climb. The first unwelcome surprise is that the *chemin* out of Estaing is a long, steep climb in the woods. I would guess at least 300 metres vertical. I have to stop at least ten times to catch my breath on the way up, in the rain and the cold. There has been so much rain that the path, one person wide, is a busy stream, running downhill past me as I wade through it. After I have finally reached the top of this very steep, wet, long climb in the woods, there is, happily, a T-junction on a paved road, and I follow the signs to the right, the red over white rectangle marking for a GR (Grande Randonée). Perhaps half an hour later, I catch up to a family of four: two adults, Daniel and Arlette, and two children, Victor and Cassandre, who turn out to be a couple from Paris with two of their grandchildren.

The next, and much more unwelcome, surprise is that I am not going where I think I am going. As we walk, Daniel asks me where I am headed today, and I tell him "Golinhac." He stops dead and says, "But this is not the way to Golinhac. We are heading for Campuac." It turns out that I am on GR 6, not GR 65, miles out of my way, and I have no idea where I went wrong. I did not realize that there was an option for GRs. (It turns out that my error was immediately after crossing the bridge in Estaing.[14]) And since it is pissing down cold rain, this is not a good time to pull out my guidebook and see. Later I discover that I am actually off my map completely. As I stand there dumbfounded, he asks me what I will do. I tell him that I will go on, then see what I can figure out to get to where I intend to be. I don't want to walk down that long climb out of d'Estaing then have to climb out on another trail. After a few minutes of walking together, he asks if I have booked a bed in Golinhac. I tell him that I have not. He then suggests that I walk with them as far as Campuac, which I agree to do. What else am I going to do? I am effectively lost in this wet cold hilly wilderness.

Cassandre walks with me. I have told them that I am Canadian, and she, Cassandre Fouques Duparc, wants to practise her English and, like most kids, is not shy about another language. She is actually very good. (Her mother is a translator.) She tells me that she is eleven, and the boy, who is her cousin Victor Vasseur, and taller, is ten.

At one point, we come across a little hamlet where there is a man doing something rural in an open shed by the road, and Daniel stops to talk with him. It isn't raining at the moment. The discussion is friendly and animated and has to do somehow with Daniel knowing someone or is related to someone here and it all ends up with us being invited into Jean Radalié's "cave," his wine cellar, which is at road level and where we are invited to have a little wine for the road. It's only just past eleven here, but the sun is over the yardarm *somewhere*. Arlette has a rosé, Daniel and Jean and I have some red wine from a barrel marked 18–4–12, which means the wine is six days old. And it is just fine. At this point, Daniel asks me if I would like to stay where they are staying overnight, at the *gite* of a friend in Campuac. Yes, I would—these are kind and friendly folk—so he calls and makes the arrangement. We are so appreciative of Jean's winemaking efforts that he offers a little taste of a fortified wine, Apéritif Ratafia, which he has made. This is also just fine, and just what we need as the skies open up

---

14 This is exactly the same mistake, even the same routes, GR 6 and GR 65, that I made a year ago in a village with Francine.

again and off we go. Just before we leave, a whole herd of cows walks by us on the road. The kids are delighted.

Yesterday, I noticed, walking into Estaing, that the sign was bilingual, French and—I am guessing here—langue d'Oc. I seize the moment here and ask Jean if he speaks langue d'Oc. He laughs and tells me, in French, "Yes, but you won't understand a word." Then he launches into the ancient local language and he's right. None of us understands a word. But I find it fascinating that an old local language is still being spoken here. It turns out the local language is called "Occitan."

An obstacle on the chemin.

The path veers off the road after a few minutes, and we descend in another steep brook to where it joins a larger, muddy stream about fifteen feet wide, which is surging over the path; there is no way to avoid walking through it. Daniel tries to walk over the place where the slope drops rapidly away, but it does not look safe and if he slips he will be fifty feet downstream and way downhill. About ten feet above that, it's fast but flat, so I test with my poles, discover that it is less than a foot deep, and walk smartly across. I figure less time in the water is less water in the boots. And it works pretty well. My boots and lower pants are soaked but my feet feel dry. (It's an illusion, which I will discover later when I take my boots off.)

After another arduous climb, we stop for something to eat in a farmyard. The path here, just as in Spain, goes through people's property. It has stopped raining for a few minutes. We sit on a low stone wall and share what we have: some bread, sausage, cheese. It's not much but it hits the spot. Again, the trail descends into a ravine with rushing water at the bottom, but it is narrow enough for us to jump it. Of course, the descent is followed immediately by another hard ascent. I am getting tired of this . . . and I am getting tired. At last we see a sign for Campuac, and Cassandre shouts out, "We are here!" Well, it turns out that we ARE in Campuac, where the only bar is closed and for sale, and the friend's *gite* is about two kilometres the other side, out in the country. So we walk and walk . . . and walk in the steady rain.

Just before we arrive here, we meet with two pilgrims, brothers, Pierre and Jacques Vuillet, who Daniel tells me are friends of theirs. They are coming to the same *gite*, where they will meet their older brother, Guy, who is bringing all three wives by car to meet the pilgrim pair. They started from their home, just this side of the Swiss border across from Geneva, and intend to walk to Santiago.

At one point, the rain turns to hail. As if it hasn't been miserable enough! At least the path is mostly level and all paved, but I sure am glad when we turn right into a long country lane. It is the Gite d'Etape du Barthas, a farm complex, and Emilienne, known as Mimi, the gracious and tiny host, makes me feel like part of the extended family. As soon as we arrive, we are offered hot drinks to warm us up. I have a tiny room of my own. It is Victor, the ten-year-old, who stamps my pilgrim passport.

Cassandre has borrowed my book and after reading about forty pages (her mother is a translator), with a very serious voice pronounces it "super." In French, it sounds like "soo pair," with the accent on the "pair." This good review from a French eleven-year-old warms the cockles of my heart. At dinner, I promise them that

Victor and me and Cassandre.

I will send three copies: one for Cassandre, one for Victor, and one for Daniel and Arlette.

It is sunny for a little bit, then back to rain . . . and always cold. I see a newspaper headline that reads, "The Weather Makes a Mockery of Springtime." I would agree.

I tell Mimi and Daniel that I feel very lucky that I got lost today and ended up here with this family. Daniel tells me that it is Saint Jacques who got me lost today. I can scarcely argue.

We have an excellent dinner, starting with an aperitif, then quiche and salad, sausage with baby peas and carrots, cheese plate, crème brûlée, all accompanied by red wine. After dinner, people want to take photos. Mimi, the *hospitalière*, stands next to me (standing, she is about three inches taller than me when I'm sitting) and holds my hand. I love it. It is like being an honoured member of the family—such love.

Mimi and me at Campuac.

While I am here, I think about the unintended consequence of my error this morning. I am here in this loving family environment with people who actually care about me, even though they don't know me. Then I think about unintended consequences in general.

Many decisions made with the best intentions in mind end up with horrifying consequences. I think about a couple of examples, one from history and one from the present day. The historical event had to do with the slave trade from Africa to North and South America. Abolitionists in England—with whose intentions I entirely agree—had for a very long time tried to get Parliament to outlaw the transatlantic trade in humans. Finally, in 1807, they succeeded in their quest, and the government of the day charged the Royal Navy with enforcing the ban on ships flying the Union Jack. But the impact was not what they expected. The intended consequence was that slave ship owners and captains would turn to other cargo for their profit.

But some, more greedy and more daring, and certainly more ruthless and immoral (or amoral), continued the hugely profitable trade. If a slaver was in serious danger of being overtaken and boarded by the crew of a Royal Navy ship, the draconian solution was to bring all of the slaves up on deck, chained together, and throw them, every man, woman, and child still living, into the trackless ocean. When the slaver was boarded, there was no live evidence that they were carrying slaves, even though it was perfectly clear that slaves had been in the holds very recently. No evidence equalled no charges and no conviction. It was not until slavery itself was outlawed in North and South America and the Caribbean that the trade withered and died. This was the unintended consequence of a well-meaning law. Oh, and what happened to the slave ships? The British ones ended up anchored in the Thames and used as floating prisons before transporting their live cargo off to populate Australia.

More dangerous and more recent is the development of laws, usually during a perceived or real crisis, that end up curtailing the rights of individuals. Since 9–11, with the downing of the World Trade Center Towers, national governments in Canada, the United States, and Britain have passed laws that are intended to help prevent terrorist activities. These laws have been used for that purpose but they have also been used to limit the rights of individuals who have nothing to do with terrorism and in fact aren't criminals in any sense of the word. Passed with the best of intentions, the anti-terrorism laws cast a very wide net, and the police, also with the best of intentions, are happy to use any tool at their disposal to make their job easier. Every individual freedom has been hard-won and it is alarming when I see these freedoms being eroded as an unintended consequence of the laws against terrorism.

A more current example has to do with the banning of hand-held devices for talking or texting while driving. We already know that a driver is four times as likely to be involved in an accident if he or she is distracted by a cell phone or similar device. We also know from the research that it is the mental distraction, not the physical one, which leads to the increase in accidents. The lawmakers—at least in Ontario, where I live—have decided that the solution is to ban the use of these handheld devices while driving. Using them hands-free is still legal.

The impact? Most drivers will comply with this seemingly reasonable demand. Some drivers, however, will choose to continue to use the device illegally but hold it below the window line of the vehicle so that it cannot be seen from outside. Before the ban, drivers would hold their device up in front of them so that they could see the road while they were punching numbers. Now they will do the same thing while looking down and away from the road in front of them. My prediction is that they will be involved in more, and more serious, accidents than before the ban.

So what? I hear you say. It is called the Law of Unintended Consequences and it is invoked all the time. Now, it isn't always bad. As an individual, it just makes sense to *think through* the likely consequences of a decision before making it. When someone does this for a lifetime, it is called wisdom.

But when governments and organizations make decisions that affect many people or the environment, it is morally imperative that the potential outcomes be examined to identify all potential, unintended consequences. A "sunset clause" is always a good idea when enacting legislation for a problem that was previously not recognized. This clause allows the law to expire automatically after an agreed number of years after enactment, if it isn't deliberately renewed. That way, if the unintended consequence turns out badly, the law can just die a natural death or be amended to fit the new understanding of what works. The expression, "It seemed like a good idea at the time," doesn't seem to cut it. But my unintended consequence today has brought me new friends, both young and old. I like it.

I go to bed, warm, dry, and full of good food and red wine, hopeful that my clothes and my boots will be dry in the morning. It is raining and blowing as I go to sleep.

25 April—Campuac to Sénergues

There is a fierce, cold wind this morning, but at least it isn't raining. My boots, which I thought would be dry this morning, are not. I bring them into the kitchen area and prop them near the stove, where everyone else's boots have been all night and are now toasty dry and warm. Daniel asks me if I would like to go with them today. They are heading toward Conques, but plan to do it in two easy stages, thirteen kilometres today and nine kilometres tomorrow, which will give them . . . and me . . . most of the day tomorrow in Conques for sightseeing. It will also put me back on the GR 65.

We have a French country breakfast—coffee with hot milk, orange juice, baguettes with butter, and a variety of homemade jams. Mimi is a resourceful cook, as well as a superb host. When we leave, I hold her face in my hands and tell her how lucky I am to have gotten lost yesterday and to have been brought here to meet her and share her hospitality. We do the mandatory three kisses and off we go.

The "we" is a larger group than I expect. It includes not only

The chemin *winding through a wood.*

Daniel and Arlette and the two kids, but also the three brothers and their wives, so there are eleven of us. The path today is much easier than yesterday's (it would be hard-put to be more difficult), not so steep and mostly on small country lanes with perhaps two cars every hour. The call of *"voiture, voiture"* rings out, and everyone crowds the side of the road. Interestingly, almost all the pilgrims walk on the right side, not the left. Perhaps it's because the road is really only one car wide, so they stay on the side nearest the driver.

The wind diminishes and it gets warm. Off with the fleece; and, later, off with the rain jacket.

Sometimes the group is small and dense, but more often we break up into smaller groups, either chatting or just walking together. I learn that the two brothers will walk on, while Guy, the oldest brother, along with the three sisters-in-law, will walk to Conques, visit there for a day, then Guy will get a ride back to Campuac to pick up his car and return for the ladies.

When we go off the road, it is usually a path down the side of a ravine to the brook below (although these brooks are dangerous, they are so full and fast) then across on a footbridge and inevitably up the other side of the ravine. I had rather naively expected that after we came down off the Massif Central, the way would be fairly flat. Wrong.

I have been told about the Appalachian Trail in the U.S. that there was never a hill that the folks who laid it out would go around rather than over, and that certainly holds true here. The GR 65 seems to go over every hill that it can find, which means that there are a lot of stunning vistas, accompanied by a lot of equally stunning climbs and descents.

Here is one explanation: this pilgrim path from Le Puy was lost for hundreds of years. In the 1970s, when the *camino* started to become popular, the folks in France, bless their hearts, decided to simply declare that an existing hiking trail, the GR 65, was the Chemin de Saint-Jacques. But while the pilgrims look for the most available direct route, hikers, with different motivations, want to get exercise and see the sights, so their path goes over everything and avoids villages, to boot. So we get to take the most scenic, circuitous route possible. I do not have any qualms about taking the road if I can see that I will end up in the same place. I enjoy the scenic views as much as anyone, but not at the expense of my legs and lungs.

My concern last year about the condition of my heart has been put to rest. If anything were going to bring on a cardiac crisis, these hills would do it. I have learned to take much shorter, slower steps and to stop for a rest whenever my breathing gets too fast and deep, say one deep suck of air with every step. At the same time, I can hear Cassandre singing — SINGING! — as I plod wearily up the slopes. Oh, for just a little of her energy . . .

As we pass one old homestead, I discover the origin of the roofline so familiar in Quebec: the steep roof and the shallow part near the eaves, used to let the snow slide off the roof and be thrown clear of the walls of the home. It's the same here, but with stone tiles rather than the red metal so often seen in Quebec. This homestead has "1791" carved over the doorway, and near it, on the same piece of wall, there is an old arch, the entry into a farmyard. The keystone has "1316" carved into it, barely visible, it is so worn by age.

Think about it. That's almost 700 years ago, or more than thirty-five generations ago. To write that, one needs scientific notation (grandparents x 35). At about noon, we stop for lunch. This is the first place that we have seen for food since we left this morning. In this aspect, the *chemin* is very unlike the *camino* in Spain, where there were frequent places to stop for sustenance. Not so much here.

We have only about three kilometres to go, but there is consensus for lunch. In addition, I am flying blind. I don't know where I am going but I do know that Daniel has called ahead and reserved a bed for me, so I am sticking with him. Lunch is a generous slice of hot, cooked ham in a tasty sauce, pasta, bread, and wine on the side — all for ten Euros.

We finally get under way again. The fleece goes back on, since it has gotten colder. Only three kilometres on, and we arrive at the *gite* Domaine de Sénos in Sénergues.

As we are walking this morning, one of the brothers' wives gives me a little lesson in pronunciation. I probably learned this in French class but, if so, I have forgotten. At the end of a word such as Sénergues, the "u" is not pronounced but it has an impact on how the "g" is pronounced. Without the "u," the "g" is soft (as in the second "g" in garage), so Sénerges would be pronounced "Saynergh." With the "u," the "g" is hard, so Sénergues is pronounced "Saynerg." There may be a test later.

I am installed in a room with four beds, by myself for the moment. My benefactors are next door. My room has a spectacular view. The room quickly fills with three men: two Frenchmen, and a Flemish-speaking Belgian from Antwerp, from where he has walked for the past seven weeks. He plans to go to Santiago, another nine weeks, for a total of four months on the road. I feel like a piker with my planned 750 kilometres.

The *gite* is full, and now people arriving are told they have to go on to Conques, about nine kilometres farther. I am seeing that there are a lot of walkers on this section of the *chemin*, and having a daily reservation is a really good idea. Daniel has already told me that they have a reservation at the monastery in Conques and asks would I like to join them. They are very companionable and kind, and the kids are fun; so, "Yes I would." He will see what he can do about that. I am not actually concerned about getting a bed in Conques. If the *gites* are full, there are always hotels, and one only has to pay enough to get a room. (This turns out to be quite naïve. Many of the villages are tiny and have little accommodation.) He manages to reserve me a bed before we go to dinner.

Dinner is, of course, excellent. A vegetable soup followed by a type of thick hamburger patty on a huge bed of lettuce. I discover that this is the appetizer! A dinner of sausage, baked potato, and baked tomato follows, ending up with a soft, rich custard in a tall glass. Good thing I am walking or I would be gaining weight every day.

As I go to bed, the wind is howling outside, and our hosts tell us that the forecast is for rain tomorrow. We shall see. Everything I have is now dry, so I can brave the elements.

26 April—Sénergues to Conques

The wind howls most of the night, which is quite alarming, but it drops off about dawn to absolutely calm, and, I discover when I stick my head out of the door, it is quite mild for a change . . . and it is not raining! I also discover that my boots, which stayed in my room last night rather than near the heat source, are still very wet. I stuff them with newspaper and put them near the stove, which helps dry them sufficiently so that I can wear them today. We, the family Borzakian and I, eat our breakfast in the well-equipped dining room and are off at nine a.m., which incidentally is when we are required to leave the *gîte*. The timing for leaving and arriving is much more civilized in France than in Spain, since it is normal here to reserve one's bed a day or two in advance, so no need for early departure. We leave Sénergues and immediately embark on the usual steep climb out of the valley. Before I am halfway up, I have both my fleece and my rain jacket off and I am sweating, perspiration dripping off my face. Cassandre, the bright, chatty eleven-year-old, is singing as we climb. I may have to strangle her. (Just kidding, Cassandre! The last thing I would do is silence your cheeriness.)

It is overcast, but not raining, and the rain keeps off all the way to Conques. The path is often on quiet, mostly flat, winding roads; but as we approach Conques, we veer off the road and descend just under 300 metres in a very steep and slippery descent on a narrow trail in dense woods. It is quite dangerous because the rocks are slippery and I have to place every foot carefully before I put weight on it. It is slow and treacherous, and I have a very firm grip on my poles, planting them in front of me as I descend. We eventually reach almost the bottom of the gorge of the Dourdou River and come into Conques and the 950-year-old Abbaye de Sainte-Foy.

This is where I notice that my ring finger on my left hand is numb, and when I look at it, more than half the finger, down almost to the second knuckle, is discoloured—a cyanotic blue. It takes about an hour before the sensation and colour come back, which is a relief. I was really holding on tightly. And now I know where the term "cyan" comes from.

This extraordinary village is old, old, old and is built into the steep side of the gorge. It is also a huge tourist attraction, and it is easy to see why. It is so vertical, that it makes me think that I am in an Escher drawing. I can see where I want to go, but I have to figure out how to get there, up or down several levels of stone steps. The only level place in town is the small square immediately in front of the abbey. Inside the abbey are huge columns and a dome high overhead. It is almost unadorned, natural grey stone walls, columns, and floor, and wooden pews.

We eat lunch in a restaurant above the abbey and it is, as always so far in France, excellent. They take their culinary arts very seriously here. The French are proud of French cuisine and have every right to be. I pay my share of the bill then head off to the bank machine, since I am down to loose change. To my horror, the machine is not working at the moment. It tells me it is *désolé*, but not as *désolé* as I am. I have no cash and it is the only machine in town. An hour later, it is working again, so I am able to get some Euros.

The abbey is huge and the *gite* is physically part of it. I am sleeping in *Dortoir* 1, on a lower bunk. Daniel has called ahead and made sure that they give me a lower bunk. I don't know exactly what he told them, but I am treated with great care when I arrive. One of the good things they do here is to provide each pilgrim

Shelves of pilgrims' footwear.

with a large, clear plastic bag into which they spray anti-bedbug stuff, then drop your backpack into it. The backpack stays in the plastic bag, so bedbugs don't stand a chance here. I have noticed this same type of care generally in the *gites*. They are very aware of the bedbug problem and do everything they can to keep the bugs under control. For example, there is an iron-clad rule everywhere: no backpacks on the beds.

They can handle 100 pilgrims here and, to my relief, are able to take Visa to pay my accommodation and dinner, which total twenty-seven Euros. I decide to stay over for another day and am able to keep my bed.

In the street in Conques, I meet a *hospitalière*, Penelope, from Vancouver. The way the people here say her name, it rhymes with

Street scene in Conques.

antelope. She has given up correcting them. She says it is usually quite busy here. There are six volunteers to handle all the pilgrims, although they have cooking and cleaning staff to do some of the labour. I find out later that three of the six volunteers are Canadian: Penelope and two women from Quebec, all cheerful and happy. They work very hard for the two weeks or so that they are here. They tell me that there are lots of Canadian pilgrims, almost all from Quebec.

The family with whom I have been walking the past few days, Daniel and Arlette, the folks who rescued me on the GR 6, will not be going on. The Easter school break is finished, and the two children, Cassandre and Victor, have to go back to school in Paris. I have two Ziplights with me, attached to zippers on my jackets and, since I also have a headlamp for those dark nights in the *gite*, I remove the Ziplights from my zipper pulls and give one to each of the children. I tell them that each time they turn them on, they can remember me. They are properly delighted. Cassandre switches hers on and off repeatedly, just to be sure it works as advertised.

At dinner we sit in a crowded, noisy, happy, dining room with about 100 people. I think that the *gite* must be full. Dinner starts with tabouli on a bed of lettuce, followed by an excellent ratatouille of eggplant, tomatoes, and ground beef. Of course, there is lots of bread, water, and red wine. With us sits a family of six from Paris, the young mother and father, Anaïs Damame de Prunelé and Pierre-Alexandre Damame, their three children, Gaspard, four and a half, Aurèle, three, and Maxime, eleven months; and their grandmother Danièle, Pierre's mother. I may not be the oldest pilgrim—I am hearing about a man a day or so behind us who is eighty-two years old—but I believe that Maxime is definitely the youngest. I do not know whether this is the guy reported as ninety-two, or another older pilgrim.

So I am sitting with five adults and five children from eleven months to eleven years. I think that they cannot possibly be walking the *chemin*, but they are. The baby girl, Maxime, travels in a backpack carrier on either father's or mother's back, depending on who is less tired. But how do the little boys manage?

The secret is Cadichon, a rent-a-donkey. They started about forty kilometres back from here and will continue on another twenty kilometres before they say goodbye to Cadichon and return home. I ask how they managed the steep, difficult descent into Conques. Anaïs tells me that Cadichon is very sure-footed, although slow. She tells me that they have to do short stages because the donkey is old and slow. Each night, they have to find a place that can look after them and stable the donkey. Both parents look a little worn, and no wonder. This is a major enterprise every day, but they all seem very happy. The boys are happy, active, rambunctious. The older one has walked almost the entire way, the younger rides on the donkey when he tires.

I am reminded again of Robert Louis Stevenson's book, *Travels with a Donkey*, which he wrote as he travelled for almost two weeks south from near Le Puy-en-Velay about 150 years ago. He had better weather than we are experiencing at the moment. He also noted the slow speed of his donkey, who was named, if I remember correctly, Modestine. Over the two weeks, he became very fond of her. If I were a donkey, I wouldn't be in a hurry, either.

There is a pilgrim service in the abbey after dinner, and I am asked if I will read a short benediction in English as part of the service. I inform the person asking that I am not religious, but I am told that's not a problem as long as I don't object to doing it. Actually, I feel very honoured to be invited to speak, even for a few moments, in this 750-year-old abbey. The short service is in French, with four Benedictine brothers singing in Gregorian chant. Perhaps sixty people are seated in the cold, damp abbey, all with our fleeces on. Three of us, French, German, and English, go up to the lectern and read our benedictions. I find out later that I am the only native English-speaker here, so I am preaching to a very small choir. (It may also be why I was asked to read the benediction.)

One of the brothers blesses the pilgrims who will be leaving in the morning. He asks if there are any English — there are none, which is how I know that I am the only native English-speaking person.

Other people come forward, in French, Flemish (there are three), and German. He gives each one a small card with a pilgrim's blessing on it. It seems to me that the pilgrims here are more often walking for religious reasons than those I met on the *camino* in Spain. When I think about how far some of these people have walked or plan to walk, it's not a surprise.

It's off to bed at about nine-thirty.

27–28 April — Conques to Descazeville

I am staying a full day in Conques. It is very small but such a fascinating place that I decided on a rest day here. I wander around the little town, up and down the narrow roads. I stumble upon a store where the young, very tall and dark owner, Nicolas, makes beads and jewellery from stones of every type. I buy a tiny pendant in the shape of a scallop shell — what else? — and he arranges to send it home to Canada for me. He spends six months out of the year here, and the other six months exploring the world and picking up strange and beautiful stones of every type.

In the afternoon, two young women arrive: Fanny from Switzerland, and Joemie from Quebec. I met them in Aumont-Aubrac at La Ferme du Barry a few days ago. We sit outside a charming little café, have a coffee together, and get into a discussion about relationships. I tell them about my marriage and its longevity. They are in their twenties and are very concerned about serious long-term relationships with men. They both know people who have been very badly hurt in their

Roofline in Conques.

relationships and don't want to go there. I suggest to them that one key indicator is mutual respect. Of course, in any long relationship there will be times when the relationship is strained, but there should never be a loss of respect for the other person.

At breakfast this morning, 28 April, I discover that a sixty-nine-year-old pilgrim, a man from Marseilles, has died in the *gite* overnight. It is not announced, and most people remain unaware. I am told that he had been acting extremely stressed for the past few days and I wonder if it was the stress that brought on the cardiac crisis or whether his stress was the result of not feeling "right" and not being able to account for it. I will never know anything more about him except the time and place of his death. *Memento mori*.

I also discover that perhaps only half of the people who arrive here continue on the *chemin*. Apparently the ten-day walk from Le Puy to Conques is extremely popular, and Conques is certainly a destination by itself. That makes me feel quite confident about accommodation for the next few days. I am about to be disabused of this confidence.

I pay five Euros for a picnic lunch and off I go. It is sunny and quite warm, although the

In Conques—memento mori.

weather forecast is for rain. I have packed my fleece, my long johns and my rain gear, so I am wearing my usual: pants, shirt, undershirt, hat, etc. The exit from Conques is steeply downward to the Roman bridge over the narrow river Dourdou, then a savage climb for the next kilometre. I climb 267 metres in a dense woods on a narrow switchback trail of over a kilometre. That's a 27 percent grade and, to give you an idea of the height, it is the equivalent of climbing stairs for about ninety storeys. This is something I am not planning on doing every day! I take a lot of oxygen breaks on the way and I finally reach the top. This is the section that is described in one of the English sites I found on the Internet as ". . . *bit of an uphill hike leaving Conques* . . ." A bit of British understatement!

Climbing out of Conques.

It occurs to me that if I had continued last year, this section would have really frightened me, because of the evident risk of incurring a cardiac crisis like the one that (probably) carried off the pilgrim in Conques last night. I am really happy that I went home and got reassurance from the medical community that there that is nothing wrong with my cardiovascular system. What IS wrong with me — diabetes — I can manage.

I come out into a highland pastoral scene, cattle in the fields and extraordinary vistas. The trail is wide, crushed stone, and feels like a reward for making it to the top of the gorge. It clouds over in the next hour, and the wind comes up, but the rain holds off.

I catch up to an older pilgrim talking to a local woman on an open section of the trail. She has a plant in a wheelbarrow, but is in no hurry to plant it. I stop to chat. When she, Sylvie, discovers that I am Canadian, I get a sharp lecture on the evils of the seal hunt and the whale hunt. I explain to her that we do not have a commercial whale hunt and the only people in Canada who hunt whales are the Inuit of the far North, who hunt them only for food. I am not sure that she is convinced, but we part friends.

The man with whom she was speaking was the eighty-two-year-old (not ninety-two as earlier reported) pilgrim that other pilgrims have told me about. He is carrying a full backpack and a wooden staff . . . and I cannot keep up with his pace. He does, however, stop every few minutes, so we speak for a few minutes, then separate. He tells me that he has been walking on the *chemin* since he was sixty-two — for the past twenty years. Other pilgrims who have spoken with him have been told, by him, that one of the reasons he walks here is because his home life is less than stellar. I want to announce right here, right now, that my home life IS stellar and that is NOT why I am here, in case any of you were wondering.

The trail goes up and down a lot of relatively small ravines, so over the course of the day, I probably double the height of the first high climb out of Conques. Every hilltop is a personal victory.

I can tell you here that I have had a few psychological crises over the past few days, usually at some point on one of these long steep climbs. They run along the lines of: *Guy, what on earth are you doing here? You are sucking for air, your heart rate is out of sight, your legs hurt, this mud sucks (and it DOES suck), you wonder when the knees are going to fail and your fingers are going numb and blue because you are holding the poles so tightly. And you don't even know why you are here. Why don't you quit?* And I don't have an answer. Then I eventually get to the top, and in a few ("few" varies directly with the duration of the climb) minutes, all is well.

The wind comes up to a gale. Happily, it is warm and dry, but it is sufficiently gusty that it blows me around. I have to be very careful to keep my footing. Today, for over five hours of walking over trails and on country roads, I do not hear or see a car until I am almost in Descazeville. The absence of vehicle noise is quite precious to me. I can hear birds, the wind, water running (sometimes I am in it), and my own footsteps, sometimes squishy in the mud. But my boots are excellent, and my feet are dry and comfortable.

Eventually (after six hours for twenty kilometres—which should give you an idea of the difficulty of this section), I descend into Descazeville, a town on the other end of the attractive scale from Conques. It is industrial, not ancient, but when almost every small town in France is losing its children to the cities, Descazeville is thriving. It is not pretty but it's working. I arrive at the Gite Volets Bleus (Blue Shutters) to be greeted warmly by Jean, a young man who has been expecting me. Daniel gave him very clear instructions about looking after me, apparently. I have a lower bunk in a small room with three bunks, so it is quite cozy.

After getting myself settled in (laundry and shower), I ask Jean if he will call ahead for me to get a bed for tomorrow night. He does . . . and I learn about the first of May weekend in France. It is a major, major exercise to get a bed or a room anywhere. I had not anticipated this problem. After several failed attempts, he gets me a bed in a *gite* about eight kilometres from here in Chaunac, with breakfast, but no dinner. Not where I had planned to go, but I will have a bed. I will need to pick up dinner en route tomorrow. He is also trying to find me a place in Figeac for the next night. I am confident that I won't have to spend the night on a park bench somewhere. I could, of course, be quite wrong about this. I shall see.

Jean has just told me that he has a confirmed place for me near Figeac for the night after tomorrow. I tell him—and I mean it—that he is a gentleman. It is actually about five kilometres outside of Figeac, in La Cassagnole, which is in the wrong direction from my intended path, but I don't care. I will likely take a taxi from Figeac to get there.

This Blue Shutters *gite* is a little oasis in a mostly industrial town. I dry my clothes on a line in a big garden—the wind has them dry in fifteen minutes. I discover when I am undressing from my walking clothes to my in-the-village clothes that it looked as though I had inadvertently stolen someone else's sock, since I have three heavy socks in my bag, where there should have been two. The mystery is made clear when I take off my socks prior to washing them. On my left foot, I have the correct combination: light sock under, heavy sock over. On my right foot, however, there is no heavy sock to take off because I had never put it on. I have walked all day in a very light under-sock on one foot—with no ill effects (apparently).

I have noticed that the ring finger on my left hand is a little numb and a little bruised again. I have discovered why. When I descend, I have the poles in front of me and I use that finger on each hand to control the top of the pole. I am trying to use the other fingers to take the pressure off this one or I will have the honour of naming the latest medical phenomenon, the "Chemin de Saint-Jacques amputation." I am hoping to avoid this. But it really is weird.

Dinner with, mostly in one group, fifteen French, one Swiss, and one Korean, is interesting and fun. The Swiss woman is German-Swiss and speaks little French (so we speak German); the Korean, who speaks no French, comes in late, bows, and sits at the very far end of the table; and the fifteen French and I carry on an animated conversation, of which I understand anywhere from 5 to 50 percent, depending on who is speaking and the topic. One of the things that I have noticed is that as I tire, my level of comprehension steadily diminishes, until it extinguishes in a last little puff of light. They are all properly amazed by my age—as am I. It is a wonderful meal, and I really enjoy myself. One of the Frenchmen has walked the *camino* in Spain and thumbs through my book, exclaiming at the photos. Of course he recognizes most of the places. When the wine runs out, we go to bed. Good move.

29 April—Descazeville to Chaunac

This morning, I wake up in my bunk to the sound of breakfast in the adjoining room. It is seven-thirty; the room is full of people getting ready for their day. I get Jean, our young and very helpful host, to call ahead for me so that now I have confirmed quarters for the next three nights. Today, I have a bed in a rural *gite* in Chaunac, tomorrow in another just outside Figeac, and the next day in a *chambre d'hôte* in Lacapelle-Marival about twenty kilometres in the direction of Rocamadour.

Just after I start off today, on the apparently inevitable long climb out of Descazeville, I meet three of the people from last evening, who tell me that they are staying in Chaunac today as well. We walk together for a bit, but I have to walk at a pace that I can maintain, so much of the time I walk alone, but always in sight of them, ahead or behind. The *chemin* is hilly, sometimes dry, sometimes very wet in the woods, so I have to take great care when walking the wet, slippery descents. The views when we are on top of the hills are breathtaking—or perhaps that's just me trying to catch my breath. After two hours for four kilometres, I arrive in Livinhac-le-Haut a few minutes ahead of my companions and spot a bench in the tiny town square where there is another pilgrim sitting.

I join him and we talk—in English, which is very unusual here. Jacques is sixty-nine, very lean, a little shorter than me, from Vichy and spent three years in London, where he learned English. Last year, he started the *chemin* in Le Puy with his sister, a year older than him and very close. They got as far as Descazeville, where her cancer and her diabetes made it impossible for her to continue. They returned home, where she has since died. Now he has returned and is walking alone, in her memory. He tells me that he needs to have both knees replaced but wants to complete the walk to Santiago before he has this done. We bid each other *"bon chemin"* as he leaves.

The three from last evening arrive. They turn out to be two sisters, Annie from Lyon, and Odile from Albertville, with Bernard from Lyon as well. Bernard is sixty, swarthy, huge grin, smiling eyes, the two sisters perhaps a little younger . . . or perhaps not. I am not going there. We buy provisions in the tiny stores for lunch and for dinner, find an open pub where we have a draft beer with a touch of peach syrup—this is new for me and I quite like it—and have a picnic lunch on a bench in the square as the town shuts down for its afternoon nap. We share our food and plan to do the same for dinner this evening. The *gite* we are heading for does not offer dinner.

Based on our experience from this morning, we decide to walk on the road to Chaunac. We are hoping to avoid the mud and the hills. We succeed in one of these. There is no mud, but the road climbs steadily, not steeply but consistently, practically all the way for the next four kilometres, all the way to Chaunac. I cannot imagine what the *chemin* is like. We see the sign for Chaunac (it's about 600 metres off the road) at the same time as we see the exit from the *chemin* here. It is muddy, so our instincts are right.

The *gite* is an isolated farmhouse on what appears to be a working farm. There is no one here when we arrive just after two, but there is a hand-printed sign welcoming us by name and telling us where to sleep. Each of the sleeping spaces exits directly outdoors. Mine has no windows and a big door; probably used to be a storage room for something dry. The beds are clean and there are pillows and blankets. That has been consistent in the *gites* so far this year. It is a nice touch.

We take off our boots and sit in the garden under a mature chestnut tree. When the sun is out, as it is now, it is just perfect. In the shade, one needs the fleece. Bernard makes coffee using the truly ancient gas stove (it has an external tank sitting on the floor and one uses a match to light the burner).

I have a sleep for about forty-five minutes, which is enough to rejuvenate me. Afterwards, I sit outside and make my notes for the day. I also copy all my photos from my camera to my iPad. It allows me to see them better, and it's good security if I were to lose one or the other device. What I have lost, I discover (or fail to discover), is my little headlamp, so I will have to acquire a small flashlight when I can find an open store. That is one of the really exciting parts of this journey. Which stores will be open, when?

The weather in the late afternoon is beautiful but cool. A huge thunderstorm rolls past us to the east, making a superb and menacing display. An hour later, another rolls over us, bringing marble-sized hail but little rain. This is a good thing, since my clothes are still on the line drying.

Supper is another shared experience. Since there is no dinner here, we have brought our own supplies. Besides us, there are four other people for dinner, a Swiss couple, who have walked from Geneva, and two French guys. She has a wonderful, open smile. The Swiss woman, from the German-speaking region of Switzerland, makes a big pot of pasta and potatoes. I have brought cauliflower, carrots, zucchini, and onions, which I boil up in a big pot. Sausage and ham magically appear, as do two bottles of red wine. There is lots of bread and even dessert! It is like the loaves and fishes—a little bit from each and we can't finish all the food. We do, however, finish the wine with dispatch.

At some point in the evening, I tell the gathering about my Hike for Hospice. I have to explain the idea of palliative care, since not everyone has heard of a hospice. This is tricky for me in French, but we manage. They all think it's a great idea when they understand it . . . and I tell them about a donation of fifty Euros that a dear friend in Germany, Ginette Parent, from the Berlin area, has made to a German children's hospice as part of my hike.

It's off to bed before nine, because it is cold, there is no diversion, and we have a long walk, about twenty-one kilometres, tomorrow. The sisters Annie and Odile finish tomorrow at Figeac. Bernard will continue on a different route for another month. I am going to a place, La Cassagnole, a few kilometres south of Figeac. It is where Jean from the *gite* in Descazeville was able to find me accommodation.

30 April—Chaunac to La Cassagnole

The day dawns overcast and it has evidently rained all night. And it still rains. After breakfast, I say goodbye to my three companions of yesterday and I head out, dressed in full regalia, rain pants, jacket, and rain-cover on my pack. I decide to walk the road today, not the GR 65, because the road goes directly from here to Figeac, while the GR meanders back and forth, perhaps adding 50 percent to the distance. After about fifteen minutes, off comes the fleece, and, after an hour, off come the rain pants and jacket.

Over the next several hours, the rain gear is donned and doffed perhaps four times as the weather changes from sunny to overcast to wet and back to sunny. The road is all country, the sounds of cows lowing, birds singing, the water running and, often, the pitter-patter of raindrops on my trusty Tilley hat.

At one point, I stop for a few minutes in a sheltered spot, take off my rain gear, and, before I can get going, have to put it on again. At this shelter a fellow pilgrim has a different guidebook, which cautions about the possibility of flooding—an *"inundation"*—on one section of the GR for today, which is another really good reason to take the road. After a month of rain, that possibility is likely very high. The brooks and rivers here are full.

There are quite a few people like me who have chosen the road as a better option, here. It is mostly flat, winding, and not busy, except in a few sections. After almost five hours, I am on the eastern outskirts of Figeac. For the last hour, I have watched an enormous storm front move from left to right across in front of me on the far side of Figeac. The problem is that it is slowly getting closer as I approach Figeac and it looks and sounds big and menacing. It has been my plan to walk into Figeac, then get a ride to Cassagnole, but this storm alters my plans. I hail a car, and the young driver takes me a kilometre into Figeac and deposits me at the train station, where we both believe that I can get a taxi. He leaves me there and drives away.

Storm over Figeac.

After four phone calls and no takers, it appears that we are both wrong. The taxi companies are not interested in this fare. I go back outside and sit on a bench, contemplating what to do next. There is little traffic, and no taxis in sight. A decrepit van pulls up and two guys get out. I approach them and ask if they can tell me how to get to the Chemin de Saint-Jacques. I tell them where I am heading because I figure that I will be walking the last five kilometres after all. They have a little discussion and determine that they know where I am going. My mistake has been that I think that La Cassagnole is a village and it is actually just a single point. That is why the taxis aren't interested. They do not know where it is.

But these guys do, and the driver is quite prepared to take me there. It's on his way . . . and he does not want payment for the ride. Germain turns out to be an organic chicken farmer (*ferme bio*) and is a very interesting guy. He does not hold out much hope for the future of the human race. He sees more and more pollution and the business money talks . . . and the politicians listen. Sound familiar?

The road to La Cassagnole winds up and down and goes all over the place. It is only about five kilometres out of Figeac but it might as well be on the moon. The storm clouds have gotten darker and more menacing as we drive, and by the time we pull up in front of the *gîte* Saint-Jacques (what else?) the heavy rain has started. I ask him if he will take payment, not for the ride but for the organic farm. But he won't, and after I unload my pack and poles from the back of his little van, he drives off with a "*bon chemin*" and a big smile. A gracious man.

I am first here and there is no host in sight. It is a two-storey *gîte*, five single beds and a bunk on the first floor, some more singles and bunks in the loft. Since I am first here, I get to choose my location and I select the bed nearest to the toilets and shower, planning ahead for tonight. The night traffic won't bother me, and it will be a short walk to the toilets, which I will undoubtedly need to make some time tonight. I change into my "village" clothes and have my afternoon nap under a blanket. People start to arrive, but since I can turn my hearing aids off (thank you, Julia Robillard!), the quiet talking in the *gîte* does not bother me. I figure that I have earned this nap today.

As people slowly drift in, the weather worsens. Over the next hour, three separate thunderstorms roll through, each with its load of hail. I am very happy that I am not out in this. Four of the people who come in are the same women who had walked the road just ahead or just behind me for a few hours. One of them, a short woman, had me concerned a few times because she walked as part of a group of three down the centre of the road. Since this road is

Dortoir *at La Cassagnole.*

shared by people driving big black Mercedes at speed, I was concerned for her safety. But here she is.

There is lots of chatter, mostly in French with a smattering of German. There are quite a few Swiss on this section of the *chemin*. I speak at length with a Belgian guy, Corneel, quite young, Flemish from the northern part of Belgium. To my relief, his English is better than my French, and we have an extended conversation in English about the bilingual nature of our two countries and the way the politicians manage to botch it. It sounds as if theirs are worse than ours.

Later, he assists me as I try to add time to my cell phone. The problem is to understand the recorded voice giving instructions on the phone — in mechanical French. I think we sort it out.

At dinner, I sit with Corneel, Stefan from Munich, Frans from Holland, and Johanna, who is Swiss. There is no single common language, so the animated conversation drifts from language to language, depending on topic and speaker. If the speaker can't find a word in a language, someone else offers a substitute. We range in age from Johanna, who is barely twenty, to Frans and me.

Frans, perhaps sixty, left his home near Eindhoven on 5 March and is halfway to Santiago. I am amazed at how many people on this route have started from home and intend to walk all the way. He tells me a story about the early part of his journey.

He was in a small town in Holland at about five-thirty in the evening and had not found any place to stay. He was sitting on a park bench when an older woman walked up and asked him if he needed a bed for the night. He said that he did. She told him to wait there, she had a hair appointment and she would be back in half an hour, which she was. She collected him in her car and off they went. He asked if there would be a problem with her husband. She assured him that there would not. When they arrived at her place, they went in and met her elderly husband. It turns out that she had walked the *chemin* years before and had recognized his scallop shell as the mark of a pilgrim. She looked for other pilgrims that she could help — and this was one of the ways she could do it.

Jésus, the genial host here, in his sixties, white beard and a ponytail just like Hollis Morgan's,[15] arranges accommodation for me in

---

15 Hollis Morgan is the warm and thoughtful sound recording engineer, dobro player, and much more from Constance Bay in Ontario who recorded the audio version of my earlier book, *A Journey of Days*, at his studio, Constant Sound Studio (**constantsoundstudio.com**).

Rocamadour. He also volunteers to drive me back to Figeac in the morning because he figures that I won't make Lacapelle from here. It is just too far and too difficult. I accept his offer with alacrity and go to bed to the sound of quiet sleeping noises in the *dortoir*.

1 May — La Cassagnole to Lacapelle-Marival

It is very misty when I wake up in the morning, but the sky clears, and it looks like it's going to be a very nice day — which is how it turns out. At breakfast I say farewell to the folks from last evening. They are heading west toward Cahors; I am heading north about twenty-one kilometres toward Rocamadour. Jésus, true to his word, finishes up his breakfast chores and collects me for the ride to Figeac. It's only five kilometres, but it takes about fifteen minutes, the road is so narrow, windy, and hilly. I am extremely glad that he has offered this ride. He deposits me in the surprisingly empty town at an intersection where the signage for GR 6 is obvious. I offer him some money, which he turns down. It is just part of his service to pilgrims.

This is a fifty-kilometre diversion from the GR 65, which I am making because I specifically want to see Rocamadour. I have known about it for decades. It is a very popular tourist attraction, and, from what I have seen of photos, it is no surprise as to why. It appears to be built into the cliffs overlooking the river.

I hump my pack on, cinch the belt tight, grab my poles, and off I go into the unknown . . . again. It is the first of May, a big holiday in France, so there won't be much open, and there likely won't be much traffic, either. It is also my daughter Meredith's birthday. I hope she will have a good day. She is such a good person and works so hard. She has become a brilliant futurist, like her mother.

The walk out of Figeac is beautiful, due north, a quiet road that becomes a bridle path. No vehicles, only a couple of joggers here. Trees line both sides of the road, and there is a noisy, very full brook on my left. The sun is shining, the road is flat, and it is very peaceful. For the first hour, it stays this way; then the path starts to climb. I am on the east side of a narrow river valley, and as I climb, I can see behind me farther and farther.

Eventually, I am so high (another of those breathtaking climbs) that I can see about 270 degrees of rolling hills and a mix of farms and forest and small villages for miles behind me. Of course I can. The

Pastoral landscape.

folks who laid out this path have made sure that I am cresting the top of every hill in this part of France.

Then I reach the top, another small victory, and start to descend into the next valley. As the view to the south disappears, the view to the north opens up. The roads are narrow, and the *chemin* uses them when convenient and diverges whenever it suits. I can see on the map that the path winds a lot, but so do the roads, so there is no direct path to where I am going. The frequent directional changes also tell me that the countryside will be very hilly. At the halfway point, I reach Cardaillac, which sounds almost like cardiac, which is what this path is a superb test of; yet another of the prettiest villages in France and yet again, one of the most closed. Nothing open, here.

Today is like a day outside of time. I get a sense of the grandeur of this magnificent countryside. I walk, I feel good, I feel healthy, and when I climb, I take small steps, very, very slowly. If someone were to see me, he would think; "*That's an old man walking up a long hill.*" And he would be right. When I get to the top of these climbs, however, the recovery time is shorter and shorter, so the body is responding well to the stresses that I am putting on it. Within a couple of weeks, I will discover that all the experienced people, young and old, walking up hills take very small steps and walk very slowly. Only the inexperienced walkers walk uphill fast.

I walk from nine a.m. until three p.m. and meet exactly one fellow pilgrim en route. He is from Luxembourg, this is his first day, and we end up staying in the same elegant little hotel in Lacapelle-Marival. I am tired when I arrive. I check in—they are expecting me—find out that they can wash my clothes for me, then I have a shower and sleep. The view from the room is spectacular: a fifteenth-century gothic church and the twelfth-century chateau, known as Château Cardaillac. And I am looking at them from my room across a lovely little park with a brook down the middle.

There is an interesting psychological phenomenon going on. While I am on the path, I seem to have lots of energy. When I get into a town, the energy drains away as I get closer to my destination, so when I arrive at the lodging, I am dragging. There is a market in town today, even though it's a holiday—but by the time I manage to get outside after a short sleep, the market is being torn down. And everything in town is closed. There is not even a place to get a beer.

At dinner, the service is excellent and elegant. The food is as good as, but no better than, that at any *gite* but it is served on china, and the wine is served in a crystal goblet. I sit with the pilgrim from Luxembourg. This is his first day and he has spent way too much of it in the sun without a hat. His face is red and burned. That has to hurt.

He talks about the immigrant problem in Luxembourg. It's the usual litany of complaints. They won't work, they steal, they take all the government money. I don't know what an immigrant is supposed to do. If you work, the complaint is

Moss-covered stone wall.

that you are taking all the jobs. If you don't work, you are taking all the tax money. He is anti-immigrant, far right of centre politically. I do not agree with him on much but I don't argue with him because it would be near impossible with my level of French, and frankly, I don't need the stress. I bid him goodnight and head off to my room with its ensuite bath, towels, and personal light switch by the bed.

2 May—Lacapelle to Rocamadour

Today, 2 May, is my grandson Cian's fifth birthday. Five years ago, I was in Spain, sitting in the garden at an *albergue* feeling sorry for myself (I was injured, self-inflicted) when I found out that I had a grandson. Everything got better for the rest of the day! Happy birthday, Cian. I see him every day because his picture is wallpaper on my iPad. The other wallpaper picture is of his little sister Isabella, known as Bella—and she is.

The hotel in Lacapelle loses one of my expensive liner socks in their laundry. So much for the five-star service. They tell me they searched to no avail. I guess this is why I have been carrying an extra pair all this way. If they were going to lose something, why couldn't they lose something heavier? Later today, I discover that they hadn't lost the sock—it was stuck inside some other laundry—so I take all my bad thoughts back.

My plan today is for a day off in Rocamadour, just thirty kilometres from here, and I am going by taxi. This is a place that I have wanted to experience for years and I want to do it fresh, not after having walked all day. The drive up is pleasant, the driver is careful, the countryside is gently rolling hills . . . and very, very green. There's been lots of rain here, too. The weather today is perfect, sunny, about seventeen or eighteen degrees Celsius, just right for a walk or a cab ride.

We arrive in Rocamadour but have a little trouble finding the hotel. My guidebook calls it the Comp'hostel (a little word play for pilgrims) but it has been recently renamed the Hotel Amadour. The cab driver charges me less than what's on the meter and won't accept a tip. This is one of the advantages of being a pilgrim. I am here by eleven, but the hotel doesn't open until noon, so I drop my backpack at the entry, obscure it as much as possible behind a bush, and walk

Rocamadour.

around a little bit while I wait. In the event, it's not a problem.

I visit the tourism office and sort out how I am to get to Cahors tomorrow. There is a bus that runs from Gramat, five minutes by car from here, to Cahors in the morning, so that's the plan. The hotel orders me a taxi for the morning and also books me a bed in Cahors for tomorrow. So now I can go explore Rocamadour.

The site at Rocamadour is every bit as good as in the photos that I've seen over the years. The town is perched on — actually it's partially built into — a huge cliff, a wall of rock 400 feet high on a bend of a tiny river. About 600 people live here. And since the buildings are made from the same rock, it's hard to tell where the building ends and the rock begins. The town lies above the river and the narrow flood plain, the church buildings lie above the town, then there is a rock face above that with the chateau on top of the cliff. It has been a major pilgrimage site for about a millennium — Jacques Cartier came here sometime before 1534 to pray for success on his first voyage to what became Canada. It worked for him. So, too, earlier in 777 or 778 did Roland, one of Charlemagne's generals, but it didn't work so well for him — the Basques defeated Roland's forces and killed him near Roncevalles.

It reminds me a bit of what it might look like if you took the Barron River Canyon in Algonquin Park and, on a bend in the river, built a town up the side of the canyon with a chateau on top of the cliff. It might be hard to get government money for that project.

Rocamadour fell on hard times for several centuries when pilgrimages fell out of favour, but the tourism folks have been spectacularly successful in reviving the town. It is now the second most-visited site in France, after Mont-Saint-Michel, 1.5 million people a year. I am glad that I am here in the off-season.

There are many resemblances to Niagara Falls. The site is spectacular, and the trashy tourism stuff is everywhere, including the full length of the main street in town. There are no cross streets — too steep. My hotel is just back from the edge of the gorge, around a river bend from the old town of Rocamadour, and, from the other side of the road, the whole vertical town is in view. I take pictures here and I walk down a steep road into the village area, taking pictures as I go. I then walk down to the flood plain, across a bridge, and along a road on the far side so that I can get a shot of the whole panorama. Then back up into the village — quite a climb — and walk the length of the

Rocamadour seen from below.

main street, where I find dozens of little shops selling treasures to tourists, of which there are lots. I am ambivalent, here. I don't feel like a tourist, but I don't feel exactly like a pilgrim, either.

There is a family taking pictures—mother, father, three kids—and I ask them if they would like a picture of the whole family. They look to be Indonesian but when I ask them where they are from, they tell me, "Madagascar." I learn that Madagascar was settled by people from Indonesia—I didn't know that. I had always thought, when I thought about it, which wasn't often, that they would be African.

Later, I sit in a little brasserie and have a glass of beer with peach syrup and a small salad. Together it costs ten Euros, which does not feel like much of a rip-off. It's nice just sitting here in this mythic town and watching the tourists go by.

Next, I take an elevator up to the chapel level, visit there briefly, and end up walking a paved switchback path that represents the Stations of the Cross. At each switchback point, there is another station. This feature is about 130 years old, which, incidentally, is about how old I feel when I finally get to the top. There is a little more climbing—I thought that I was going to have a day off from this—and then I am out on the flat road on the edge of the canyon that leads me for a kilometre or so around a bend in the valley and back to my hotel. There are parking lots for buses up here, but only a few buses today. This place must be a zoo in the high season.

I also visit a grotto here that has some wall drawings done about 20,000 years ago. It is a short visit, because the entry is right near my hotel and the little cave is only about ten metres underground. Altogether, it is less than thirty metres in any direction and from two to five metres high. It is cool and damp. The guide takes a long time to get to the interesting stuff. There is a negative impression of a left hand; some really primitive drawings of horses done in black and ochre; perhaps an elk—you have to have a lot of imagination to see some of these. These are not anything like some of the cave paintings in other parts of France, but they are genuine. Twenty thousand years translates roughly into a thousand generations. I can't imagine how to make a thousand generations make sense for me. When I think about the hand negative, I think about Og's partner when he gets home from a hard day in the grotto: "Og, what have you got all around your mouth? It's all black—and your left hand, what a mess. What have you being doing? Get outside and clean up. You can't let the kids see you like this!"

There is no one here I know, so I eat dinner by myself on the terrace of a small restaurant overlooking the town. Beer, a salad with a piece of local goat cheese—delicious—and a vegetarian crepe are as much as I can handle. As the sun sets, it cools rapidly, so I head back to my room. I would love to stay up and see the town lit up at night, but I cannot stay up that late. I would also like to get up early and catch it in the early morning sunlight, but that will only happen if I can get up early.

3 May—Rocamadour to Cahors

I do wake up early, about 6:20, and am relieved to see that even though it's light, the sun has not yet risen. I realized last evening as the sun set behind the old town that when it rose it would paint the vertical surface of the town in sunlight. So after checking my blood glucose (I do this first thing every morning), I leave the little Hotel Amadour and walk 200 metres to the Esplanade Restaurant, where I had dinner on the terrace last evening. There is no one here but me—it isn't open yet—and it is a perfect viewpoint for my planned photos.

The sun has just illuminated the chateau and the top of the rock face as I arrive. I place the camera on the top of a flat wooden fence, use maximum zoom, and over the next forty-five minutes, I sit and wait patiently and about every five minutes take another photo as the sunlight creeps down the surface of the town. When I leave, there is still no one around. I am quite surprised that I am the only person today who seems to have realized the photographic potential of this sunrise.

It reminds me of an early morning in Ottawa about twenty years ago when I went to Remic Rapids with a stepladder. The artist John Ceprano[16] had created some wonderful forms out of rock in and near the shallow water, and I wanted to get some photos of them. One problem that I had noticed earlier was that, when I stood on the ground and took a picture, the horizon line of low trees on the Quebec shore always showed up and I didn't want the shoreline in the image. I had figured out that using a stepladder and shooting down would likely solve the problem.

So there I was, almost alone. The only other person there was Ceprano, fixing up some forms that thoughtless people had damaged. I set up the ladder and took my photos. After a while, Ceprano came over, and we talked for a bit. He said that I was only the second person that he had ever seen use a ladder for the photos. He also said that I was in very good company. The only other photographer was Malak.[17] I was in very good company, indeed! Sometimes comparisons are odious, but not this one.

Today is our fifty-fourth wedding anniversary. It seems simultaneously a very long time and no time at all. I remember with absolute clarity the twenty-one-year-old I married in 1958. I see her all the time in the elegant woman she has become. Later today, I will call her and tell her how I feel about her and about our wonderful and enduring relationship. I won't call her now, because with the six-hour time difference, it is two in the morning in Ottawa, and calling now would put a little strain on our relationship.

It is now just after eight. I am going to have breakfast and get my gear together for the trip south to Cahors. Oh, yes . . . the hotel does not have a stamp for pilgrims for the pilgrim passport! So we find a more generic stamp for the hotel that indicates Rocamadour, and that's what we use.

The taxi arrives at nine, and I am on my way—I think. (I am wrong but I don't know it yet.) Yesterday, the Tourism Office in Rocamadour found the bus schedule, showed it to me, and gave me one. It shows a bus going south from Gramat, about five minutes by taxi from here, at 9:35, arriving in Cahors at 10:45, just over an hour on the bus. So I expect to spend the day in Cahors. I wonder

---

16   See his sculptures on the Internet at ***http://jfceprano.com/natural-rock-sculpture***.
17   Malak Karsh (1915–2001) was a well-known and respected Canadian photographer, brother of Yousof Karsh.

idly what I will do all day. The taxi drops me at 9:15 at the station in Gramat — it's for both buses and trains — and I wait . . . and I wait. Usually the public transport in Europe is deadly accurate.

At about ten minutes to ten, I ask someone in a local café across the small parking lot if there is a bus today. They think so but suggest I ask in the station. I didn't see anyone there before but in I go and find someone who eventually comes to the wicket. I ask about the bus. He looks confused. "But sir, there is no bus today." Now *I* look confused. I tell him about the schedule, which I left in the taxi. He insists there is no bus today, and I ask if there is any way to get to Cahors today.

Yes, I can get a train to Cahors at noon. It takes a very devious route going north and east, then west, with a stop and a train change and then goes south to get to Cahors just after four p.m. Well, I have the whole day. I just wasn't planning on spending a chunk of it on a train. There go those pesky expectations again.

So now I am sitting under a shade tree in the outdoor patio of a café just across the parking lot from the station, waiting patiently until noon. I have a *grande crème* and a glass of water to sip on. I have lovely weather, a sunny day, birds chirping, a gentle, cool breeze to keep me company. It is very pleasant. The train arrives at noon, and I get on for the short trip north, an hour's wait, and another short trip south.

The first stop on the train is — you guessed it — Rocamadour. So I paid twenty Euros for a taxi, waited three hours for the train, and I could instead have gotten on at Rocamadour and spent the morning in the town. On the other hand, the wait at the café was very pleasant, the staff was congenial and helpful, and they let me use their WiFi for free.

And twice in the past twenty-four hours, a cab driver has charged me less than the meter reading and has refused any more payment. Toto, I don't think we're in Kansas anymore.[18]

At the halfway point, I sit on the terrace of the restaurant at the station and have a beer and a small salad. Two tables away, facing me, is a young man, slouching, face set in a frown, cigarette dangling, and a chip like a two-by-four on his shoulder. He is not eating or drinking, just slouching there. When the waitress asks him what he would like, he says he wants nothing then ignores her. She tells him politely that if he isn't going to have anything, he has to sit elsewhere. He pointedly ignores her; then, after a few minutes, he takes something from a paper bag and eats it. Another twenty minutes passes before he

---

18 Dorothy's line from *The Wizard of Oz*.

gets up, leaves his garbage, and walks off. A lout is still a lout in every culture and in every language.

The train down is fast, quiet, and almost empty except for a couple of young guys with a two-month-old kitten who does not like the ride and is very vocal about her distress.

At Cahors, I ask at the station for directions to the *gite*. It is on a road directly across from the station and about 400 metres away. When I arrive, it's a big building with no one at the welcome desk, so I sit and wait for a few minutes. Someone arrives and checks me in. He doesn't seem very organized, which is explained when I discover a few minutes later that everyone is in a meeting and he is part of the cleaning staff. But everything works. He gives me a room key (in a *gite*? That's a first), and sheets and a pillowcase—another first.

I organize dinner here for tonight, and they call ahead for me for the next two nights, so that is all arranged. I have discovered that I like the assurance of a bed reserved for me when I arrive.

I speak to Carroll on my cell and we exchange anniversary greetings. I am looking forward to seeing her in less than a month in Barcelona.

Dinner is different. I am the only pilgrim having dinner here. There are other pilgrims staying here but they are all eating in town. Good choice. There are a bunch of teenagers in the dining room to whom I am apparently invisible. They all chat animatedly with each other, simply ignoring the fact that I am seated here in their midst. The age gap, from their side at least, must appear to be a chasm; in addition, they are all chock-full of raging hormones that have absolutely nothing to do with a fossil when there are young members of the opposite sex nearby. Seated kitty-corner across from me is one man in his thirties or forties, who, I discover the next morning, is actually one of the staff, and in any other place would be a *hospitalier*—but not here. Hospitality is not his strong suit. For me, it's a very disconcerting feeling, to be invisible in a group of people. It is psychologically disturbing. They can see me but they don't acknowledge my presence.

And the food, for the first time in a *gite*, is really institutional. Overcooked chicken legs in what purports to be a curry. At least the fresh, raw veggies are good and plentiful.

After dinner, I walk into the main part of town. Big, tree-lined main street. There are 23,000 people living here, so it is much larger than most of the towns and villages on the *chemin*. I sit on a bench and watch the interplay of people, but I don't sit down at any of the outdoor cafés. I am feeling a little—no, a lot—rejected, so I would not be good company for anyone, least of all a stranger.

It doesn't help that I cannot avoid comparing this anniversary to the one five years ago in Boadilla in Spain, where the whole atmosphere was warm and welcoming. But I am here by choice, so stiff upper lip and on with tomorrow.

4 May—Cahors to Lascabanes

The weather forecast for today is partly cloudy in the morning, with thunderstorms and hail coming in the afternoon. So it looks as if getting out in good time might be important. In the event, I am out of this *gite* by eight-thirty. At breakfast, I discover that they have picnic lunches available for today. That is great, because everything I have read about this next section says that there is no place to get food for over twenty kilometres. When I ask about buying the lunch, I am told that, *désolé*, I had to have ordered it the evening before.

I do surreptitiously create a little picnic of my own with a chunk of bread and butter wrapped in a napkin and a couple of small, hard pears. I say surreptitiously because the breakfast Nazi—the man from last evening's dinner—is standing there, checking that everyone has actually paid for breakfast. Another first in a *gite*. I smuggle it out of the breakfast area and I am out of here with the rain cover on my pack, just in case. Frankly, this is not a *gite* that I would recommend for its warm and welcoming spirit.

I walk by myself through Cahors and across its landmark, the thirteenth-century bridge over the Lot River, the infamous Valentré Bridge.[19] On the far side, there is a paved road running left and right at the foot of a cliff, but no people walking. Where are they? I cannot at first see where the path goes and then I see, to my horror—why am I surprised?—that there are pilgrims practically overhead on the face of the cliff in front of me. I gird my loins, figuratively. In places, the local authorities have installed steps, which is a good idea, except that the rise of each step is well over a foot.

---

19 It took seven decades to build the bridge. The story is that finally the builder made a deal with the devil to help in the completion of the bridge, but when it was finished, the builder tried to go back on the deal by refusing to place the last stone onto the bridge. In the 1800s, during a restoration of the bridge, a carving of a devil was added on one of the towers.

The devil's bridge at Cahors.

In addition, the path switches back and forth as it climbs, with only a narrow screen of brush to give the climber the illusion of safety. I am under no such illusion. If I were to trip off the edge here or slide on the wet, rounded stones, the fall could easily be fifty or 100 feet onto a very hard surface. I am not afraid of heights, but, as you may have gathered, this bit concerns me. This is the first place on the *chemin* where I use or need handholds to help me up the incline.

After I reach the top, I leave the valley of the Lot and walk into an area of small farm holdings, lots of small woods, and a path that is wide, well-surfaced, and often on narrow, little-used country roads. The vistas here are short, not long, but the air is clean and smells of spring. So much rain has taken any pollution out of the air, if there was any here to begin with. I am still in a sparsely populated area and expect that will continue.

Frans, the Dutch guy walking from his home, overtakes me, we talk for a couple of minutes, then off he goes with his long legs and long stride. We are heading to the same town, so maybe we will meet later. Then Fanny, the young Swiss girl whom I last saw in Conques, catches up to me, followed by Johanna, another Swiss with whom I ate in Cassagnole. Everyone passes me, since I am bent on walking at my own pace. I am glad to be meeting people who recognize me. I start to get a feel for how powerful the need for connection is and why the threat of exile or shunning or, as the British so quaintly put it, "sending someone to Coventry," is avoided. I did not like what was going on in my own mind last evening.

The weather is good until noon, when the promised thunderstorms start to appear on the horizon. Eventually it starts to rain, and I arrive at the *gite* very wet but not thundered on.

And here is Jacques Parmentier, the guy from Vichy with whom I shared a bench in Livinhac-le-Haut a few days ago, along with a couple of guys with whom I have been sharing a *gite* for some of the past few days. When I first saw them, my gaydar fired off, and every time I see them, it continues to signal me. They are in their fifties—I am guessing—and are close all the time. I don't mean cuddly close, no sign of that, but just a quiet attachment that looks like more than friendship; it looks like a long-term relationship. I could be entirely wrong and I don't care what they do—or not—together, but it is interesting that the signals seem so clear to me. They seem like nice guys, and we see each other often for the next few days on the *chemin*.

The lady who runs this *gite* is somewhat distracted. She is doing what is necessary but not much more. I find out later that her husband recently killed himself and has left her with this *gite* and a mentally challenged teenaged son. No wonder she's distracted, not able to focus on what she's doing. Suicide will come up again later on my walk. It's a curse everywhere, it seems.

I have a bed in a room that I share with three others: one a quiet, older guy who doesn't participate much, and a couple. Now, here is a *chemin* love story. He is Henri-Pierre from Toulouse, fifty-something, movie-star handsome with dense, black, curly hair just starting to grey at the temples. She is Brigitte from Holland, small, blonde, attractive, also fifty-something. I don't know why he is on the *chemin*, but I have a pretty good idea about her. She is a psychiatric nurse and has also been a volunteer at a hospice for years. Now she is considering changing her career path and becoming a palliative care nurse. I think making this career decision is why she's here.

The story starts back in Le Puy-en-Velay on 21 April, when they are both there and notice each other, although they do not speak. The next day, after they have both started walking, he passes her on a steep incline, making a smart comment about being careful here, because it's quite steep and you could fall—which he promptly does, hard on his butt, injuring himself right in front of her. He laughs as he explains that he fell for her—literally. Evidently, they have been nearly inseparable since. A few days ago, he had to leave to go to Paris on business and did not intend to return, but he called her from there and told her that he needed to come back to her. She told him that she would be in or near Cahors. When he arrived back, he called her and told her that he was in Le Hospitalet, a tiny town near Cahors. So was she, and they reunited. They have been together since.

Now they have another few days together on the *chemin* until he really does have to go back to work. Will it work? He is a computer consultant, speaks only French with tiny bits of English; she speaks Dutch, English, and French and wants to work in palliative care. Holland and Toulouse are not that close together; where would they choose to live? I have no idea if I will ever learn what happens to them, although I would like to. She is a warm and sincere person. I am a little suspicious of his movie-star looks, but that is unfair. He seems to have really fallen for her as she clearly has for him. I really hope that it works for both of them. If I find out more, I will let you know.

5 May — Lascabanes to Lauzerte

I have a good night sleeping. Since I lost my headlamp, I have not had a night light, nor have I needed one. Here, however, there will be a problem. In the middle of the night, I wake up, need to go to the john, and it's dark — as it often is at night. My solution? I turn on my cell phone and use its faint glow to keep me from bumping into things and to keep from waking the other sleepers. Yes, I know, everyone else in the world has already figured this out, but I did do it on my own! Much later on, I discover that there is a flashlight app.

The weather forecast is for storms later today, so after the usual breakfast of bread, butter, *confiture,* and coffee in a bowl, I am out of here by eight . . . and I am the last of the dozen who slept here last night. It's twenty-four kilometres to Lauzerte, so I figure on being there by one or one-thirty. At first, that's doable. The path is clear, the weather is good, and it looks like a lovely walk along country lanes — until I hit the white mud. I have become today a connoisseur of mud. The black mud is smelly but does not stick. The brown mud is slippery but does not stick. You can see where I am going with this, can't you?

The white mud is clay and it sticks to my boots like a desperate child clinging to a parent's leg. This stuff will not let go. I am sure that it's sent all over the world to potters who want to throw something on their wheel, and this stuff is just the right consistency. What's worse is that it looks like an ordinary stretch of path. It's just that when one walks on it, it accumulates rapidly on the bottom of one's boots, sliding around and up the edges of the boot like an alien creature. I think that it may be laughing at me. The first reaction is to try to kick it off or slide it off on some grass. But nothing works. I can see places where other people have tried this and it didn't work for them, either. The only solace is that this section of white clay is only about two kilometres long, although it seems much, much longer at the time.

For a couple of kilometres, I am on a road, with other pilgrims away off in the distance. Then gradually the skies start to darken and the rain starts to fall, a few drops at first, then slowly in increasing intensity. I stop, put on my rain pants and jacket and put the rain cover on my pack. It's quite warm, but the promised thunderstorms seem to be just a kilometre or so away. I walk like that for about half an hour, just light rain and at one point it stops, as do I. I start to take off the rain gear . . . and the rain starts again. I am wondering if this is cause and effect. I test this hypothesis for a while and it does seem to correlate. Rain gear off, rain starts. Rain gear on, rain stops.

A rare level section of the chemin.

Eventually we—the rain and I—get it right. I have all my rain gear on and the storm breaks over me. I am in a woods, walking uphill, not on a road, it is coming down in torrents, and I have to remind myself: *Guy, you are here by choice, you are here by choice.* Then it hails—I think that's a little unfair. The good news is that the thunder, which rumbles endlessly, is cloud-to-cloud lightning, not cloud-to-ground—and eventually it ends, and the sun comes out.

As I walk today, I think about my time in the military. When I was a young tank officer, we used to sit around the mess arguing about how best to employ tanks. We had been trained in tank tactics—at the troop level, four tanks, two moving forward, two stationary and watching. It was called fire and movement. At higher levels, the same principle was followed. Some of the other young officers (we were all young) used to argue that tanks were best used fighting other tanks, much like medieval knights would fight each other. It was all about honour and personal bravery. I thought they were frankly nuts.

It seemed to me then—and it still does—that the best use to be made of tanks is to use them to punch a hole in enemy lines, push through and disrupt their rear areas, targeting communications, headquarters, supply depots, and troop concentrations. In that order. Now I recognize that this is much more a strategic view of how to use the power and protection of the tank: "shock and awe," as it was called in the first Gulf War.

One major problem that I had as a young officer was that I thought that strategic thinking was what we were supposed to be doing, in addition to tactical thinking, which was what my peers appeared to be practising. This meant in practice that you had to overtly demonstrate loyalty to the person directly senior to you who would be writing your annual performance report, on which promotion would largely be based. I wasn't smarter than they, by any means; I just had a different point of view. Some of my early peers got to be generals. I didn't. They understood the unwritten rules much better than I did.

I spent twenty-five years in the military, never quite getting this right. Loyalty like a puppy's, as I saw it, was never my strong suit. My superiors noticed. My big mouth may have had a role in this, as well. I now realize that direct and absolute loyalty is required in the military. How else do you get people to go willingly to what both you and they know will be their deaths?

Late in my military career, 1977, I was sent to the Army Staff College. I was about ten years older than most of my classmates and I suppose it was a last attempt by the military to rehabilitate me.

As part of the curriculum, we had to, in small teams, come up with a project that would stimulate and educate our fellow classmates. I ended up in a small team along with an air force pilot, Peter Krayer. Since two of us were pilots, one army, one air force, we decided to see if we could get one of the new U.S. attack helicopters for show and tell. We contacted Hughes Helicopters, responsible for the YAH64,[20] a prototype attack helicopter with enormous firepower. The Canadian army had shown no interest in his aircraft, so the Hughes representative was delighted for the opportunity to show off his prototype for the Army Staff College.

Unfortunately—or fortunately, depending on your point of view—we decided to tell the Land Operations Directorate in Ottawa

---

20 The YAH64 became the AH64 Apache attack helicopter, enormously successful in the Gulf Wars.

what we were planning. When they found out what we had arranged, they were simply livid. We were advised that there would NOT be a YAH64 landing in the square at the college and that the Canadian Army had no intention of getting into the attack helicopter business. Our wrists were severely smacked and our project's showpiece went out the window.[21]

My point, of course, is that the United States and the Soviet Union, as well as other countries, were developing these advanced attack helicopters because they were deadly weapons on the battlefield at that time. Our idea was strategic; the army at the time was thinking tactically. This little misadventure put paid to any idea of a real career in the military for me. Of course, I had not considered the political ramifications of having a U.S. military prototype land at a Canadian military school without official approval. Might have been difficult to explain in Parliament.

I was a square peg in a round hole and it took me almost twenty-five years to figure this out. Both the military and my wife had it figured out decades before I did. Happily, I never had to find out who was right because I never saw combat during my military career. There were a few anxious moments, in Cyprus and elsewhere, but I never heard a shot fired in anger.

Back to the present: I arrive in Lauzerte, about a total of 260 kilometres along my route. The *gite* here is wonderful. I have a room with two beds but I am the only occupant. The room has a toilet and ensuite shower, with towels — a first for a *gite*. The bed has sheets, pillow, pillowcase, and blanket. I have my own light switch! The food is wonderful, they have and I use both a washer and a dryer, so everything is clean for the morning. I meet Mike here, the Aussie with whom I talked in the evening in Conques, as well as an assortment of friends from various *gites* along the way.

Tomorrow is Hike for Hospice across Canada. I wish them all well and hope that it raises both the funds and the awareness that hospices need and deserve.

---

21 The army had already lost the battle for who controlled the helicopters. The air force had won that battle years earlier. What the current fight was about was the aircraft budget. If there were any interest displayed in an expensive attack helicopter, that would compete with funding from the fighter aircraft budget, and that was unacceptable to the air force brass of the time. We had inadvertently stuck our hands into the hornets' nest of an internal budget battle at military headquarters.

6 May—Lauzerte to La Baysse

This has been one of the best *gites* that I have stayed in and certainly the most comprehensive in terms of support for pilgrims. Sheets on the beds, towels, washing and drying of clothes, an excellent meal last evening. For the foodies among you, here is the menu: carrot soup, a cold pie of veal, ham, foie gras and caviar, salad, country sausages roasted with whole figs, bread and red wine as needed, caramel custard. And that is all included in the thirty-two Euros for an overnight stay.

It's a little bittersweet leaving the *gite* this morning. Most of the people here are going on to Moissac, and from there, a number of them are leaving the *chemin* to go back to work. I am going only as far as La Baysse, about eighteen kilometres, and about eight kilometres short of Moissac, so I will likely not see them again. Even those who are continuing on will be a full day ahead of me, so I may or may not see them again. Many kisses and hugs and lots of "*bon courage*." Out I go at eight a.m. into the partly cloudy weather. It's cool; there is a light breeze, threats of thunderstorms, perfect for walking. Out of Lauzerte, with great smiles and "*bon chemin*" from Michel and Bernadette, the genial and warm hosts at the *gite* Les Figuiers.

Just on the outskirts of Lauzerte, I come across a plaque in a tiny park that stops me dead in my tracks, it is so unexpected. It reads, in French:

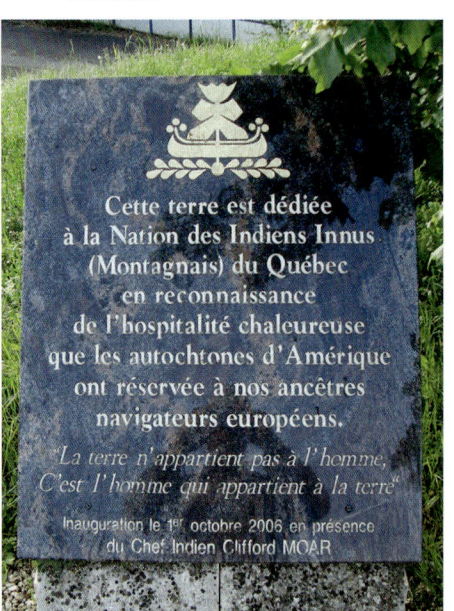

This park is dedicated to the Innu nation (Montagnais) of Quebec in recognition of the warm hospitality which the aboriginals of America gave to our European navigator ancestors.

"The land does not belong to man, it is man who belongs to the land."

The plaque was dedicated on 1 October, 2006, in the presence of Chief Clifford Moar. He was at the time the chief of Mashteuiatsh, a Montagnais First Nation reserve a few kilometres north of Roberval in

Monument to Canadian Innus.

the Saguenay-Lac-Saint-Jean region of Quebec. The plaque does not indicate who created it, but it is nice that someone is grateful and it is a lovely reminder of home.

The *chemin* continues on a paved road for about a kilometre then off onto a path that — surprise — turns sharply upwards into woods. It is a long, hard climb again, and I stop several times to catch my breath. As I approach the top, I can see that there is a tiny clearing, and, on the right-hand side, a low, backless bench. I can really use a short rest, so I decide to sit down on the bench. It looks too good to be true . . . and, like the witch's cottage in Hansel and Gretel, it IS too good to be true.

It is very low, and as I sit, I do not lean forward enough to compensate for the size and weight of the pack. I know even before I touch the bench that I won't be here long. In extreme slow motion, I tip backwards, flailing my arms and poles in a desperate and unsuccessful effort to avoid the inevitable. Down I go on my back on my backpack . . . in the mud. Then, like a turtle, I discover

Site of the Lauzerte bench incident.

that I cannot turn over or get up. Suddenly, I have a lot more respect for overturned turtles. I have to unclip the waist and chest clips that hold my backpack on, wriggle out of the harness, and turn over, now with both knees in the mud, to get up. I feel like an idiot. It is one of those things best experienced without an audience. Happily, no one comes up the trail to see any of this, so I am able to get my gear back on and get out of there, leaving the trap fully set for the next unsuspecting pilgrim.

Yesterday, I spoke for a while with Mike, the Aussie whom I first met in Conques. At that time, he had told me that his first walk to Santiago was quite spiritual for him, even though he is an atheist, but the last two have had no religious or spiritual overtones at all. I asked him yesterday whether anything had changed since then. He told me no, that this walk was for him a holiday but that the spiritual part was not there at all. He was looking for it, but it just was not there for him.

Today, as I walk I think about this. Is there a religious or spiritual element in this journey for me? Or am I just having a holiday (although it doesn't feel like one)? And as I walk on a quiet country road, alone with the morning and the birds and the wind, the answer comes to me in a flash. How could I have been so blind, since the spirituality is all around me? It is in my fellow pilgrims, as well as in the people working in the *gites*, by conviction, and often as volunteers and, by extension, also in me. Their spirit of caring, warmth, concern—yes, even love—has been all around me since I started the walk.

Imagine, if you will, a world of people who are friendly with each other, even strangers, who ask about your well-being . . . and are genuinely interested in the answer; share without being asked when a need is evident; offer help freely whenever help is needed. This is the world of the *chemin* and the world of the *camino*. The spirit of the people on it makes the *chemin*. Are they touched by the spirit of God? Some think so. I don't know, so I can't say that they are or that they are not. I think that this is what we can be when we reach for our enormous personal potential for good.

It doesn't seem to me that we need to call on a higher power to be able to treat one another with respect and value each other as individuals on the same journey, this journey of life that we are all making together. The *chemin* that I am on at this moment is just a microcosm of what the world could be like if people would give up their lust for power, for advantage over one another. I like this world of caring and respect and love a lot more than that other one of fighting and clawing each other and self-interest to the exclusion of others.

The rest of the morning is anti-climax. It's a mix of road and path, the path always muddy. One section is an uphill piece, between two farmers' fields, fenced on either side, and the mud is so slippery that it is one step forward, half a step slide backward, and so on. It is not very high but it is exhausting, especially since there is nothing to hang on to, and the probability of falling is very high. I should worry—I am already pretty muddy from what will be forever known as the "Lauzerte bench incident." In any event, I do not slip or fall and I do reach the top, where I stop for five minutes to recover.

At the fourteen-kilometre mark, there is a town with a new restaurant that is nicely placed to catch the pilgrim traffic—and there they are, five or six people from this morning's breakfast. I stop, have a beer and a couple of bananas, share a bit of dried sausage from one of my friends, and finally head out for the last four kilometres for me today. For whatever reason, the body does not want to co-operate, so I walk very slowly, and it takes me an hour to walk the distance, all on the road. I spot the sign and turn in to this *gite*. La Baysse, once again, turns out to be a single home, not a village.

I am the only pilgrim here at the moment, although two Italian guys come in later. I sleep for ninety minutes and feel much better. I wash out my clothes, hang them out to dry—and it promptly rains. However, I discover to my delight that the *gite* has WiFi, so I can talk to Carroll using Skype. The magic of technology.

I acknowledge that there is an argument that we should eschew technology while we are on the *chemin*, to allow us to be alone with our thoughts. But last evening I was able to talk to and see my two grandchildren in Canada, and today I was able to speak with my wife. I have no problem being alone with my thoughts . . . and I don't think that I have to be here to do this.

The *chemin* is just a place and time where it is easier to slow down, feel your own heartbeat, sense the heartbeat of others, and recognize that in so many fundamental ways we are the same. I think that we can do this no matter where we are. We just have to make the effort.

I use that same technology today to communicate with one of the Italians, with whom I have no common language. He speaks only Italian. But on my iPad, I have an App called "iTranslate" that allows me to communicate in writing in English, he in Italian. It's not perfect, but it allows us to communicate . . . and that is the first step in understanding. I can't figure out how he can be here without any French, but I discover that he is with another French-speaking Italian whom he met on the *camino* in Spain four years ago.

And at dinner, with our hosts, there is my friend Jacques from Vichy. Eating with our hosts is another first. All of us sit down and eat together. We eat food all produced locally, pea soup, pork from within five kilometres, strawberries produced in a nearby town. The hosts, M. and Mme Heinrich, are foster parents to troubled children. It takes a very special kind of person to take on the catastrophes that can happen when parents are not able to bring up a child, for whatever reason.

At nine-thirty, we finish an animated conversation and head off to bed. It's cold, so there will be an extra cover on the bed tonight.

7 May — La Baysse to Moissac

I am up at six-forty-five and ready to go, except for breakfast, by seven-thirty. I have breakfast with the two Italians and head off into a perfectly beautiful day. The sun is shining, there is barely a cloud in the sky, and it is cool — just perfect for walking. Maybe, just maybe, the weather has changed. I am going only nine kilometres today, the equivalent of a rest day.

The only bad news is that I have lost my power adapter again. Somewhere in the past two or three days, I recharged my camera battery and blithely pulled the plug from the wall, neatly leaving the adapter plug behind in the socket. I did this last year in Paris before I even got started, so I am improving. It has taken two weeks this time.

I have about 100 minutes still on my camera battery, so it is not an immediate problem. I am heading to Moissac today. It is a pretty big town, about 12,000, so maybe I can find an adapter there . . . except it is another holiday weekend in France, so everything will likely be closed. And so it turns out.

For the first hour, the walk is on roads and much less muddy paths, and I am, as always, hopeful that this will continue all the way to Moissac. Then I hit an incline on a path in a forest and start to climb. It is a five-rest-stop climb, and as I reach the top, there is a little clearing. I look around warily for a low bench, but there is none. Once bitten . . .

The rest of the walk is through farmland, vineyards, and fruit trees. I ask someone in an orchard what type of fruit, and he responds, "Abricots." There is a lot of white plastic sheeting over the rows of vines and low trees. I discover that the sheeting is primarily for protection from hail, with a secondary purpose of protection from bird predation.

I arrive at the *gite* in Moissac before noon, and it is a marvel: a former convent built around 1860, with an interior courtyard and garden; absolutely beautiful. The reception here is very friendly, with a young woman — another Fanny — helping me make reservations for the next four days. I discover that there is another former convent like this in Condom, where I will spend two nights a few days from now. Well, no, I won't. I have just been informed that it is full already, so Fanny is looking for another spot in Condom for me.

I have run out of Euros, so I walk down into the town centre, find an ATM, and discover l'abbaye Saint-Pierre de Moissac, a huge

The courtyard at Moissac.

abbey more than 1300 years old, founded in legend by Clovis, and located on a small square where there are little restaurants open. I spot the Italian who speaks French, with whom I had breakfast this morning, sitting on a bench in the square in front of the abbeye, and we have lunch together.

He tells me that he started in Le Puy with two other guys. The first dropped out at Conques with eye problems, the second (the one who speaks only Italian) is dropping out today with a foot or leg problem, and he himself has developed a problem leg as well. He is hanging in, but doesn't know how much farther he will be able to go. He comes back to the *gite* with me and gets a bed without a reservation, and I am thinking he is lucky. And here again is my quiet friend Jacques from Vichy.

Back at the *gite*, I meet Stephanie, a young Québécoise with a severe limp, a muscle problem in her lower leg. She is staying here a few days to recuperate. Stephanie has a power plug adapter, which I have borrowed to recharge my camera battery. Another Canadian arrives, this time with a sprained ankle. He slipped sideways in the mud and his ankle is badly swollen. He won't be walking anywhere for a few days.

It is a powerful reminder that the body works only as well as its least functioning part, so it is incumbent upon me to pay attention to my physical surroundings. You see, Carroll, I am listening, even when you think I'm not.

As I sit here, people keep coming in. Already my room of four beds has been fully occupied. This is obviously a very popular place to stay. Families come in, one group of nine travellers, some Americans on bikes.

Things are getting exciting, in an uncomfortable way, on the accommodation front. Fanny has been calling the *gites* in Condom and is having trouble getting a place. It is almost seven p.m. Apparently there is to be a big fete in Condom soon and many, many people are reserving space. She is hopeful that she can find something for me this evening. We shall see. She has been extraordinarily helpful today.

She finally, just as dinner is called, has me a spot. It's for only one night and the person at the other end of the phone in Condom tells her that I wouldn't want to stay in Condom two nights. The fete will be very crowded, the streets will be full of drunks, and the noise will be awful. What's not to like? So I will stay in Condom one night and move on the next day. I will take my break a little farther along the route.

At dinner, I sit with my Vichy friend, another who remembers me from Conques, and as dinner is finishing, here are two pilgrims whom I last saw in Estaing. It's like old home week in . . . Moissac (I have to think for a moment about where I actually am).

It's a strange environment on the *chemin*. There is this stream, sometimes a river, of people all heading in the same direction. Some drop out, some drop in, some are planning on going all the way to Santiago (and it's funny, as we get closer to the Spanish border, the names are becoming interchangeable: Saint-Jacques and Santiago, as are the terms "*camino*" and "*chemin*").

Over the past couple of years, I have walked a lot with an Austrian guy named Victor Frankl. He died fifteen years ago at the age of ninety-two, so I haven't physically walked with him, but I have often walked with him nevertheless. Frankl was a Jewish psychiatrist from Vienna. In nine days in 1946, Frankl wrote a book called *Man's Search for Meaning*, which I have read several times. He could write this book with a lot of personal authority because he was able to study the subject under the most appalling conditions. For over three years, he was an inmate in four of the Nazi extermination camps. One of the lessons that he learned, and that I have taken from him, is that even in the most extreme circumstances, one is always free to decide how to deal with whatever is going on in one's life. Something that he also recognized in the camps was that when people lose the meaning in their lives, they quickly die. He thinks that people make their own meaning in their lives.

What has become clearer as I do this walking again and again is that I, like many others here, am not actually sure why I am here, but I think that it has to do with trying to make sense of my life. Frankl says that when people do not have meaning in their lives, they actively search for it. The age range of pilgrims seems to be mostly people who are likely in the later stages of or have finished with their careers, their families have grown. The meaning that they previously found in family or career is mostly behind them and they are wondering; "Is this all there is?"

Frankl says that the meaning in people's lives is whatever they want it to be. If one is a religious person, then the meaning may be dictated by the particular faith. If one is not religious, then the meaning in one's life is a more personal thing. In his own life in the camps, the meaning for Frankl was partly that he wanted to see his pregnant wife again—he did not, she died early on in one of the camps, but he didn't know until after the war—and he wanted to publish his book. As well, he found personal meaning in helping other people *in extremis* determine what it was they wanted to live for. He argues that "our primary drive in life is not pleasure, but the discovery and pursuit of whatever it is that we personally find meaningful."

It's after nine and I have to go to bed. Another longish day tomorrow after an easy and happy one today.

8 May—Moissac to Espalais

Today it starts to rain lightly just before I leave this lovely old convent and the warmth of the people here. So I have to put on my rain jacket and rain cover for the backpack, which means that in less than ten minutes the rain stops. It stays overcast. After about twenty minutes, I have to stop and take off the jacket. It is just too hot for walking. The *chemin* today will be about twenty kilometres, of which

Canal à la Garonne.

seventeen are between a narrow canal and a larger river that is, as I discover after about half an hour, a larger canal. It is a section of the Midi Canal, connecting the Atlantic to the Mediterranean, cutting off hundreds of miles of sea journey. And it was built just in time to be made superfluous by the invention of the steam engine. I wonder if the investors ever recovered their money.

The path is dead flat, paved, almost straight, and has alongside a long parade of very large trees, *platane* in French, plane trees in English.[22] Sure. I think of them as camouflage trees because of the trunk, which is a mottled pattern of grey, brown, and a very pale green. Looks like perfect camouflage material to me. After about three hours of this I am almost—almost—wishing for a hill. A little one would suffice. Mud I am not missing.

There is a bridge over the canal at one point, and the road coming from the side is elevated so that I cannot see the canal beyond the bridge. As I climb up the tiny hill, I see that there is a table and some chairs set up in a little clearing, a wide spot just beyond on the other side of the road. There are several people here, two men and a woman, with a Volkswagen van open behind them. The table is covered with water bottles, some thermos bottles, and an assortment of fruit, biscuits, and cookies. I am invited to stop for a while and have some refreshment. With big smiles they assure me that it is free—and it really is. These three are locals who set up here every day and provide assistance to anyone who is walking the canal towpath. It is likely that most walkers are pilgrims of one sort or another, and the three people just want to help make the pilgrim's day a little easier. It's hard to believe, but they absolutely refuse to take any compensation for what they are doing. They make the meaning of "hospitality" come alive for me and demonstrate the spirituality that seems to be almost everywhere associated with the *chemin*. There is no hidden agenda here. I thank them sincerely as I take my leave after enjoying a couple of cookies and some coffee. They ask me to put in a good word for them to Saint-Jacques. I tell them that I will be sure to.

It starts to rain again, fairly steadily, and I have to put my rain jacket back on. I turn off the canal after seventeen kilometres and head south over a flat plain, following the red and white markers. At about one p.m., I arrive in Espalais at the *gite* "Par'Chemin . . ." run by Vincent and Sylvie. The welcome is genuine, and Sylvie, with a

---

22 A North American species is referred to as a sycamore.

warm voice and a big smile, asks me if I would like a basin of warm, salt water for my feet. Yes, I would. I dump my backpack, take off my boots, and settle into an easy chair under the huge overhanging roof with my feet in the basin. It is heaven. She gives off a powerful sensuality, although she is apparently completely unaware of it.

Vincent speaks excellent North American English, and I ask him where he learned it. Well, from age five to thirteen, he lived with his parents in the United States. While I sit with my feet in the basin, he tells me a wonderful, terrible story that I have to share with you. He is Swiss, and Sylvie is French — grew up about ten kilometres from here. Vincent, late forties, was a successful HR director for a large international organization after working for fourteen years with the International Committee of the Red Cross in war zones. He was well up on the ladder of success, without ever any clear intention of climbing it.

Then, without warning, his father, a successful international public health researcher, committed suicide at age seventy-seven. He left a letter explaining that there was a line between high creativity and madness, and he thought that he had crossed the line. Then he stabbed himself through the heart. The family was stunned.

Vincent's farmhouse near Espalais.

Vincent decided to go for a long, long walk on the Chemin de Saint-Jacques, all the way from Le Puy-en-Velay to Santiago, 1,500 kilometres, hoping to make sense of his father's apparent act of madness. He also decided to wear a mohair shirt that for him symbolized his father as he walked.

On his walk, he saw this empty farmhouse just on the edge of this tiny town of Espalais. He describes his reaction as a *"coup de coeur,"* literally a blow to the heart. He stopped, discovered no one here, had a picnic in the overgrown garden, and went on. As he walked, he thought about how he could convert this old farmhouse into a welcoming stop for pilgrims. He had noticed a "For Sale" sign as he left the property. But it seemed a pipe dream. He had a job, a career, and he did not have the kind of money that would be required to give everything up to realize this dream. So he walked on, thinking about his life and its meaning.

When he arrived, finally, in Finisterre, he took off the mohair shirt and set fire to it. (It's a tradition that once you get to Finisterre, you destroy, by burning or throwing it into the ocean, something that you brought with you for that purpose. Perhaps it's symbolic of turning over a page in your life.) Of course the shirt, being mohair, smouldered, just wouldn't burn. So he tied knots in the arms, and whirling it over his head, threw it as far as he could into the ocean. Then he went home to pick up his life.

At home in Geneva, his mother asked, "What are you going to do with your life?" He told her about his impossible dream. Then she said, "When your father died, he left some money. I think that he would have liked you to have some of it. It might help you." A gift from both his father and his mother, it was only 10,000 Euros less than the asking price of the property in France.

When Vincent inquired about the property, the owner wanted to know about Vincent's plans for it. It turns out that the owner's father had for years provided a welcome for pilgrims, never a *gite* in the commercial sense, just a place that welcomed pilgrims on the way. It had been empty and for sale for five years, but as the owner explained, "I have been waiting patiently for the right buyer."

He was financially comfortable, still owns a lot of land in the area. He wanted someone who would carry on the tradition of welcoming weary pilgrims as they made their way toward wherever they were heading. So the property changed hands about eighteen months ago.

Since then, Vincent and Sylvie have created a little paradise here, providing a warm welcome to pilgrims as they travel. And the price is "*donativo*," or pay what you can. They want to create an environment, not based on a certain price or expectation, where they respect the pilgrims and honour their needs, and the pilgrims respect the effort and welcome of these two delightful hosts. And each side gains from the exchange. There is an opportunity here to rest, to reflect, to meditate, or to discuss one's problems without fearing the judgment of someone else. Just a place to be. I think that they have been successful in this intent.

As both of them read the "Life's Lessons Relearned" from my book, *A Journey of Days*, about my walk on the Camino de Santiago in Spain, they exclaim as they read each one, "That's exactly it, that's exactly it!"

I am simply overcome with emotion as I embrace them both and I tell them, "It's not often that I fall in love with two people at the same time." And it is true. If there is any place on the *chemin* where the best of the spirit of true human fellowship shines brightly, this is it. This is true spirituality in action. She is weeping with emotion . . . I am close to tears.

I ask how they ended up together. Vincent tells me that they have a common acquaintance, Steff, in the village. One day, Steff asked Sylvie, who had dropped in, if she knew the Swiss guy. She said "No"; he said: "You have to know the Swiss guy," and brought her here to meet the Swiss guy. She had been interested in the use of the property in former days and was glad to see it being put to its new purpose. They met a few times, then Sylvie decided to go for a walk on the *camino*, perhaps having a life change in mind. He drove her to Toulouse; she got a train to Saint-Jean-Pied-de-Port and walked toward Santiago. She got as far as Léon, where Vincent met her. They came back here and decided to see how well it would work to be together. That's Vincent's story.

Here is Sylvie's version: A year or so earlier, she had had a boyfriend who was a realtor. She asked him to let her take a look at this house, which was on the market. She walked through it and felt a powerful, almost mystical connection to the house, but had no interest in buying it. She already had a place elsewhere. One day, she met Steff in the village and he invited her back to his house, where he was welcoming some pilgrims. She had had a friendly breakup with her boyfriend just two days before. They then came as a group out to the Swiss guy's house and she felt her heart tug as she turned into the driveway and realized that it was THIS house. Vincent was not here at the time, and they sat in the garden until he came home later.

He invited her to see what he had done so far; she was impressed and looked forward to meeting him again. There was a special connection to Vincent. They met a few times, each becoming a little more interested in the other. One morning, she woke with the urge to walk the *camino*, which had not been in her plans at all. He offered to drive her to the train in Toulouse, where she took the train to Saint-Jean-Pied-de-Port and started walking. At the station as she left, he told her that he would be waiting for her; so he was already sure.

A few weeks into her journey (they had been messaging back and forth), she had to cut her journey short to return to France. She was in Léon, and he drove 800 kilometres to pick her up and bring her back. By the time he picked her up in Spain, she was pretty sure that he was the guy for her. By the time they got back to this house, she was absolutely sure.

Vincent, Sylvie, and me.

My take on it, a year later, is that it is working just fine. (And by the way, both Vincent and Sylvie have read and approved their individual versions of the story.)

I tell them that I see in them the same kind of relationship that Carroll and I have. We have more than fifty-four years, they have one, but I am confident that this is a relationship that will pass all the tests to which it will be put. There is evident mutual respect and affection and self-respect as well. This ought to work just fine over the years.

One of the things that Vincent did early on was to plan a huge table to be put under the overhanging roof. He tells me that this table is a signal of his intention to stay. He went to a mill about thirty kilometres from here and asked for a single board six metres long, 1.3 metres wide, and eight centimetres thick. The mill owner said, "You're from the city, aren't you?" Vincent said that he was. The mill owner then said that if he were able to provide a single board, it would be prohibitively expensive, so they settled on three narrower boards that would do the same thing. Vincent sanded and varnished the surface and put it on two huge oak stumps as a base and as a sign of the rootedness of the place. I am sitting at this wonderful table as

I write. With the light wind, it is just cool enough that wearing my fleece, unzipped, is just right.

With my full permission, they will take my life's lessons from the book, translate them into multiple languages, and post them on the walls of the *gite*. I will, when I get home, send them a signed copy of the book.

Some people whom I know come in for a brief rest, and I convince them to stay, so we are about a half dozen now. There has been a fete for the past four days in the village, and four or five locals have arrived for a visit. They stay for a drink, so Vincent is being accepted here. That is very important for him and for Sylvie.

It has become overcast and quite dark and, around a quarter to six, a long series of regular, loud explosions, each followed by a whistling sound, can be heard. So far, about ten minutes' worth. It sounds like something pretty heavy being lofted into the air. It's louder than a 105 artillery round, less loud than a 155. If this were in the mountains in Canada, I would assume that someone was doing avalanche control, but it is summer here—and it's flat. Someone explains that they are firing warm air—I am unclear how it is packaged—into the clouds to break them up and avoid the hail. I gather that hail is sufficiently common in this area that this makes sense. Does it work? It doesn't hail. After a brief hiatus, the noise starts again, but much closer. It gets very dark and it rains but it never does hail.

At dinner, we are eleven, including people I have met several times: Nicolas, the French guy who speaks excellent English, and Mark, the guy walking from his home in Antwerp to Santiago. With us are Pierre and Marie Kirschner from Hochstatt, near the German border. He is a great big guy, big features, huge hands, dark, very funny, huge laugh as well. Later in the evening, he picks up a guitar and plays . . . CCR,[23] first "Proud Mary" (his wife is Marie) then, at my request, "There's a Bad Moon Rising." I never expected to hear that here, and I have to tell all of them the story about that song being the night flying theme song for my helicopter unit some forty years ago. Pierre tells me during the course of the evening that he and Marie noticed me yesterday at Moissac because I was sitting in the interior courtyard working away on my iPad. It was the only place that I could get a WiFi connection, near the *gite*'s office.

---

23   CCR = Creedence Clearwater Revival, an American rock band of the late '60s and early '70s.

Pierre singing CCR's "Proud Mary."

Even later, a shy young man, Rémi from Cahors, a fellow pilgrim, offers us a nursery song, taught to him by his grandmother in Occitan, the ancient language that was spoken in Languedoc . . . and apparently still is. I do not know at this point how important this connection to his grandmother is for Rémi but I will find out in a couple of weeks. I go off to bed quite late, almost eleven, feeling loved and loving.

9 May — Espalais to Castet-Arrouy

I wake up at about two in the morning, wide awake, and I have a genuine epiphany. I know, for the first time in five years, why I am walking here. I am absolutely clear about this. I am here to collect experiences, mine and those of others, as material for a book that will inspire readers to embark on their own journey of personal discovery, to take the next step in their lives. I have no idea how I have come to this conclusion — the process has been unconscious — but the result is clear and certain for me.

I don't want to leave this wonderful, loving environment. Eventually, after a long, bittersweet goodbye with Sylvie and Vincent, I am on my way at nine-thirty. I am so tempted to stay for another day. I did say I don't want to leave. I expect to walk about twenty-five kilometres today, to a *gite* in Castet-Arrouy operated by Clément, a protegé of Vincent's. It is quite a story in itself.

Vincent answered the phone one day about a year ago and connected with a total stranger on the other end of the line. It was Clément, who wanted to find out about running a *gite*. Vincent invited him to this place, and they met. Clément is a tall, well-built young man who has, as Vincent quickly finds out, a big dream and not much idea of how to implement it.

Vincent asked him how he would find a *gite* to operate. Clément told him that he would walk on the *chemin* and something will happen. This is the equivalent of wanting some milk and carrying a three-legged stool out to the middle of a field and waiting for a cow to come to be milked. It's possible, but there needs to be an alternate and more viable plan. Vincent challenged him to write down his values and how running a *gite* would honour them. After reading and discussing them the next day, Vincent invited Clément to come work with him for a week to see if this is really a good and sustainable idea. At the end of a very challenging week, Clément left with a pretty good business plan, and over the next few months, found an available building and started to work. Now it is running, and that is where I am going today.

The walk is mostly on a road through rolling hill country, and it is sunny and gets hot. I stop after ten kilometres for a lunch break, where I find Pierre and Marie (you will remember him; he's the big guitar player). Lunch for me is *un demi*, copious glasses of water, and a twelve-inch sandwich of real bread with ham, cheese, and tomato. Lunch costs just over five Euros, including the beer. Pierre and Marie tell me they are stopping at Clément's *gite* as well. I am very pleased. They are delightful companions.

Rolling countryside.

I head out alone for Miradoux, where I am told I must stop at Chez Thérèse for a drink. I am hot and tired when I arrive. It's about twenty kilometres already and it is hot. My clothes have been soaked with sweat since this morning, and I have noticed that my pulse has been about 120 for the past couple of hours. Some of that is effort; a lot of it is the body trying to keep itself cool.

Chez Thérèse turns out to be not a restaurant or a bar, as I had expected, but a kitchen where Thérèse gives pilgrims drinks, food, cheese, whatever they need—always free. There is no way to pay for this. She looks after pilgrims just because she can. Thérèse is a short, chunky woman, a year younger than me, walks with a sailor's roll (it's her hips) and is a force in the region. She is a friend of Vincent's, of Clément's, and, as I will find out later, of Philippe's, where I will spend the night tomorrow. I ask if she can make mocha and I have to describe what that is (chocolate, coffee, milk, all hot—delicious). She has never heard of it but puts it all together for me. This is all before I find out that this is not a paying establishment. I find out much later that she runs a tiny *gite* here, as well.

I am sitting here really tired, hot, sweaty, having walked for just over six hours, and I ask her if it is possible to call a taxi to carry me the last five kilometres. She immediately responds: "No, I will get my car and take you. It's only a few minutes." And that is what she does. When we arrive in Castet, she asks me if I would like to see the church before going to the *gite*. I am in her car—of course I would like to see the church. We walk in; it's a very pleasant, smallish church, lots of colour—nice. Then she starts to sing. It is a sublime transformation. Her superb voice fills the church, which has near-perfect acoustics. She is simply a wonderful singer, without shyness or braggadocio.

I am reminded of an experience that Carroll and I had in Cyprus some forty-odd years ago. I had taken her to Bellapais Abbey, the ruined abbey that Lawrence Durrell wrote about in *Bitter Lemons*. We walk in to the roofless structure, just stone walls crumbling about us. It is a little disappointing. We are just leaving when four young men come in. I think they were German, Carroll thinks they were English, but it doesn't matter, so I let her have this one. They start to sing in Gregorian chant, and the place reverts to what it might have been like hundreds of years before. It is another transformation, like the one happening here in this little church.

Thérèse stops singing, and the church goes back to being a nice little church. Back in the car, off to the *gite*, where I meet Clément. He is tall, well-built, young, and wears a baseball cap backwards. My first impression is a little negative, but that doesn't last long. I think it's the cap. His *gite* is called "*Le Lièvre et la Tortue*," The Hare and the Tortoise. I think that the name has to do with his eagerness to start the *gite* and Vincent's good advice, which slowed him down. Of course, with this name, I have to tell him the story about my unfortunate experience with turning turtle off the bench after Lauzerte. It's a delicious irony to be here in a *gite* with this name. Nicolas is here, camping with his tent in a field. At six-forty-five, Pierre and Marie come in. I really like these two. Because it's so late, I had given them up for lost, so I am delighted to see them here.

There is a family of five here as well, parents and three girls, ranging in age from five to thirteen. The parents tell me that they have two grown children who elected not to come. The oldest child here, who is just transforming from a little girl into a stunningly beautiful woman—girl's body, adult's face—never says a word, sits here quite solemn and still.

We have dinner in the garden—well, it's a small field—behind the *gite*. Clément barbecues sausage and, I think, zucchini, and serves it with an enormous bowl of pasta. We sit, just the few of us, talking as it gets dark and the candles get lit. The red wine keeps coming, and the conversation keeps vivid. My French gets worse as I get tired but better with the wine.

Shortly after ten, the red wine, the conversation, and my endurance all fail at the same time. Off to bed; another longish walk, about twenty-one kilometres, tomorrow.

10 May — Castet-Arrouy to Marsolan

I leave The Hare and the Tortoise on a sunny, cool morning with Pierre and Marie. They are very *sympa*—which is a lot more than congenial, it's more like soulmates. It's good walking, partly because of the weather, partly because when I am on the path, off road, the mud is mostly gone. At eleven-thirty, we three stop for lunch. After we eat, I go to pay, only to find out that it's already paid for by Pierre. That's very generous of them, and I tell them that I appreciate it.

They tell me that they have space reserved with a friend of Clément's in Marsolan. I already have a reservation in Marsolan,

Marie, me, and Pierre at lunch.

but I ask if there is room for one more with them. I want to stay with these people as long as possible. It turns out to be an inspired—and controversial—decision.

Pierre calls, finds out that there is room, reserves a spot for me, then, at my request, calls the place where I have already reserved and cancels my reservation. His face gets red and his voice gets louder as he speaks with the owner of the *gite*. Apparently, the owner thinks that I should pay even if I am not coming. Given the pilgrim traffic here, he is not going to have any problem filling the bed, but he is adamant. So is Pierre. He is furious.

He is a businessman, the director of two medical supply centres where he lives, so he understands business needs. But he says that providing services to pilgrims is different. It is more than just a business, and you have to respect the pilgrim as well. He tells the *gite* owner that it's not going to happen and ends the connection. If there were going to be a problem renting out the bed, I would have no problem paying, but this is a form of gouging. At the same time I have some sympathy with the *gite* owner because I have heard about people who call and make multiple bookings wherever they can, then just pick one and ignore the others—not good pilgrim behaviour.

After a walk of more than twenty kilometres on what turns out to be a hot day, we arrive in Marsolan, a tiny, tiny village on a steep hillside. Actually, we arrive separately because they are walking a few hundred metres ahead of me and miss a shortcut that I take, so I arrive a little ahead of them. It doesn't buy me much because I realize that I have no idea where we are staying, except that it is NOT at the *gite* where I was booked. We meet a local and ask him the location of the *gite* Bourdon. He has no idea. We ask him how many people live in the village. He says, "Thirty-five."

Resting on a stone bench.

How on earth can he NOT know where the *gite* is? The mystery is solved when Marie goes off on a brief reconnaissance, leaving Pierre and me sitting on a bench in the shade of big trees in the town square. When she returns, she tells us that the *gite* is the very last house on the left on the way out of the village. It is a brand-new *gite* in a very old building and it is under construction. Part of a wall in the kitchen is actually part of the original wall that surrounded the fortified town.

Philippe, the owner, is a friend of Clément's and Vincent's . . . and of Thérèse's. He welcomes us warmly, repeats that the *gite* is under construction—it certainly is—and shows us to our beds. He takes dust covers off the beds. There is a toilet, wobbly, no seat yet, a working shower, and construction materials and dust everywhere. But it doesn't matter. The welcome is genuine. How new is this *gite*? We are pilgrims seven, eight, and nine to stay here—ever. I am the first Canadian; Pierre and Marie are the first couple. Philippe tells us with a wry smile that he is going to stop counting after ten.

I have a little sleep while Pierre and Marie walk back up the hill to the *épicerie* for some food for tonight's dinner. While they are out, Philippe tells me that he spent several months in Canada some twenty years ago but did not learn much English. He was always with French speakers who spoke better English than he did, so he depended on them. He also spent several months in the very far north of Quebec in the James Bay region with the Natives of that area. I never do find out what he was doing there. I can usually get the drift of the conversation but remain a touch hazy on the details.

The *gite* is not yet sufficiently advanced to offer dinner, and Philippe offers that he is not much of a cook. Marie and Pierre prepare dinner. We end up with a huge salad, sausages, and pasta carbonara. It is all excellent. We four sit together at the kitchen table, enjoying each other's company and talking into the evening. I don't know quite how it happens, but Philippe asks if we would like a little whisky. Marie declines, but Pierre and I think that's a good idea, which sounds good and gets much better very quickly when Philippe pulls out a bottle of single malt scotch. I find the atmosphere and the company just entrancing.

Philippe is a successful businessman from Grenoble who decided that he wanted—probably needed—to operate a *gite*, much like Vincent and Clément the past couple of days. He found this building with assistance from Thérèse, bought it, and is just starting up. His wife is in Grenoble and will come here in a year when the reconstruction is complete to help him run the *gite*. I find these dedicated *hospitaliers* just fascinating. They have a passion for *le chemin* and for the pilgrims who travel it. This is not a get-rich-quick scheme; it's not even a get-rich-ever scheme. He charges sixteen Euros for the night, and that includes breakfast.

We have discovered that accommodation in Condom is going to be a problem for Pierre and Marie. I booked mine several days ago, when I booked four days in a row, using the kind services of Fanny from Moissac. Marie, using the magic of her cell and her considerable persuasion skills, has found a place for them in Condom at an equestrian centre a couple of kilometres out of town.

We talk for hours, just the four of us, about the *chemin*, our lives, our families. Marie, a young and attractive forty-one, is an emergency room nurse with twenty years' experience; she has three children from a former marriage aged from seven to seventeen. Pierre, forty-eight, is the director of two medical supply centres back home in Alsace and has two children from a former marriage. They are clearly very happy together. They often walk hand-in-hand, Pierre getting to carry all four hiking poles.

They started this walk in Montcuq and will finish in Condom. Pierre, with a delicious and wicked sense of humour, points out that Montcuq, as pronounced and then translated, sounds like "my ass" in English, and Condom needs no translation. I suspect that he may have chosen these points on purpose, although he assures me that it has to do with train connections. I am saddened that we will part so soon. I was hoping to spend longer with them, but tomorrow will be the last day. I am very fond—that's not strong enough—I am in love with both of them, and it's not driven by lust. Well, perhaps just a bit . . . she is very attractive and warm . . . but it is much more than that. Sometimes in my life I meet people with whom I make an immediate and deep connection. Pierre and Marie are two of these, as are my recent hosts Vincent and Marie.

Off to bed quite late—after eleven, which here on the *chemin* is really late. The three of us share a room. I go to bed first and am asleep when they come in a few minutes later—they tell me later. And it's off to Condom tomorrow. Should be good for a joke or two in poor taste.

11 May — Marsolan to Condom

It dawns warm and sunny, should be a good day for walking. It is lovely in the morning, gets a bit oppressive in the afternoon. As we leave Marsolan, Philippe walks with us for a few hundred metres to make sure that we are on the right road. There are at least three ways to get to Condom from here. The first is a direct walk for seventeen kilometres on the road, no place for food or water along the way. The second is via the *chemin*, about twenty-three kilometres, wandering over hill and dale, much like a dog's random trail as it tracks down fascinating smells.

The third option, which Philippe recommends, is a compromise between the two. It is about twenty kilometres, through La Romieu, which has places for food and drink and is also, he tells us, the village of cats. He does not explain further — says it will be obvious. As we are standing at the point

Philippe, Pierre, and me.

where we depart, along comes Alberto, an Italian with whom we have spent some time in the past few days. We say goodbye to Philippe and head off, four of us, on the quiet, winding country road to La Romieu.

We arrive in about ninety minutes, and it is indeed the village of cats. I had imagined a village full of little old ladies with their twenty-seven cats each. I couldn't be more wrong. There is not a live cat to be seen. But there are whimsical sculptures of cats, more than life-size, on windowsills, disappearing into or emerging from little crannies in the walls. There are more than a dozen just in this one small square where we are sitting having a coffee.

Along comes Nicolas, who has been camping in his tent on the way. He tells us that he cannot sleep unless it is perfectly quiet, so a *dortoir* in a *gite* does not work for him at all.

At La Romieu, we have sandwiches made in an *épicerie* for later, the usual butter, ham, and cheese on a perfectly wonderful piece of bread. As we walk on toward Condom, it starts to get hot and oppressive. My clothes are soaking wet with sweat . . . again. I have filled my three-litre soft plastic water bottle at Marsolan, and it is a good thing. It is empty just as we reach Condom. As we walk, we talk. Marie tells me about her children. The youngest, seven, is concerned about her mother's absence for ten days. Marie's solution is to prepare a small wooden box of kisses, one for each day, every one a piece of paper with a lipstick kiss and some words of comfort. She says that the kisses are working well.

She also tells me some of Pierre's background. He had a brother, two years older, who died two years ago at age forty-eight, Pierre's age now, of heart failure. The brother was also schizophrenic, although that did not figure in his death. We talk about mental illness and its devastation on all those in the extended family. I tell her about my own experiences with a suicide and a devastating mental illness in the extended family.

As we get close to Condom, we have to decide how to deal with what little time we have left together. Alberto goes ahead, and I know that I will see him tomorrow, since we have booked the same *gite* in Montréal-du-Gers. The equestrian centre where Pierre and Marie will stay is two kilometres on this side of Condom, while my *gite* is somewhere in the city. The decision is for all three of us to walk to my *gite*, where I can drop my backpack, shower, then walk back with my friends to the equestrian centre. Just as we enter the populated part of Condom, there is a sign for my *gite*, eighty metres ahead. Bliss!

Pierre and Marie settle down on the grass while I go inside and sort myself out. After I have located a bed and have showered and changed into clean clothes and sandals, we walk back to their accommodation, where we hope that I can get dinner. My *gite* does not offer it. We think that since the equestrian centre has sixty-five beds, one more mouth to feed won't be an issue. Marie showers first,

Marie in Condom.

while Pierre and I sit outside and enjoy a cool drink. Then she comes out, looking radiant, and Pierre goes for his shower. We sit and talk for a couple of hours until we are called for dinner. We are in a little dining room, just four of us — we three and another Frenchman who speaks fluent English. He learned it in Wales. Again, we sit and talk and sip on red wine until it gets dark.

I don't want this day . . . or this relationship . . . to end, and clearly neither do they. Eventually, I decide that I have to leave, and Pierre insists on walking back with me the two kilometres into town. I embrace Marie — she has tears in her eyes, as do I, as we say goodbye. None of us knows where, when, or if we will meet again. Pierre has a headlamp and waves it around with huge, sweeping gestures as we walk along the edge of the busy highway. He tells me, in jest, that he is blessing all the drivers.

When we arrive back at my *gite*, we embrace and promise to keep in touch — and we will. I ask him to give my love to Marie and he says that he does — often. Then off he goes into the dark. They leave tomorrow morning by bus back to Cahors, where they will pick up their car for the eight-hour drive back to Alsace.

Why so busy here? There is a big festival in Condom this weekend. The town of less than 8,000 is more than three times its normal population. This is the fortieth anniversary of this Banda festival. Banda is folk music, big bands, accordions, and large, noisy, and energetic crowds. This festival has over time been corrupted to be a huge, drunken brawl, mostly young people, mid-teens to mid-twenties, for a full weekend.

The noise in the city is incredible. Even in my *gite* at the very edge of town, close to a kilometre from the city centre, I can hear the noise without my hearing aids. It does not keep me awake for long, although it clearly has a negative effect on some of the other people trying to sleep here.

Okay, I know that you want to know what is going on with Condom. First of all, the accent is on the second syllable, not the first, so it's conDOM, not CONdom. And the word in France is *préservatif*. Second, guess what they make here. Well, you're wrong, although it was a good guess. What they make here and are famous for is Armagnac, a strong liquor similar to cognac, but unlike cognac, distilled only once.

However, catering to popular demand, there IS a museum here of population control devices. I do not visit the museum. At my age, nature pretty well takes care of that for me.

Tomorrow, I am off to Montréal, where I expect to take a rest day. No, the other one, Montréal-du-Gers. It is much, much smaller, and even more French. I am just short of 400 kilometres so far, so more than halfway.

12 May — Condom to Montréal-du-Gers

I am out of the *gite* by eight a.m. The other pilgrims tell me that they had a poor sleep last night because of the noise. It takes me about forty minutes to walk out of Condom and it is an amazing, amusing, and horrifying walk. As I walk through the centre of the town, I see at least a dozen young men who are in really advanced stages of drunkenness. I see one whose stance against a wall reminds me of the scene in *Cat Ballou* in which the gunslinger, on his horse, is leaning against a wall, completely drunk. The evidence of a really big party is all around.

The local authorities have barricaded the whole of the city centre to keep people safe from vehicle traffic, although nothing can keep them from self-inflicted damage. These guys aren't aggressive; they are in fact quite friendly and, when they are able to focus on me, wish me "*Bon courage*" or "*Bon chemin.*" As is quite common, the signage for the *chemin* is less conspicuous in the town, so I have to keep asking if I am on the right route. The tables are turned once when one of the drunks asks me if this is the Chemin de Saint-Jacques, and I tell him that I hope so, but I don't know.

Out of town, the countryside is gently rolling hills, the farms look prosperous, there is haying going on, the strawberries are already ripe and in the stores, and the barley is high.

It is overcast and cool with a haze that supports my guess that humidity is close to 100 percent. I have refilled my water bag and sip from it every time I think of it. I have my hat attached to my belt, since there is no sun, and it's cooler with the hat off.

I meet Alberto soon after I leave Condom and we walk together for the day. He is companionable and sufficiently garrulous that I don't have to carry my end of the conversation. Yesterday, Pierre and Marie said about him, with fondness: "Alberto is SO Italian!" He tells

Solitary pilgrim.

me at one point that the Italian term for the scallop shell, a symbol of the pilgrim's walk, is "*La concha,*" which he also explains, in passing, is the less-formal Italian term for female genitalia. It creates quite a vivid image for me.

We walk past vineyards, and at one point, I see a man checking his vines and I ask him, naively, what kind of wine he makes. It's the kind of question that must make a winemaker's hair turn grey. He responds, after a pause to think of an appropriate answer to a dumb question; "*Vins de Gascogne,* the best wines in France." He produces both red and rosé, and it looks to be a good year.

We arrive in Montréal-du-Gers at about one p.m., find our *gite,* deposit our backpacks (it opens for pilgrims at two), and walk back 100 yards to the town square, where there is a bar with outdoor seating under an old arcade. We have a little aperitif and wait until two, being entertained by a small group of young men, clearly survivors of last night's bacchanalia in Condom. According to the bar owner, they have been here for several hours, drinking. That is perfectly obvious.

They are loud, boisterous, but not obnoxious. Just before two, they leave to go to their car and drive—horrors, they can barely walk—back to Condom for more revelry. I am so glad that I am not there. I have never been fond of groups of drunks, because they can get nasty so quickly, and for no reason apparent to anyone but them. As they walk away, one of them has his pants down around his knees and is mooning, probably inadvertently, scandalised little old ladies. I say inadvertently because I doubt he or any of the group could form a coherent intention.

At two, we return to the *gite* and get our beds. Since we are the first here, we have our choice. I pick a lower bunk with a window shelf next to it. That gives me a place to put small but critical bits of gear, such as my hearing aids, at night. Better than on the floor, where I might step on them as I make my nightly trip to the john. Alberto picks the bunk above mine.

The place is lovely. It's on the edge of town, up high—actually it's hard not to be on the edge of town—with a view over farmers' fields, woods, and a couple of small villages or large homesteads. There is a tractor cutting hay in the distance. It is the only noise besides birdsong.

One of my first moves is to ask if I can stay here another night. They are happy and obliging. It turns out—this is a newly opened *gite*, only six weeks old—that I am the first pilgrim to ask to stay over for two nights. The owner, Anita, is German, slight, friendly, of indeterminate age, speaks French with a delightful lilt. She walked the *camino* three years ago, then decided that she wanted to open a *gite*. But she had little money, only a flat in Spain, worked two years at various *gites* in Saint-Jean-Pied-de-Port to learn how to operate a *gite*. She would have liked to sell her flat, but the economy was dreadful. Then, out of the blue, she got a call from a neighbour. Someone wanted to buy her flat. She sold it and that gave her enough money to buy this place and open the *gite*.

Late in the day, two young Norwegian women arrive, both twenty-four, both in teacher training. They are Anna and Tone—pronounced, approximately, "Toone." I tell them about my love affair with Norway and they tell me about their experiences on the *chemin*. They are walking from Le Puy to Santiago and have planned ten weeks to do it. They tell me about being in the snowfields on the Aubrac plateau and realizing, even for Norwegians and used to winter conditions, that this was a very dangerous place to be. They got lost one day for three hours and were very concerned. I am surprised that no one died up there. Over the past three weeks, I have heard a number of real horror stories about the conditions there. When I was driven through in a taxi, it looked like a scene from Napoleon's winter retreat from Moscow.

I ask them about the mass killing in Oslo, and Anna tells me that her mother, who is a priest, lives very near the island where most of the killing took place and she went there to help immediately after the killing. There was not a lot that she could do except console the survivors. They are both very proud to be Norwegians, as they should be, and tell me that the population has just passed five million.

We enjoy a lovely dinner, all thirteen of us, and get to bed in good time. Everyone except me will be leaving in the morning. Alberto will walk for a few more days in France, then take a train to Spain and walk the Camino del Norte along the northern coast.

13 May — in Montréal-du-Gers

A rest day today. I have walked about 180 kilometres in eight days without a break, and the idea of a rest day really appeals. I am just at the 400-kilometre mark. This is a lovely *gite*, spotlessly clean, roomy, with really good toilet and shower facilities, even a washing machine, and I am happy to be here. I have breakfast with the group who are leaving, then they are gone, and I am alone. It is a strange feeling, kind of like having the whole family emigrate to a faraway country. I might catch up with some of them, perhaps not. The weather is good for the walkers today, light overcast, light breeze, warm, not hot.

I keep out of the road as Anita and Michel do their daily cleanup. Then I am invited to have a small midmorning snack — coffee and a sweet pastry — with them, sitting outdoors and looking out over the fields. Anita tells me that they are heading off to a nearby village for a flea market and asks if I would like to go with them. Of course I would. Into the car for a ten-minute drive to Fourcès, where the market is.

The old town is very unusual, since the main square isn't square. It is round, planted with pollarded plane trees, and with five stone benches down each side of a pathway through the centre of the circle. All the stores around the "square" are fronted with a deep arcade. It is very attractive. The town is also on another of the *chemins* de Saint Jacques, this one running south from Vézelay. The route merges with the one I am on a day's walk south of here.

The flea market is under the arcade, in the stores and in the centre area under the plane trees. It is a typical flea market, an awful lot of it appears to be junk, but it might be treasure for someone else. The dress of the treasure-seekers is indistinguishable from that at a typical flea market in North America. We are far from Paris, where elegance is still the norm. I sit on one of the benches and watch the world saunter by.

I am enthralled by a tall, elderly man who sets up four trestles and two flat surfaces immediately in front of me. It takes him a full twenty minutes to do this, moving the trestles a centimeter at a time. I don't think that I have ever seen OCD in action before, but this has got to be a textbook example. By the time he gets the tables arranged and the goods displayed, the buyers will have all gone home for the afternoon. When I leave, he has just gotten the white plastic cover on the tables. Fascinating; and so far as I can tell, he is completely oblivious to my sitting there not five feet away. I never do find out what it is he intends to offer for sale.

Anita finds me sitting here and asks if I will join them to taste a local wine. Hardly needs an invitation, does it? We taste an aperitif wine called Ladevèze made from Armagnac. According to the bottle it is the "authentic apéritif Gascon de Ladevèze." It is 18 percent alcohol and is made locally in Montréal-du-Gers. I buy a bottle as a gift for my hosts, who tell me that they will re-gift it this evening for the pilgrims who arrive today. Once again, it is like being an honoured member of the family. It's a good feeling.

Back in Montréal-du-Gers, I am further invited to join them with a friend, Hervé, here for lunch. The friend turns out to be a seasoned pilgrim who frequently acts as a *hospitalier* at various *gites*. He has dropped in here today and will be returning in a few days to give Anita a hand. Michel has been here just two weeks. He walked for four weeks from the north of France to be here to help. He met Anita four years ago on the *camino* in Spain, and they have remained in touch ever since. A retired air traffic controller (so we have aviation in common), he will be here for two months helping Anita establish the pattern for this *gite*.

Pilgrims arrive throughout the afternoon: three Germans, two women and a man, then five more, all French. They all have reservations here.

Just before six p.m., the phone rings. Anita answers it, then passes it to me, saying, "It's for you." I am dumbfounded. How could anyone call me here? I scarcely know where I am. But it IS for me. It is Pierre calling me to tell me that he and Marie are safely home, that they have been reading and enjoying my blog, and that they have put a couple of comments on the blog. I had not seen them, so I have to go and look.

There is a joke about Condom (I did tell you that there would be tasteless jokes about Condom), and another about Alberto, my Italian travelling companion. Pierre wants to make sure that we have a solid electronic link, and I couldn't agree more. It is deeply moving for me to have this couple go to the effort of figuring out where I am, then calling me.

About six-thirty, after having talked to Carroll on Skype, I and the rest of the pilgrims here walk up to the enormous, dark, and imposing old church for a brief pilgrims' ceremony, led by Anita's friend Hervé. The church's square pillars are seriously over-engineered, about two metres on each side.

Then we come back here, and the three German pilgrims sit outside and start to sing. It sounds like a missionary meeting, and I foresee a long evening. But I would be wrong. They sing a couple of hymns, then they switch to Frère Jacques, and the like. They just like to sing. We all, three Germans, five French pilgrims, our hosts, and I sit outside and break out the fortified wine that I bought this morning. I discover that not only is this wine local, we can see, on the distant crest to the south, the actual farm where the wine is made.

The Germans don't speak much French, the French no German, Anita is busy, so God help us all, I am enlisted as the translator between the two groups. Scary. We each have a little shot of wine and make toasts to the *chemin*, to our various countries, and to the peace between them.

Dinner proceeds at the same happy pace . . . lots of laughter and bad translations. One of the people has been to Canada and visited friends in Vernon, BC. Bear stories appear, and I try, with appallingly little success, to tell the joke of how to tell regular bear scat from grizzly scat. It's the bells. After dessert, we are all out of the dining area by nine, including me. It's off to bed for a seventeen- or eighteen-kilometre walk tomorrow to Eauze, pronounced Ayooze.

14 May — Montréal-du-Gers to Eauze

I wake up this morning raring to go. The day's rest has rejuvenated me, and I am anxious to be on my way. It helps that the day promises to be gorgeous, sunny, and not too warm; and the *chemin*, I am told, is easy all the way to Eauze. I have discovered that the three Germans will be in the same *gîte* as me, Chez Nadine, in Eauze, which is good to know. They are good people, and I would like to spend more time with them. I say goodbye to Anita, Michel, and Hervé, and walk out of the *gîte*.

Pilgrim walking on a narrow path.

I know where the *chemin* is as I leave, but as soon as I get to the bottom of the hill, I lose track. I meet young Rémi from Cahors at the bottom of the hill, but he is heading the other way. However, I see a sign for the road to Eauze, which promises to be much shorter than the *chemin*, so I head off on the road. I am feeling really good, physically and psychologically. I am walking through vineyards, gently rolling hills, the weather is co-operative, and I am right with the world.

As I walk, I see a sign for "*massage pelerine.*" I stop, think about it, decide against it, walk on 100 metres, stop again, and decide: "What the hell—why not?" I walk back to the sign, turn in, and walk a couple of hundred metres to a house. I knock on the door, a short woman answers, a little hesitant. I ask if this is where the massage is. She calls out to someone; it turns out to be her husband, who comes to the door. He is the masseur. I drop my backpack and poles at the door. We discuss what he can do, what the price will be, and we agree on terms.

Then we walk through the house and out another door into a garden. There is a blue tent-like structure, about twelve feet square, and it is where he does the massage. It is effectively outdoors. I strip off everything except my shorts (I am North American, after all), even my MedicAlert bracelet. Onto the massage table for perhaps one of the best massages of my life. The birds chirping and the light breeze make it wonderful. When he is done, I am just about asleep on the table. He covers me with a sheet, tells me to take my time. It's good advice. I don't want to move, it feels so good. I get up, get dressed, and he asks me if I would like to have tea with him. Of course I would.

Back to the house, he makes green tea, which we drink together on the stone patio. He is Denis, a pilgrim from four years ago, not from this region. He loved this area as he walked through, and eight months later, he and his wife and their blended family of seven children had moved here so he could serve pilgrims as they walk through. I am amazed at the dedication, almost obsession, of so many of the people whom I meet who are providing services along the *chemin* to pilgrims. Many of them are pilgrims themselves, and it shows in their welcome and their whole approach.

The path changes to a walk in farmers' fields, a lot of barley, and a lot of woods. The last third of the *chemin* today is a dead-straight, dead-flat road that is shown on the map as the ancient road to Eauze. From all appearances, this must have been a Roman road. It has been engineered to be flat, wide, and straight. At times it is ten metres lower than the surrounding land, at times up to twenty metres higher. The land height varies, the road does not. That is a lot of construction, and the Romans were exceedingly good at engineering and road-building.

It is exactly the road that I would have wanted had I been a Roman garrison commander about 1,800 years ago who needed to move troops, equipment, or supplies quickly to deal with an unruly local population. It reminds me of the Eisenhower interstate system in the United States, built in the 1950s for exactly the same reason: to move troops, equipment, and supplies quickly over large distances.

I listen to the birds chattering and singing—they are loud and insistent—and I speculate about what is actually going on. I know birdsong sounds sweet, but here is an approximate translation:

"Hi, big fellow. Got a match?"

"Sure I have, sweetheart. You from around here?"

"No. I'm just in town for the festival. You?"

"Yeah, me too. Like to have a drink?"

"Sure, I'd love one. Do you want to sit here on this branch with me or would you like to find a place a little quieter?"

"Sure. Your place or mine?"

It actually takes a little longer than that, because these aren't trailer trash, these are birds from good nests, but you get the idea.

I come into Eauze about one-thirty, discover that it is the capital of Armagnac (it's on the sign), and have great difficulty finding the *gite*. The town centre is a square next to the church, and there are a number of roads leading off. I get differing opinions on where the specific street is. Part of the problem is that it is Monday, which seems to be synonymous with "closed" in this part of France.

I eventually get sent off on a road that is leading me quickly out into the country, and I have little faith that I am actually on the right road. However, when I get to number 43, I am very relieved to see the *gite* sign and turn in. I stand in the driveway, not sure what to do next, when the lady hanging up laundry calls to me and welcomes me in. I have arrived at Chez Nadine—she is Nadine, and the *gite* is just fine. It is the bottom floor of a house and I have a bed in a two-bed room. The three Germans from yesterday are in the next room. We embrace like old friends.

After washing up and doing the necessary laundry, we walk back into town and sit in the square and have ice cream and beer. But first, I have to tell you about the shower incident. You will remember, I'm sure, from any number of movies, the shower scene in which the man inadvertently—or advertently—walks in on the twenty-five-year-old woman in the shower. She is, of course, like a deer in the headlights and, depending on the movie, biology takes its course . . . or not. Well, fast-forward fifty years. The seventy-five-year-old man inadvertently walks in on the seventy-five-year-old woman in the shower. She is, of course, like a deer in the headlights but, unlike the movie, this is more like soft horror—or soft humour, depending on your bent. After a brief flurry of "*Pardons*" and "*Je m'excuse*," and so on, the man withdraws. The incident is not discussed again.

As we sit in the square, we get to know each other. He, Wilfried, is a couple of years younger than me, from the Constance area. The two ladies, Inge and Helga—Inge is his wife of forty-eight years—are good friends. He tells me that he worked for the company that makes the Airbus, but that isn't his area of specialty. He is an engineer specializing in secure military airfield communications, so we have aviation in common. The couple has spent at least six weeks each year for the past fifteen years in India working with orphaned children.

When I go to pay for my beer, I discover that it is already paid. The attempt to pay is funny. I ask the young waitress for the *rechnung* and she looks at me and says; "*J'n'comprends pas*" and of course she doesn't understand. I just asked for the bill in German. When I ask for it in French, she tells me that it is done. When I ask again, she says, "Stop, stop, *c'est déjà fait*." Stop, stop, it's already done. Well.

Back at the *gite*, I have a roommate. It's Weird Harold. I first saw him a kilometre before Eauze on the trail. He was standing over his pack, very lean, about my age and height, complaining that the pack was too heavy and that he was too hot. Of course, he was wearing a heavy fleece at the time and it was warm out. The next time I see him is here. This could be a long day. He spends all of his time poring over his maps and his schedule. He is my second OCD in two days! He doesn't drink, doesn't smoke, doesn't eat most things, etc. He is quiet, which is good, and we don't have a lot to say to each other. I don't want to trigger any hidden murderous impulses. I find later that he has already walked for two months from somewhere north of Paris and he is a few months younger than me.

At dinner with the family—Nadine, her husband, and eighteen-year-old son—we have an aperitif, couscous salad, roast pork, *frites* (that's a pleasant surprise), and finish with a drop of thirty-year-old Armagnac. During dinner, I am again pressed into service as a translator.

Nadine and me.

When Nadine finds out where I am staying tomorrow, she is horrified. What has happened is that I have by mistake selected a *gite* that is not in Nogaro, but about eight kilometres this side. She suggests another *gite* on the far side of Nogaro that will give me two reasonable days of twenty-four kilometres each day rather than one short day and one very, very long day. A couple of phone calls—she is efficient—and it's all fixed. She also insists on a photo with me for the next book. "It's very important," she says with a big grin.

Off to bed at nine-thirty. Harold is a quiet roommate.

15 May—Eauze to Arblade-le-Haut

I had a pretty good night, but not as good as some. My roommate, whom I will call "Weird Harold" for the time being, although that will stop soon, gets up several times in the night. He is considerate and quiet, but I still wake up. He rises very early and has finished breakfast before I get up. Then he spends an hour packing his backpack. I watch him as he folds his towel just so, and I can only imagine what his life must be like. I have no idea how he manages.

The three Germans and I eat together, then they are organized and gone while I am still getting myself ready for the day. They are going to Nogaro, and I am going a few kilometres beyond, so I do not think I will see them again. When Wilfried asks me if I will be staying at the *gîte communal* in Nogaro, I tell him yes, even though I am not going to be there. I have no idea why I tell him this; perhaps it's me not wanting to have a farewell scene.

As I sit putting my boots on, Nadine is here starting to clean up. I comment that my roommate is interesting. She tells me that they talked yesterday and when I hear the story, I am so ashamed. My quick judgment is dead wrong.

He had a wife and two children, lived north of Paris, apparently a happy enough life. Then one child was killed in a car accident. Not long after—I don't know the details—both his wife and the remaining child committed suicide. It is an appalling story.

His name is Jean-Marc and he is absolutely lost. I think that he finds solace in familiar and repetitive processes, which looks to me like OCD. Of all the people on the *chemin*, he is perhaps the one most in need of understanding—and I couldn't be bothered to find this out.

I leave the *gîte* just after eight with the promise of a lovely day. My walk will be about twenty-five kilometres in gently rolling country. I think that for the moment I am out of the big hills and the mud. There is lots of evidence that it was very muddy here as well, so I am grateful for the sun and lack of rain.

After two hours, I stop in a little town, Manciet, to buy a banana and some local strawberries, called "*garrigette*." They are long and narrow and delicious. I leave the store, walk about 100 metres, and realize that I have left my poles behind. When I turn around, there is the attractive—very attractive—store clerk hurrying after me with the poles. The people here are so kind and thoughtful! I continue to where I was headed, a nearby restaurant where the attractive—very attractive—server makes me a *grande crème* (coffee with hot frothed milk—it's a latte).

Now one attractive woman is anecdotal, two is a trend, and I am waiting with interest to see what the next data point is.

While I sit here, a big truck stops on the busy highway, the driver puts on his flashers and gets out of the cab. I expect he's going to offload something. Wrong. He is going into the bakery to pick up a long baguette, after which he gets back into his truck and drives away. I am absolutely in France. And in southern France—I am seeing stands of bamboo and the occasional palm tree.

Off I go to Nogaro. The first part out of Manciet is on a busy road, so I am pleased and relieved when the *chemin* turns away from the road and back into the vineyards and through farmers' fields. At one point, I discover that I know exactly where I am. There is a wooden sign, "Greenwich Meridian,"[24] so I know that I am at zero degrees, zero minutes, and zero seconds neither east nor west. I am directly south of the Royal Observatory in Greenwich, England, which is where the world's time is measured from east to west.

I am walking through Nogaro, thinking this would be a good time for lunch, when I spot Jean-Marc sitting alone in a restaurant. I think that I will join him, perhaps undo the damage of yesterday. I ask if I can sit with him, but that doesn't fly. He indicates a table next to him, and that is where I sit. He tells me that the *gite* in town is not good. If I understand correctly, it is one big dormitory.

I end up ordering the same salad that he is already having. When mine comes, he indicates that his salad is not so good. I imagine that everything he sees, everything he tastes is like ashes in his mouth. He is deeply grieving, and it is just not possible for me to have a meaningful conversation with him, so I ask for my bill, pay it, wish him "*Bon chemin*," and leave. It tastes a little like ashes for me, too.

Another few kilometres, and I am in this lovely *gite*, where I have brought greetings from Nadine for the owner. This is the only *gite* where we have dinner on china plates and drink our red wine from crystal glasses. I could get used to this. There are several Dutch people here who all speak English. They tell me it is a nice change for them to speak English, since they find French more difficult.

I am able to get WiFi and Internet here. I have a look at the Hospice website, where the donations have stalled. I can understand this. It's called "donor fatigue." People get asked to donate to so many worthwhile causes that they just eventually turn off.

Let me tell you about a different kind of donor fatigue. Since 22 April, I have travelled almost 500 kilometres, the vast majority of it on foot, carrying my backpack as I go. I have been through rain, mud, hail, and some seriously steep long hills, as well as some steep psychological climbs. And I have physical donor fatigue.

---

24 The French wanted the Prime Meridian to pass through Paris and lobbied for Paris Mean Time at the International Meridian Conference in Washington, DC, in 1884, but that didn't happen. The English won that argument. The time is known as Greenwich Mean Time (GMT) or ZULU time, or, more recently, Coordinated Universal Time.

But I believe with all my heart that what I am doing is worthwhile and I hope that you do, too. If you have not yet made a donation to this or another hospice, please consider doing it now. And please tell your friends about the blog and the Hospice website: *http://www.hospicemaycourt.com*. I will continue this walk to the end, whatever happens. Okay, barring apocalypse. If that happens, we are all on our own.

16 May—Arblade-le-Haut to Aire-sur-l'Adour

Today I walk twenty-five kilometres from Arblade-le-Haut to Aire-sur-l'Adour. It is an easy walk, gentle, rolling hills in farmland. At first, the crops are mostly vines and barley but it changes to mostly corn as I get nearer to Aire-sur-l'Adour. The last seven or eight kilometres are flat, almost dead straight on an old railway right-of-way.

And I have to admit an embarrassment. That Roman road that I walked on the other day? I was out by about 1,600 years. I mistranslated *"ancienne"* as "ancient" rather than "old" and I failed to translate *"voie ferrée"* at all. A *voie ferrée* is a railroad and an *ancienne voie ferrée* is an old railway right-of-way. I still think it would have made a great Roman road.

As I walk today, alone again—this is the third consecutive day of walking alone—I think about Eleanor of Aquitaine, helicopters, and sex, and about the three stages of being.

Why Eleanor? Because today I entered the province of Aquitaine, one of the ancient provinces of France, and, in the twelfth century, a duchy. Let me tell you about Eleanor of Aquitaine. Although she lived in the twelfth century, she was a thoroughly modern woman. In an age when daughters of noble families were but pawns in their fathers' games of dynastic chess, she stood alone. Anyone would recognize her type today: powerful, smart, confident, used to success, used to having her own way. Today she would be CEO of a Fortune 500 company. She was tall, blue-eyed, reddish-blonde hair, beautiful throughout her long life. She was born to wealth and nobility—her father was the Duke of Aquitaine, an area ten times the size of the small French monarchy around Paris. But without the Camino de Santiago, she might be just another footnote to history. Her father, the Duke of Aquitaine, made a pilgrimage to Santiago and died from having drunk polluted water. Her wise and cautious father had taken the precaution, before he left on his doomed pilgrimage, to have all of his vassals swear allegiance to her, made her a ward of the King of France, and betrothed her to the Crown Prince of France, young Louis. At fifteen years of age, Eleanor became Duchess of Aquitaine. Less than four months after her father's death, Eleanor and the crown prince married. While on their honeymoon, his father (the unfortunately named King Louis the Fat) died, and she was now Queen of France at sixteen, married to Louis VII for the next fifteen years.

She then found her husband incompatible and uninteresting and arranged for an annulment on the convenient grounds of consanguinity. She had met the man that she intended should be her second husband, Henry of Anjou—and eleven years younger than Eleanor.[25] After adding insult to injury by defeating Louis in battle in Normandy, Henry invaded England, and, after a small war, was crowned King Henry II. Over the next twenty years, Eleanor bore Henry eight children, but only two of her sons, Richard the Lion-Hearted and John (Bad King John) survived to occupy the English throne. This was the beginning of the centuries-long succession of Plantagenet rulers in England. The lesson? A person can overcome almost anything, even being born a woman in twelfth-century Europe, if he or she is determined enough.

The helicopters? Because yesterday—I think it was yesterday—as I walked out of Manciet, a French military recce helicopter flew overhead at less than forty metres above the village. As well, I saw then and again today a small helicopter flying circuits. It turns out that there is a military flight training base near here. So that is what triggered the thoughts about helicopters.

What I think about is a story I was told years ago at a party at the home of an American helicopter pilot in Germany. All of the Americans at the party were guys who had survived at least one tour in Vietnam. One of them was a young guy who by any reasonable standard should not have been alive. He should have been one of the more than 55,000 Americans who died in Vietnam.

With a big smile, he showed me a picture on the front cover of a Hughes Aircraft brochure. It was a photo of a Hughes OH5A, universally known as the Loach (LOH, Light Observation Helicopter).

---

25   He was nineteen, she was thirty, and really tired of being married to Louis, a man she described as "a monk." Louis was very religious and had been brought up with the intent of entering religious service. It was the unexpected death of his older brother that propelled him into service instead as the king of France.

It was battered almost beyond recognition. The blades were twisted and bent with chunks out of them. He was flying the aircraft when it sustained the damage.

Here is his story: He was in Vietnam flying low-level, just above the jungle along a road where the Americans were advancing. His job was to reconnoitre the road to keep the American column from being surprised or ambushed.

He flew around a bend in the road and suddenly he was directly above a large unit, hundreds of men, either North Vietnamese or Viet Cong. Either way, it was a very, very bad place to be. The aircraft and its crew had no effective protection from small-arms fire, and the Vietnamese had learned how to deal with aircraft overhead. Rather than everyone trying to aim at the aircraft, which didn't work—almost everyone would shoot behind the aircraft—everyone simply pointed his weapon straight up and fired. The pilot had to fly through a hail of bullets and the odds of getting away without many hits were remote.

So he used one of the peculiarities of the Loach. When you pulled up hard on the collective control, the helicopter had a strong tendency to turn hard to the left. He pulled up very hard in desperation, and the helicopter turned hard left—directly into and through the top of a large tree. He was pretty sure that he was dead, but the aircraft flew clear of the tree, shuddering and shaking—but still flying. He looked for a place to land, then realized that the shuddering and shaking had stabilized. It wasn't getting better, but it wasn't getting any worse, either. Landing here was likely going to result in a very unpleasant encounter with the guys on the ground.

He declared a "mayday," but continued flying and he was able to fly about forty kilometres to a friendly airfield, where he landed and shut down the engine. He and the other member of the crew were unhurt. The aircraft was not even salvageable, but the Hughes Company recognized the marketing possibilities of using the photos of this terribly damaged aircraft as an example of the survivability of their product.

So why is this story running around in my head? I haven't thought about it in years. Perhaps it is the idea of the possibility of life changing in an instant, which happens to people all the time. And perhaps I am thinking about that poor, desperate pilgrim who has lost his entire family.

The sex part is easier to explain. There is a big difference in young men thinking about sex and old men thinking about sex. Young men think about sex about 100 times every day. Then they act on the thought as often as possible. Old men think about sex about 100 times every day. Then they act on the thought as often as possible. The difference is in the definition of "as often as possible."

I am reminded of a wonderful scene from *The Bucket List*, in which Jack Nicholson's character explains his three most important rules for getting old:

"Never waste a hard-on,
"Never trust a fart, and
"Never pass up a toilet."

Anyone else out there recognize these truths?

We know that survival and the urge to reproduce are two of the most fundamental biological needs for every species. But I don't think young men sit around saying, "Hey, I think that I'll go out this evening, find a girl past puberty, of symmetrical features and childbearing hips, and satisfy my primal urge to reproduce the species, since I know how important this is to the future of Homo Sapiens." What they think is: "I really, *really* want to get laid!"

For girls, I'll bet they also don't sit around thinking, "I'll go out this evening and find a man who has enough power to protect me and the child we will create together for the period while I am pregnant and for the next fifteen to twenty years so that the species can be continued." I think (apologies to Cindy Lauper) that girls just want to have fun.

My roommate last evening was Franz, a genial and recently retired theology professor from the universities of Utrecht and Nijmegen. He is the author of several books about theology but he told me that I was very lucky because I write in English. He writes in Dutch for a *much* smaller audience.

We sat for a long time discussing the phenomenon of the Chemin de Saint-Jacques. There are so many people walking it for so many personal reasons; but they are, according to medieval philosophers, in one of three stages of being. The stages are not necessarily sequential, nor are they all achieved by all people.

The first is the sense of being at one with the universe: Everything is all right with the world, or for a person who believes in God, being in a state of grace. This is the feeling that I have at the moment, the sense of being okay with the universe. It gives me a strong sense of inner peace.

The second is the sense of meaninglessness, of terrible solitude: for a Christian, the "dark night" when there is a sense of abandonment by God. This, I think, is where the unfortunate man who lost his entire family is at this moment. I hope he can survive it. I think that a lot of people have this quietly desperate sense of meaninglessness in their lives. I certainly have at times in the past.

The third sense is that of simply being: "The imperturbable stillness of mind after the fires of desire, aversion, and delusion have been finally extinguished,"[26] the state of being that Eastern religions and Buddhism, which is not a God-based ethical and moral system, seek to achieve.

We also talked about positive and negative reassurance, on which I will have more to say soon.

I am in another lovely *gite*. This one is quite special. André has walked the *camino* nine times, his wife, Odile, fewer, but still several times. This *gite* is reserved solely for pilgrims on foot, carrying their backpacks, and carrying a credential (the pilgrim passport). There are some strict rules, here. One is that the *gite* is closed at 9:30 p.m., so if you are out on the town after 9:30, you might as well stay there. A second is that while dinner is offered, it is expected—actually required—that the pilgrims be involved in the meal preparation. I help by chopping vegetables but mostly by keeping out of the way.

There are two parties of women, here, both from the area of Lyon. One group of three is finishing here, and the other of four women started yesterday in Arblade-le-Haut and will be walking for four days. The second group is four friends who are wives and mothers, in their late thirties, early forties. Between them they have—are you ready for this?—twenty-six children.

One of them, Valérie, sits across from me at dinner and becomes very alert when she discovers that I was once a helicopter pilot. She says that her first husband was a military helicopter pilot as well. I ask, "First?" She tells me that he was a French Marine pilot, and when I ask what happened, she says simply, "He fell into the sea." That kind of ends the discussion for the moment, but we will pick it up tomorrow.

André, our host and a nine-time veteran of the *chemin*, has what sounds to me like really good advice for the pilgrims going beyond

---

26 Richard Gombrich, *Theravada Buddhism: A Social History from Ancient Benares to Modern Colombo* (London: Routledge and Kegan Paul, 1988).

Saint-Jean-Pied-de-Port over or through the Pyrénées toward Pamplona.

His first bit of advice is to go over the high route only if the weather is good and your pack is light. He points out, correctly, that the ancient pilgrims walked the easiest route, not the most photogenic one, so the valley route is more closely aligned with the ancient route.

Second, if you really want to see the far vistas, pack a light bag, climb about eight kilometres up the path, take your photos, come back down, and next day walk the valley route.

Third, don't stay in Roncevalles. It is like a herd of animals leaving there every morning, hundreds of people together. He suggests taking the valley route, staying in Valcarlos overnight, then walking through Roncevalles and staying in, I think, Espalion the next night. In the morning, it puts you hours ahead of the Roncevalles crowd.

As it turns out, when I get there in a few days, I won't take any of André's sensible advice. I will walk over the high route with my pack and I will stay in Roncevalles. Of course, if I were being sensible, I likely wouldn't be here at all, would I?

17 May—Aire-sur-l'Adour to Miramont-Sensacq

Well, not a good night's sleep. We are three in a room, and the other two guys are fine, but I have a sodium street lamp about fifteen metres from the window, and it glares all night. It isn't until the morning when someone asks how I slept—the universal question in the morning is, "*Avez-vous bien dormir?*"—and I say "poorly" and explain why, they ask me why I didn't close the shutters. "Because we don't use shutters in Canada and I don't remember shutters in the usual course of events." It does, however mean that I can get up at night—twice—and head to the john without needing my newly purchased, trusty little LED flashlight.

After breakfast, most of the others leave, and I sit with André and Odile for a few minutes. He tells me that one of the pilgrims asked him this morning why they don't have any children. He refused to answer because he finds that type of question both personal and intrusive. He says—and I agree—that people need to respect each other's privacy, and that includes the privacy of the people who have chosen to operate *gites* for the pilgrims. It is a matter of reciprocal respect for privacy. For many people, this is a deeply moving experience, and personal questions can be quite damaging. He also tells me that he doesn't think that the four women from Lyon are real pilgrims because they walk for only four days each year.

I walk up the long hill out of Aire-sur-l'Adour, and at the crest, I see the Pyrénées on the southern horizon for the first time. They are big, and there is a lot of snow on the slopes and summits. I expect to be seeing them for the next two weeks as I walk south and west. This turns out to be dead wrong, but I don't know that yet.

I expect an easy walk of eighteen kilometres, and it is — flat farmland, cultivated fields, tractors doing their thing. I meet the four ladies from Lyon, and we share a coffee by the side of the trail. I note that they carry small Testaments with them — with twenty-six children among them, I am pretty sure they are all Catholic, which they turn out to be and are very serious about the pilgrim aspect of their walk.

I walk with Valérie for an hour or two, and we have a long talk about her first husband. They were stationed in Germany, with their three young children, and he had been gone for two months for an extended exercise in the Mediterranean. His helicopter was performing the safety role for night carrier operations, hovering off to one side, and something failed catastrophically in the aircraft. It really did fall into the sea, and the crew was lost. It was 1998 or 1999. She was thirty, with three children: four, three, and twenty months. It was a terrible blow, and yet at the same time, as the wife of a military helicopter pilot, just like my wife, she had conditioned herself to be able to handle it if the unthinkable happened.

That didn't change the grief or the horror of facing life without her husband, but she tells me, in retrospect, it became one of the happiest periods of her life. She said to God: "Well, it is all in Your hands, now. I don't understand it at all. I don't know what You have in mind, but there is nothing I can do to change it." And that was the way it worked for a long time. She put her absolute trust in God and, for her, it worked and continues to work. After some years, she found another man.

Their meeting is a story in itself. It had been about five years since her husband's death, and she had moved with her children to a place near Lyon. Her parish priest talked to her one day and told her that he knew a man that he thought she should meet. She told him she wasn't interested. A couple of weeks later, a good friend of hers told her that she knew a man that she thought Valérie should meet. So

Valérie met the man, a widower, and they quickly connected. When the parish priest met the man Valérie would marry he laughed because this was the same man that he had thought she should meet. Her new husband had three small children from his previous marriage, and they have since had three more children, for a total of nine.

This annual walk for four days with her friends is, for them, total liberty. André back at the *gite* told me that he doesn't approve of this four-day pilgrimage and that when they walk together, it is not a pilgrimage. In fact, they don't walk together, they walk mostly alone and the four days is the most that they are able to pull out of their busy lives. They are walking from their homes near Lyon to Santiago, four days each year. It is a multi-year commitment. They tell me that they understand that André doesn't understand and that it is just his point of view. Seems to me that they are better and more genuine pilgrims than most of us who are out here.

And since I am on the topic, let me tell you my views about authenticity. People make their journey on the *camino* for a very wide variety of reasons and in a very wide variety of ways. Most walk, some cycle, a few ride horses or donkeys (I saw horses on the *camino* in Spain, a donkey on the Chemin de Saint-Jacques in France). Some of them are pilgrims travelling the route for religious or spiritual reasons. Others walk the *camino* for sports, for culture, for architecture, or for the history of the region. Most carry a backpack with whatever they think they will need en route. For those who cannot or choose not to carry their pack all day, there are companies set up that will transport your backpack from point to point on the *camino* for a modest fee. They will also carry you, if you are tired or bored or disabled.

The *camino* is also a popular active tourism route, in which travel companies set up an itinerary, often a week or ten days, for small groups of travellers who travel by bus, walk a portion of the *camino* each day, carrying only a daypack, then retire to a comfortable hotel for the night. I don't think that these folks see themselves as pilgrims, more as tourists or travellers, but they seem to enjoy the experience. Sometimes the tour leaders are pilgrims who have walked the *camino*, others are enthusiastic walkers and adventurers who enjoy spreading the word about what the culture has to offer.

In recent years, there been a disturbing trend, fostered by a few—a very few, I think—of the dedicated walkers about how the *camino* is "supposed" to be travelled. Here are the rules: First of all, "real" pilgrims on the *camino* start in Saint-Jean-Pied-de-Port (or farther away), in order to traverse the Pyrénées on their first days of walking. They must carry their own gear, they must not accept a ride, or allow their gear to be carried for them, they must stay in hostels (*gites* in France, *albergues* in Spain), they must stay on the trail; above all, they mustn't cycle. It is the cult of authenticity. I am a little surprised that they don't require that you flagellate[27] yourself as you walk.

I heard about one American pilgrim cyclist who was told, by someone who had walked the *camino*, that he had only had a "shallow" experience because he had cycled. I also talked to a Canadian pilgrim who had cycled the route, but was reluctant to tell others how she had done it, because of her expectation, frequently met, that the walkers would look down on her or seek to diminish her experience. It seems to me that if these dedicated "real" pilgrims thought about it, they would not be so disparaging of others.

First of all, the trail we walk today is generally not the trail that the early pilgrims walked. They walked on what was then the road and is now the path of heavily travelled highways. If they really want to be authentic, they should walk on the highways . . . and take their lumps.

Secondly, one of the things that I relearned on the *camino* was not to judge others. Who knows why someone has his pack carried for him or why he accepts a ride? My recent experience in France taught me that when you hit your personal physical limits, which I did on several days, it would be foolhardy and perhaps risky to continue walking. If there had been a place available to stop overnight, perhaps I would have, but there wasn't. I sought out a ride to my planned destination and I don't feel any less of a pilgrim for it.

Thirdly, if the church authorities who dispense the formal document at end of the journey in Santiago accept cyclists, why wouldn't other pilgrims? I thought that completing the pilgrimage would teach tolerance and compassion, not closed-mindedness and bigotry.

People have to make their own *camino*, and if that includes having your pack carried or yourself carried or staying in hotels rather than *albergues*, well, it's their *camino*, not yours. I find nothing wrong

---

27 Self-flagellation is the medieval practice of whipping yourself with an instrument called a "discipline," a cattail whip made with knotted cords and flung over the shoulders to mortify the back. Some members of conservative monastic orders and the lay organization "Opus Dei" practise self-flagellation today, as did Pope John Paul II. There is a scene of self-flagellation in the 2010 movie *The Way*, starring Martin Sheen, about walking the Camino de Santiago.

with people wanting to have the most authentic experience possible for themselves, based on their perception of what is authentic, but that does not give them the right to denigrate the experiences of others. Pride is not a good pilgrim emotion.

So the next time you hear someone extolling her "authentic" experience, congratulate her. But if she continues on to point out the shallow or false experience of others because they didn't do the "authentic" *camino*, stop her gently and remind her that each person has to experience his or her own *camino*, just as each one of us has to experience his or her own life.

And you could mention casually in passing that the Bishop of Le Puy who followed this pilgrimage in 950 certainly didn't walk and didn't carry his own gear . . . and *everyone* thinks that he was a pilgrim.

We arrive together in Miramont-Sensacq, a tiny village, at around one p.m. We stop in the churchyard, and I go off to find my *gite* and get rid of my backpack. It doesn't open until 2:30, so I leave my pack there and go back to the churchyard, where the ladies are preparing their lunch. I sit with them and for a while lie back on the grass and almost drop off to sleep. Around two, they get organized, because they have another fourteen kilometres to go, and we say goodbye—another bittersweet goodbye.

I sit in the little courtyard of the *gite*, Maison Helene, until 2:30, when a woman, black-haired, opens the door. I tell her my name, and she looks a little nonplussed. She checks her sheet; I am not on it. And she has no beds, not one. I know that a few days ago, one of the *hospitalières*, Fanny in Moissac, called ahead for me, because she wrote down the name and address for me, but something has gone haywire, here. She calls the other possibilities in town. No one has my name and no one has a bed.

Now I start to get a little concerned. I know that beds right now on the *chemin* are a scarce commodity, and not having a reservation could be catastrophic. My plans do not include sleeping out under the stars, of which there will be few tonight. Possibility of rain. She asks if she could get me a ride back to Aire-sur-l'Adour and bring me back here tomorrow to continue. It is a reasonable solution if there is a bed in Aire-sur-l'Adour. I actually don't care. I just want to have a bed for the night. Finally, she calls a place not in my guidebook, the two-year-old and apparently out-of-date 2010 *Miam Miam Dodo*. It is a farm *gite*,

Ferme Nordland, a couple of kilometres off the *chemin*. Do I care? She calls, they have one bed left, and it is mine.

Then she pours me an aperitif, no charge, and her husband brings up the vehicle and he drives me a couple of kilometres on winding roads to my next spot. Except he doesn't. He drops me in the middle of nowhere at an attractive farmhouse that he says is the *gite*, bids me "*Bon chemin*" and drives away. He is happy that he has been able to help a pilgrim.

I schlepp my backpack into the farmyard and put it by the door. I try the door; it's locked. I make friends with the dog and sit down to wait. I find it strange that a *gite* would be locked at this time of day, especially since the phone had been answered earlier. I find it even stranger that there is no sign for a *gite* at the entry to the yard. That is a first. There is always a sign. As I sit here, I become more and more suspicious that I am not where I am supposed to be.

So after some minutes, I leave my pack and I walk down and then up the road—it is winding and hilly—for a few hundred yards until I see two men working in a barnyard. I ask them if there is a *gite* on this road. One of them—I find out later that he is Gilbert, a duck farmer and the owner of the *gite*—says, "Yes, it's a little farther along. My wife Christine is waiting for you; you will see the scallop shell at the entry." What a relief! So back I go, pick up my pack, say goodbye to the dog, and head for my *gite*. There on the right is the building, a woman is standing in front, and I am here.

It's a miracle. This is my bed of last resort. I have a double bed in a private room, glass patio doors looking out on a rural landscape, with an ensuite shower and beer in the communal fridge. The place is modern and spotless. There are four more people coming but they have not yet arrived. A shower, a quick wash of some clothes, and I am ready for the rest of the day—which is what I am doing now.

The other four people have arrived. Two men retired from the French military, Guy and Christian, and their wives, Agnes and Christina. Christian commanded an infantry battalion, Guy was a military engineer. They met at Saint-Cyr, the French equivalent of the Royal Military College, as young cadets. Christian is very tall and imposing, which reaffirms my belief that it is easier for a tall man to assume a leadership position.

Christine has tried to find me accommodation farther down the *chemin*, based on available accommodation. My walk for tomorrow is less than nine kilometres, but more than thirty the next day. She tries a number of places, but everything is *"complet."* There are large numbers of walkers. They think it is because the twenty-six consecutive days of rain—of which I only got the last half—delayed the plans of a lot of people and they are all playing catch-up. Also, yesterday was Ascension Thursday and another French holiday. A lot of *gites* are closed because of family events.

Dinner is at seven at the farmhouse, just up the road 100 metres. Gilbert and Christine welcome us into their home, where dinner is set for all seven of us. We start with an aperitif, Floc de Gascogne, then foie gras with toast, several courses—and end with thirty-year-old Armagnac. Now this is country living. And to think I could have been in a room in Miramont-Sensacq with several other people, one of whom would snore, and with no light of my own.

18 May—Miramont-Sensacq to Arzacq-Arraziguet

I have a really good sleep in my double bed with comforter. I wake up just before seven and am dressed and in the farmhouse kitchen by seven-fifteen. The two French couples are already there, almost finished with breakfast and ready to go. I have a short walk today, less than ten kilometres to a fairly large town. I say goodbye to my hosts and strap on the backpack—it is like an old friend by now. It is fairly heavy to lift but once it is on my back and cinched down, the weight disappears.

I have a couple of kilometres to walk to get me back on the *chemin*. It's a left out of the farmhouse and another left ten minutes away. Can't see the Pyrénées today, though. Too much haze. The road takes me into Pimbo, which is on the edge of a high escarpment . . . wonderful view to the south.

Funny name for a quiet little town, but it has been here for a very long time. It was here in 778 before Charlemagne took his troops south to consolidate the southern borders of his kingdom and to try to stem the relentless northward push of the Muslims. The myth about Charlemagne making this pilgrimage is just that—a myth. The bones that were found and declared to be those of St. James the Elder had not yet been found, so there was no pilgrimage destination and no pilgrimage for Charlemagne, at least not a Christian one.

The church in Pimbo.

Here in Pimbo, I encounter Jean-Marc at the church. I would prefer to walk alone, but he clearly wants to walk with me. I do not know what is going on, but I walk with him for a few hours. Over the next hours, he tells me a little bit about himself. He is from a village in the Ardennes, from which he has already walked 1,600 kilometres with just under 1,000 left to go. Then he intends to walk home, although he doesn't know if he will be able to make it. He has a hernia that is giving him some grief; he finds his pack too heavy, and the belt of his pack aggravates the hernia.

As we walk, he talks about the plants on the side of the road. We pass what appears to be a huge young orchard, but he says that the trees, only about three or four feet high inside the protective sleeves, are oaks, so this is a tree nursery, not an orchard. Then he tells me about some of the small wildflowers that we see. I ask him if he is a biologist. He looks at me, laughs and says no, but his older son loved plants and knew all about them. Then he says, sadly, "But he is no more." I repeat this as a question, although I already know a bit of the story.

We stand together at the side of the road at an intersection with traffic going by on the busier road and it all comes out. His wife of many years developed cancer. By the time it was diagnosed, it was inoperable and had spread throughout her body, including into her spine. She was in agony, and the medical profession did what they could, but nothing worked. The elder son in desperation shot his mother as a mercy killing, then himself. Jean-Marc had already lost a younger son in a car accident, so he is quite alone. I listen as hard as I have ever listened in my life. He needs someone to hear his story and to help him understand. I can listen — that is all I can do. He needs to talk it through until it makes some kind of sense for him. So I guess this is why he wanted to walk with me today.

He tells me that he no longer believes in the benevolent God of his youth. It is not clear whether he still believes at all or just does not understand what has happened in his life. He decided to walk to Santiago but so far he has not had any breakthrough. In Le Puy he had a long talk with the bishop. He tells me that many people on the *chemin* have been very kind to him, but like me, all they can do is listen. He talks about a Sufi mystic of some centuries ago who said that you could not find God in the heavens or in the churches, that God is found only within the self. It seems to resonate with him and it sounds a lot like my theory of the human spirit.

I am sitting at a table outside La Vieille Auberge, a little restaurant/hotel in Arzacq-Arraziguet. It's one p.m., and the communal *gite* doesn't open until two. They have seventy-seven beds . . . and they have WiFi, if I sit very close to the *gite*'s welcome centre. It is overcast, just warm enough to sit without a fleece. I keep an eye out for any pilgrims whom I might recognize. So far, none that I know.

And then who walks up but Rémi, the young guy who sang the Occitan lullaby a week or so ago in Espalais. I saw him yesterday in the churchyard at Miramont-Sensacq but don't know where he went after that. I find it fascinating how individuals keep popping up in the most unexpected places. Jean-Marc and Rémi are both staying here in my room in the communal *gite* tonight.

My left ring finger continues to give me a little grief. The last section goes partially numb and pale or bluish at the slightest excuse. When I mentioned it to André at the *gite* in Aire-sur-l'Adour, he immediately said, "That's Raynaud's syndrome." When I got Internet access today and looked it up, it certainly fits. That would also explain why the infection on the side of the finger has taken so long to heal. Everything is good now, the finger isn't in any danger of falling off or, worse, rotting in place, but I have to continue to be aware of it.

I recall that a couple of days ago at Manciet, I noted that the women—at least two of them—were stunning and I thought that it might be a trend. Today at the *gite* here, the Centre d'Accueil, the woman staffing the front desk is stunning. Karine is young, lean, tall, long legs in tight jeans, blonde, and has an engaging smile that makes me weak in the knees. So it's more than a trend and I am going to work out a hypothesis to support my observations. It might take a lot of research. She is chewing gum, which takes the edge off just a bit. She is also engaged.

I am in a small room, the Salle Angleterre, with six beds, very close together, but it is indoors, and the toilet is just down the hall. I have taken the bed closest to the door. And Jean-Marc is in the bed next to mine.

I ask Karine about helping me book rooms beyond here. She tells me that she is allowed to book only one, for more than that I need to go to the Bureau de Tourisme. So she books me for the twenty-first, and I go to the Bureau de Tourisme—turns out it's part of my research—where the quite lovely young woman (who is married) wants to practise her English and gets me a bed for the nights of the twenty-second through the twenty-fifth. So I am good for seven days out. That takes me as far as Saint-Jean-Pied-de-Port, where I will have to get a guidebook for the Spanish portion. It is very reassuring to have accommodation booked in advance when there is so little of it.

At dinner, seated at one long table for thirty, I sit with a woman, Christine, who tells me that she is from Normandy, near Caen. I tell her that I am familiar with Caen because during the Normandy invasion in 1944, my regiment, the Fort Garry Horse, came ashore near there (I wasn't there; I was just seven years old at the time, living in Winnipeg, and my military service was years in the future). She gets quite excited and says, "The Canadians came ashore at Bernieres-sur-Mer. I know this because that is where I live, and every year there is a ceremony honouring the Canadians."

I am going to have an early—even earlier—night tonight because I expect a long day tomorrow.

19 May—Arzacq-Arraziguet to Arthez-de-Béarn

When I checked the weather last evening, today's forecast was not promising. Overcast in the morning, showers in the afternoon, storms in the evening . . . then continuing on with wet and stormy weather for the next several days. I went to bed at nine and I was the last of five in our room to go to bed. Jean-Marc sleeps in the bed next to mine and he is a snorer, but a quiet one. Rémi, the shy kid from Cahors, whom I first met in Espalais, is here as well and in the same room.

They are all up earlier than me, but I am still on the road before eight a.m. I am full of piss and vinegar and ready to tackle the thirty kilometres ahead of me. I do, however, have a backup plan. The folks who run the *gite* in Arthez-de-Béarn where I will be staying have

A downhill section of the chemin.

offered to pick me up at the twenty-kilometre mark in Pomps (you pronounce the "s") and transport me to their place. What I do depends on the weather. If it is good, I will walk all the way. If it is as forecast, I may call for the ride.

Jean-Marc packs and unpacks his backpack several times. First time, he forgets to put in his sandals. Second time, he forgets to get out his medications. It must take him an hour. While he is sorting out his pack, I organize mine, go have breakfast, come back, get my boots on, and leave. He is still repacking. I wish him "*Bon chemin.*"

It is misty and raining lightly as I leave Arzacq-Arraziguet, so both I and my pack have our rain jackets on. After an hour, the rain stops, so off comes my jacket, but it's still threatening, so the pack cover stays on.

The countryside is gently rolling, then seriously rolling, hills. And the *chemin*, of course, goes over every hill rather than around, so I get several of those long arduous climbs today. The *chemin* is either on small country roads or on good, packed surface, so that isn't a problem. By now, I have a good operating procedure for hills, either up or down. Shorter steps, slower pace, stop whenever I feel like a breather. It works. I don't get really short of breath and it doesn't seem to take much longer to get to my destination.

Twelfth-century chapel.

At one point, I am at the crest of a hill when I hear what I think at first is cowbells. Then I realize that it is the bell of a church that I can see on a distant crest to my right front, which chimes ten times. I wonder how many hundreds of years that church bell has chimed out the hours for the people around here. Certainly long before the clock was invented.

Later, I hear a cuckoo whose mainspring has been severely overwound. He counts to ten and for a split second I think he is echoing the church, but then he continues. I quit counting at thirty-seven. He is overdue for an overhaul.

I have what amounts to a tense moment that could have been a pretty serious problem. I have stopped for a breather at a point on the road in a woods where there is a millstone on its side as a table, some stone benches, and a little watering point. I take off my backpack, lay aside my poles and sit down for a few minutes. When I get up I put on my pack, suddenly there is water running down my left leg. Where is this coming from?

What has happened is that the mouthpiece of my water bladder has come adrift and is nowhere to be found. This is a potentially serious problem. I am depending on the water in that bladder to get me through each day. Without the mouthpiece, it will be essentially useless. Finally, I spot the mouthpiece lying half-hidden in the grass. I pick it up and push it firmly onto the hose. It is a reminder of how important small things are.

I remember a story my mother used to tell when I was young:

> *For want of a nail a shoe was lost,*
> *For want of a shoe a horse was lost,*
> *For want of a horse a rider was lost,*
> *For want of a rider a battle was lost,*
> *For want of a battle a kingdom was lost,*
> *All for the want of a nail.*

It makes more sense, now.

For a while today, I walk with Rémi. He has a large photograph fastened on the back of his pack. This is new. I ask him about it, he tells me it's his grandparents. Since it is dated 17 May 2012, only a couple of days ago, I assume that it is a recent picture, but it's not. That is just the date he had it printed. I ask if he is close to his grandparents.

He tells me that they were very close and that his grandfather is now dead, his grandmother very ill.

They wanted to walk the *chemin* to Santiago but were too ill and old to do it, so he is walking it for them and with them. So I think that explains why a young man in his early twenties is walking here. He is probably forty years younger than the average pilgrim.

Before I get to Pomps, all my piss and practically all my vinegar has drained away. For twenty kilometres, there is no place to get a coffee or anything to eat. There are several small villages but they have not yet caught on to the idea of marketing to the pilgrim trade. Given the numbers, I would think it would be a good seasonal market.

The last hour into Pomps seems to take forever, and I am dragging, so when I arrive I make the phone call and sit in front of the closed library under threatening skies until my ride arrives. Rémi has come into Pomps with me, because we are looking for a place for a drink, but nothing is open. He leaves before my ride arrives, and I expect to see him again somewhere down the road. When a vehicle pulls up in front of the library, it's Laurent, who picks up my pack and places it in his vehicle, then takes me on a hair-raising ride up and down and around winding roads until we arrive at his place. I am the only guest today. Someone else has been injured and has cancelled.

The *gîte* is their former one-bedroom home. They have built a larger one next to this to house them and their four children. It is clean, well-equipped—I can make myself coffee with hot milk. They have WiFi, so I can communicate easily, and I have an excellent double bed in which I sleep for two hours in the late afternoon. Murielle takes all my clothes away, washes and dries them, and brings them back neatly folded.

I expect that I will be eating in the house with the family, but that is not what happens. Laurent shows up with a long baguette, a plate of homemade pâté, which he has made (it is really good), and a bottle of red wine. This is the appetizer. We have a little drink together, then he goes off and returns with the main course, a local sausage on a huge bed of home fries. Fruit yogurt for dessert. All of this I eat in solitary splendour. They figure that with their four young children plus a couple of others and her sister, it will be pandemonium in the house, so I get to eat here. I would prefer to eat with them, but that is not offered as an option, and I don't pursue it.

He also brings all the makings for breakfast and promises to show up tomorrow morning between eight-thirty and nine-fifteen to take me back to Pomps, so I can walk back here. He can't believe that I don't want to just continue on from here. The *chemin* is right beside his place. It is quite clear that he thinks I am nuts . . . and perhaps I am, but tomorrow I go back to where I got picked up today and I will continue to walk the *chemin*.

It is just coming up to nine p.m., so I am going to go to bed in the big double bed with a comforter and a light switch and see what happens next.

20 May — Arthez-de-Béarn to Pomps to Arthez-de-Béarn

I wake up during the night to the sound of rain, and it is still raining when I get up. The forecast is for several more days of this. The high today will be twelve degrees, so I don't have to worry about overheating. The plan is for Laurent to take me back to Pomps, from where I will promptly start walking back to Arthez-de-Béarn.

This is one of those moments when I could wish to have a little less of that authenticity thing going on. The place where I will stay tonight is just two kilometres from here. I could just walk out the door, take the *chemin* for about half an hour, and present myself at the next *gîte*. No one would know except me. The trouble is, *I* would know. And I am the only person whom I have to face every morning in the mirror.

Laurent still thinks I'm crazy. Before I get out of the vehicle, he tells me that if I have any problem on the *chemin*, just call him and he will come pick me up. It is a very gracious offer that I hope not to have to accept.

So it's back to Pomps and I walk, wearing all of my rain gear, for about three hours in the cold and wet. I wanted the experience; I'm having the experience that all the other pilgrims go through. Except for those who get a ride.

The rain is steady, though light, most of the time; occasionally very heavy. There won't be any view of the Pyrénées today. I start with my fleece on but have to take it off after half an hour. The weather isn't hot, but I am just too hot with it on. Almost all of the way today is on road, for which I am quite grateful. The only part off-road is downhill and slippery with surface mud. At least it's not deep.

I stop in Arthez-de-Béarn to have a coffee, and there in the little café is Jean-Marc, eating a pastry and having coffee. We talk very briefly; I have my *grande crème* and walk on. The place I am going to, the Lawrensons', is about two kilometres farther down the road. Eddy is a school classmate of Les Foster's,[28] at whose home I stayed in Victoria when I was there in April 2011 to speak to the Victoria chapter of the Canadian Company of Pilgrims.

I arrive, quite soaked, at around twelve-thirty and am greeted with a warm welcome. Eddy and Irene are gracious hosts . . . and they speak English. This is the most English that I have heard or spoken in a month. I get off my really wet rain gear and change into dry clothes. Everything gets hung up to dry. I also stuff my boots with newspaper so they will be dry by morning.

I am offered hot coffee with hot milk, which I accept with alacrity. Irene asks me if I would like to have lunch with them—paella. I cannot think of anything I'd rather do, so she makes their regular Sunday—this is how I find out it's Sunday—paella, but more than usual, to account for the extra place at the table.

While we have lunch, the rain really starts to come down and it pours intermittently for about half an hour. Folks still out walking will find it difficult and I am extremely glad that I am watching it pour from inside a dry, warm space.

We talk about the history of this area. There is lots of it. For example, in a nearby town called Orthez, in February 1814, Wellington fought and beat French Marshall Soult in the Napoleonic wars. It was the beginning of the end for Napoleon. This is also the area of the Cathars, who were the subject of the first Crusade by Christians against other Christians and were people who suffered dreadfully at the hands of the Inquisition. More about that later.

Two other wet pilgrims arrive, a Québécoise and a Swiss. I am hoping that it will be Joimie and Fanny, but it's not. They are likely way ahead of me. This Québécoise is Sylvie, from the Montreal area.

The first thing I ask Sylvie, after the introductions, is if her last name is Parent. She is a dead ringer for Ginette Parent, a dear, long-time friend, a Québécoise, who now lives just north of Berlin, and Sylvie is about a generation younger. But it's not.

I sit and talk with Eddy and Irene through the afternoon. We talk about the history of the area, man's inhumanity to man, religion and

---

28 Les is married to Mary Virtue, a two-time pilgrim on the *camino*.

spirituality, how they love to walk in France and Spain, our families, our children, and how we are all fans of Bill Bryson and the Flashman books. They tell me how they got into the *gite* business. The French family next door, who were very kind when the Lawrensons moved in ten years ago, run a small *gite* with four beds.

After they got to know each other better, they asked if the Lawrensons could occasionally take an overflow person or two—just provide an extra bed once in a while. Eventually, it got so busy that Irene and Eddy set up a four-bed, two-room operation of their own. I have a room to myself with two beds, and the other pilgrims share a room. It works out very well.

I have dinner with the two ladies and I get complimented on my French by Sylvie. This I don't expect but I am very happy to hear it. She also suggests that I should make my book known to the Quebec equivalent of the Canadian Company of Pilgrims.[29] They have over 10,000 members, which is a couple of orders of magnitude larger than the English group. She also says that many of them in the Montreal area speak and read English.

The weather clears up, and it looks quite lovely, although the weather forecast for the next two days remains wet and cool. We shall see what the morning brings. I am off to a place called the Abbaye de Sauvelade, where there is apparently a *gite* called Le P'tit Laa. I say "apparently," because Eddy tells me that there is nothing there but the ruined abbey. I guess I'll find out tomorrow. It is only about twelve to fourteen kilometres—ought to be an easy walk. (I should know better than to tempt fate by thinking like this.)

He also confirms something that I have been suspecting for some time. When they moved here ten years ago, the GR 65 passed by their door on a quiet, paved road, the D275. Several years ago, it got changed so that now the pilgrim path heads off into the hills, adding about four kilometres and a lot of off-road hill climbing. Two possibilities spring to mind: One is that the municipality asked for the change to get the pilgrim traffic off the road for safety reasons. The other reason, and in my mind a more likely one, is that hikers want to walk in the woods, not on roads, so the route was changed to accommodate them, which, by accident or intention, inconveniences the pilgrims. While we pilgrims are happy to see the woods and hills, we also want a direct route to our next bed. Roads are good, too.

---

29 L'Association québécoise des pèlerins et amis du Chemin de Saint-Jacques.

21 May — Arthez-de-Béarn to L'Abbaye de Sauvelade

We are up early. The other two guests want an early breakfast because they intend to walk to Navarrenx today, almost thirty kilometres. So it's breakfast at seven. By the time I get down, the ladies are done and preparing to leave. I have my coffee with hot milk, eat my bread with butter and apricot jam (this is a pretty standard breakfast here), and say goodbye to them. It is raining, lightly but steadily, so it is rain gear again today. It is also colder than yesterday.

Yesterday, I found the combination of rain pants with the fleece too hot, so today I am trying a different combination: long johns, pants, fleece, and rain jacket. This way, my body will stay warm and my legs might get wet but they will be warm from the walking. This works — almost.

The weather is the first part of the story today. It is cold, wet, blustery, and the clouds are skimming by just overhead. Eddy has given me a good route to get to the road heading south and he says to just stay on D9 until I get to Sauvelade. I take him at his word, but neglect to do the obvious thing and crosscheck against my guide maps. I will pay a stiff price for this neglect. The D9 goes to Sauvelade, but not to L'Abbaye de Sauvelade. It's a long way from the village. The rain is steady, and the wind is cold, probably in the single digits. As long as I keep walking, I'm okay. I need to turn off at a crossroad, which I fail to do. Then I keep on walking close to an hour until I reach a small village and ask someone. Based on the time, I figure that I am less than twenty minutes away. I am really, really wrong. I ask a young woman who is in a hurry and who doesn't want to get wet but takes the time to help me.

I am on the wrong road, and it is at least ninety minutes from here. Back a little bit, off the main road, down a steep hill, about a half-hour walk to the wrecked car place, then it's either straight ahead or to the left, she can't recall exactly or I just don't get it right. I get to the wrecked car parts place, which is closed, and there is no indication of what to do. Nothing at all. And there is no traffic, either. I am getting tired and I am starting to get cold.

Eventually a car comes along, and I flag the driver down. I am hoping for a sweet young thing but I get the next best — a helpful young guy. He is driving a clapped-out car and he doesn't look too respectable, either—of course, neither do I by this stage—but he is very helpful. Not knowledgeable, just helpful. I tell him that I am trying to get to the Abbaye Sauvelade. He's a local, he thinks he knows where it is—he is wrong about this—and is happy to drive me.

For the next forty-five minutes, we drive back and forth over these narrow, winding, hilly roads. I am totally lost and I think he is, too. I am starting to get cold in my wet pants. We see a Poste van and figure that we have found the answer. The Poste lady will know where the Abbaye Sauvelade is. They always know. But no, the lady in the Poste van doesn't know where it is. Then we spot a sign for another *gite* and again figure that they will know where the *gite* I want is. But there is no one home. By this time, I am not only soaked, I am getting very cold. Finally we spot a sign for the GR 65, then follow the signs to the Abbaye. The *gite* can't be far now.

That's when we discover that the *gite* is physically in a wall of the Abbaye. I give my saviour twenty Euros, although he doesn't ask for money, but he accepts and thanks me and drives away. It is worth every penny. I was lost, off the *chemin*, so there was little prospect of someone knowledgeable coming along; and my psychological state doesn't bear examining. I am, in fact, hypothermic and starting to lose focus.

There are a bunch of very wet, very cold pilgrims here, crammed into an anteroom of the *gite*, which doesn't open until 3:30. That's two hours away. They, like me, are all lethargic, like a herd of cows, and I realize later that we are all hypothermic. The place looks like a Chinese laundry, clothes hanging everywhere. However, next to the *gite*, in the same building, is a little bar, which, incredibly enough, is open. It is run by the same busy lady, Maryline, who operates the *gite*.

She is severely overworked today but she's in good humour, which is a good thing since the *pèlerins* are a little grumpy (for pilgrims). What I am quite amazed at is my lassitude. I just want to sit, do nothing, and get warm and dry.

I ask for something—anything—hot and she brings me a *grande crème*, followed by a plate of pasta, with some mystery meat, bony, in a black—I am not kidding; it's black—sauce. It tastes a LOT better than it looks. I find out later that it is *chevreuil*, or wild roe deer, and is considered a delicacy. They just have to do something about the colour of the sauce.

We finally get assigned our beds . . . outside, up the metal stairs, and into the upper floor of the building. I am in a room for four. At the moment, I have one roommate, a Belgian guy, Jean-Pierre. He is a big, quiet bear of a man and, like most of the pilgrims, probably retired. Today's problem is how to get everything—anything—dry. My boots, which had not completely dried from yesterday, are soaked. Even my socks are soaked.

The really good news is that they have a dryer, so I arrange for everything I have on to get pitched into the dryer. I don't particularly care if it is clean, but I care that it is dry. The boots I tip up on a chair next to a radiator and hope that they will be dry by morning. The leather gloves, which help keep my wonky finger warm, are soaked, so they are sitting on top of the radiator. Not good for the gloves, but I need them dry.

It is several hours later. It is still raining out, but I am warm, fed, and dry and in MUCH better humour than I was a few hours ago. Getting wet, cold, and lost is not my idea of a complete good time, but I am now content. Maryline has been very kind. She likes my book and wants to know if she can buy this copy. I tell her no, but she can get one on the Internet. And I will send her a complimentary copy for the *gite*, which I do after I return home.

A couple of young Germans come in, Manuela from Munich and Hans from the Augsburg area (I think). Manuela reminds me physically a lot of my daughter-in-law TJ—she is tall and lean. She speaks good English very quietly while she looks me right in the eye.

At dinner, served at eight p.m. by the same very busy folks, we sit at two tables. At mine are the Germans, my Belgian roommate, and three French couples, friends from the Alsace, Strasbourg and Colmar. One of the French couples tells me that they are coming to Canada in September to visit relatives in Montreal and will be visiting Ottawa as well. It occurs to me that I could do something about this.

I find out that the whole enterprise is a family thing. This is a communal *gite*, run by the municipality, and the staff is Maryline, assisted by her son, her daughter, and a pretty, teen-aged friend of the son's—another Fanny. I get photos of me with the various ladies. There is a lot of laughter and shy, "*Oh, non, pas moi,*" going on. But Hans takes the photos with my camera. Maryline asks me if I can send her the photos and I tell her that I will. Now I have to figure out how. But not tonight. It has been an exhausting day, and I am looking forward to my nice, dry, warm bed. I did send the photos.

22 May—Sauvelade to Navarrenx

Since I went to bed at nine, I cannot stay in bed until seven, so I am up and dressed before the rest of the people have left. I ask if the French couple who will be in Ottawa in September have already left or are still here. They are, so I issue them a formal invitation to join me in Ottawa for a pilgrim's welcome when they are there. They—Marcel and Mireille from Strasbourg in Alsace—are just delighted with this and assure me that they will come. We exchange email addresses to make sure this can happen. Then they are off. We plan to share a beer—*un demi*," I have learned—later today in Navarrenx. It is only fourteen kilometres, a short walk, and likely about three hours.

Oh, yes: yesterday I crossed over the A64, the major multi-lane highway in this area, the one that links Bordeaux to Pau.

The weather forecast for today has changed from raining to just overcast, so when I leave, I have my rain jacket packed at the back of my backpack. When did I start trusting the weatherman? In France, they have the same abysmal track record as in Canada. So within fifteen minutes, it's raining, and I have to stop and dig out the jacket to put it on—which almost immediately stops the rain.

The walk today is all on roads, very narrow, paved, no verge, long grass to the pavement. The country is very hilly, and the roads here have been laid out by the same folks who do the GR. I am on the top of more crests than ever. By now, I have been walking for more than a month—it's the twenty-second of May and I started on the twenty-second of April, so I figure that I can climb anything; and evidently that needs to be tested. So I go up and down steep hills on winding roads. The good news is that the roads wind so much that I can't see how high I have to climb, so it always looks just on the edge of possible.

Because it has rained so much, there are puddles standing on the road and I drag my pole tips through them for fun. And I recall a moment fifty years ago when I was reassured that I had married the right person. (I was already certain, but there is no such thing as too much reassurance.) We had our first child, a son, Francis, and he was just walking. We three went out for a walk in the rain, and Carroll not only permitted, but encouraged Francis to jump in the puddles—and I knew that I had a partner for life. She wanted this little boy to get as much fun out of being a child as he could.

Perhaps it is because it is a shorter day today that it seems much longer. I look at my watch, as if that would shorten the time, and note that fifteen minutes have gone by. And there are frequent markers telling me how much longer in time it will be to get to Navarrenx. Subjective time is very deceptive, I am finding. On longer-distance days, the time seems to go by more quickly. Perhaps that is because the destination is far enough away that I am not measuring time to it.

Chemin
in the woods.

The woods here are dense, and I think about Robin Hood; only here, it isn't Robin Hood of Sherwood Forest, it's Robin de Béarn who is the local hero. Similar story, different locale. I have been in Béarn for a few days and am discovering how, for many French, their local political entity is really important.[30] When *The Three Musketeers* was written by Alexandre Dumas in the 1840s and set 200 years earlier, all three of the musketeers are from Béarn. By the way, d'Artagnan is NOT one of the three musketeers. Did you know that? I didn't. And a pertinent question: since these guys were all musketeers, how come every image of them has each of them holding an épée? How come they're not holding muskets? No one can answer me. I think the French have a lot to answer for on this topic.

As I walk alone, I feel a need to scratch my butt and, to my amusement, realize that before I do, I look back to see that no one is following me. Can't be seen scratching my butt by a complete

---

30 Béarn is one of the traditional provinces of France, located in the southwest of France in the plain and in the Pyrénées just south of here. There is a wonderful story from 1589, when Henry IV succeeded to the throne of France. At the time he was the king of both Béarn and Navarre. Knowing the pride of his people, he told them: "*I am not giving Béarn to France. I am giving France to Béarn.*"

stranger, can I? I wonder what *that's* about. English prudery? I was going to write British prudery, but a Scotsman or an Irishman or a Welshman would just scratch without looking, wouldn't he?

As I come into Navarrenx, there is a plaque explaining that the town was fortified in 1316, and later, in the sixteenth century, a wall was built protecting the town square. It was the first bastioned city in France. Béarn was Protestant at the time, and the Catholics planned to change that. It was Protestant because Jeanne d'Albret, the queen of Navarre (1555–72) and the mother of Henri IV, converted to Protestantism and, in the custom of the time, converted all her subjects at the same time. The Catholic Church was understandably perturbed. The town was besieged as soon as the wall was built—bad timing for the Catholics—but withstood the three-month siege. The wall is still intact today. I am going to go have a look at it. And see if I can find the French couples for that *demi*.

The bridge at Navarrenx.

I don't find the French folks, but I do find Jean-Pierre, the Belgian, sitting outside a little café. I have a hot chocolate (anything hot is good in this weather) with him and go off to explore the town. It doesn't take long. It is about the size of Fort Henry in Kingston.

The wall is interesting but once you've seen it, you have pretty well done the town. There is a cigar factory, the only one in France, they tell me, using Cuban workers in a fifteenth-century barracks; but watching people roll cigars is much like watching paint dry. It doesn't help that it is quite cold and still rainy, so sitting outside watching the pretty girls walk by is not an option. Any moment now, spring should spring out. It's late May, after all.

There is a big, fast river here, the Gave d'Oloron, reputedly the best salmon fishing in France. *Gave* is Béarnaise for river. There is a bridge over it here, and the fortress is situated to cover and protect the bridge.

I have now walked over 560 kilometres, and the end is starting to be significant. Up until now, it has just been a vague idea, way out there. Now it is starting to feel close.

At six p.m., there is a service for pilgrims in the large and ornate church. The service is brief, done by an old layman with a poor speaking voice who then follows with a history of Navarrenx that seems to take at least as long to tell as it did to happen. In subjective time, it is about 500 years. This is followed by a little reception in the welcome centre, and who are there but the two young German sisters, Patricia and Victoria, whom I have not seen since the early days at Estaing!

At the reception, there is a young Japanese woman pilgrim, Keiko, who plays a little recorder-like instrument. The first song is an Irish reel, the second a Japanese lullaby and the third is Ultreia, a pilgrim's hymn. Very moving. I meet here a Scottish couple who are cycling from Le Puy to Santiago. My first Scots pilgrims. More about them later.

Keiko and her flute.

Keiko in traditional dress.

Afterward, I have dinner with ten French pilgrims in a restaurant. We have the pilgrim's menu, which is lots of good food for twelve Euros. After dinner, the owner's wife gives us, without prompting, a fascinating history of Navarrenx and Béarn. Basque country starts just south of here, and it's pretty clear that the Béarnese feel that this is the outer edge of civilization.

I am tired before she is finished, but I wait until the end—it would be impolite to leave—before I pay my bill, say goodnight to my fellow pilgrims, and head back to my room. The weather for tomorrow is promising. At least rain is not forecast.

23 May—Navarrenx to Aroue-Ithortos-Olhaïby

Last evening, while sitting in the church just prior to the pilgrim service, Jean-Pierre (the big Belgian) quietly asked me, "Is religion important to you?" I answered, "No. How about you?" He said, "Not now so much. It used to be very important." And I wonder, of all the people walking this path, for how many is religion important? Certainly based on the numbers at the service last evening (about forty) and on the numbers who crossed themselves at the appropriate moments (two) there are not many Catholics here. There are lots of people with faith, just not that many embracing formal religion.

And many at the service were there because afterwards there was a little welcome with refreshments—that always gets people out. The church, we found out, was originally Catholic, then Calvinist—they would not have approved of all the gilt and colourful statues—then Catholic again.

I had mentioned the Scots couple last evening. This morning, at breakfast, in the place I am staying, there they are. They are Kevin and Linda Clarke of Stirling and they are cycling from Le Puy to Santiago for a charity for motor neuron disease, of which the best known in North America is ALS or Lou Gehrig's disease. Their website is ***http://www.justgiving.com/Kevin-Clarke6***.

I have a little experience with this terrible disease. At the Hospice at May Court, I had a home patient with ALS—Tom, a delightful man, about my age, able to speak only with his eyes and with the help of his wife, using a sheet with all the letters arranged in rows and columns. She would point to each row in turn. When she had the right row he would signal with a blink, then she would scroll across until the right letter when he would blink again. Primitive but effective.

The Clarkes have lost two friends of their own age, just turning sixty, to motor neuron disease in the past two years. They left Le Puy on what would have been the sixtieth birthday of one of the friends. We exchange contact information, and off they go. I wish them "*Bon chemin.*"

I am out of Navarrenx by around eight-thirty on a cool but promising morning. It's overcast, but the forecast is for partly cloudy, no rain. Just on the outskirts—which doesn't take long—I overtake a young couple taking off their rain gear, which is too hot and unnecessary at the moment. I recognize them from the really nasty rainy day a few days ago when I was heading for l'abbeye Sauvelade. She has a small but distinctive patch on the seat of her rain pants. We speak in French, and I can't place her accent, so I ask where she's from. "Nashville, Tennessee." Well, that explains the accent.

She is Genah (pronounced Gina) Loger and she is walking to Santiago with her French husband of almost two years, Jean-François. I ask where they met, expecting it to be here on the *chemin* or something akin. No, they met in Korea at a small, remote Buddhist temple. He was there to learn, and then teach, martial arts. At one point, he was a junior monk for about eighteen months, then realized it wasn't for him. She went there seven years ago for a few days to relax. She was asked if she would stay and teach English to the monks. She stayed five years.

They were there together for two months before they spoke to each other, both of them very shy. He was no longer training to be a monk. Once they spoke, she says that it was only days before she knew they would be together. They married in Nashville about twenty months ago. I asked her whether they had considered marrying in Korea and she laughs and says, "No, I wanted the whole white wedding dress thing."

So that's what happened. And today is his thirtieth birthday! I guessed her age but luckily I was wrong by four years on the good side. Always risky, guessing a woman's age. Just a few days ago, I did the same thing but guessed on the wrong side by four years. I think that I have been forgiven.

Today I walk on the road all the time. The *chemin* goes off into the woods, but the word coming back from people ahead of us is that the trail is very muddy, and they strongly recommend taking the road. Where the *chemin* crosses the road and I rejoin it, there is a little roofed structure with tables and benches and stacked cans of various kinds of pâté for sale. There are my five French friends; and while I am sitting there, along comes Rémi! We greet each other enthusiastically and compare notes. He walked the path this morning and is mud to his knees.

Out of Navarrenx, the road is flat through farmland and rises slowly to a crest. On the crest, the view is magnificent. Can't see the Pyrénées, too much distant haze, but the land drops away steeply into a huge, flat valley dotted with farmsteads and stands of trees. I walk down the road into the valley, talking to the cows and birds and horses—with bells on. That's got to be annoying.

I am heading for a *gite* just short of Aroue. It is called the Ferme Bohoteguia. No, I can't pronounce it, either, but we are in Basque country now. We will see lots of x's and k's in the names. For example, tomorrow I will be staying just outside Ostabat at the Ferme Gaineko Etxea. Try pronouncing *that*. I am going to have to ask when I get there.

When I crested the hill just behind me, I looked at the extremely hilly country ahead and thought, *This looks like the Afghan hill country with trees*; and the people here are just as fiercely independent as those pesky hill tribes. The Basques speak a language that has some similarities to Finnish and Hungarian, but is not Indo-European in origin. There are lots of local languages, including Occitan and Béarnese, but these are variants of Indo-European languages.

I think often about the Pyrénées as I walk. I am going to be walking over or through them in a couple of days. For centuries—millennia, actually—the Pyrénées have been a barrier against invasion (in both directions) and an escape route for people fleeing from persecution or injustice on either side of the mountains. When Isabelle and Ferdinand decided to make Spain solely Catholic in 1492, thousands—perhaps tens of thousands—of Jews and some Muslims fled north over the Pyrénées to the relative safety of France. Most Muslims and some Jews went south to North Africa.

In the late 1930s, many of the survivors on the losing side of the Spanish civil war also fled to France. In the following decade, during my lifetime, tens of thousands of Jewish refugees from the Nazi extermination camps escaped by climbing these barren hills into Spain, aided by the Basques, who mostly don't want any part of either France or Spain—or anyone else, for that matter. They just want to be left alone. I wonder when the next exodus over the Pyrénées will be; who will be running . . . from what threat . . . and in which direction will they flee?

When I am about half an hour from my destination, I spot a little roadside restaurant that is advertising to pilgrims out here in the wilderness. Finding a place like this is uncommon in France, unlike Spain, where the locals have figured out that the pilgrim traffic isn't all destitute. Here, I think that they are about ten years behind, but they will figure it out . . . or they won't. The French are pretty set on their style of life, which, frankly, is pretty good as a lifestyle. They don't take commerce too seriously—at least not here in the country.

I go in, order a beer and a sandwich and frites. While I wait, along come Genah and Jean-François. I thought that they were way ahead of me. They sit down, and next here comes Rémi. I realized, after I said goodbye to him at the roadside stop, that I didn't have a photo of him, so I take this opportunity to remedy that fault. Genah takes a picture for me.

While we are eating, along comes the Japanese girl, Keiko, who is a friend of Genah's and Jean-François's. In she comes with her tin flute and immediately starts to play . . . and she doesn't stop until the couple get up to leave. It is a little unnerving to have a conversation with a background, actually a foreground, of mostly Irish reels on a tin flute. I begin to understand how the Pied Piper got into so much trouble.

Rémi and me.

Keiko speaks English, very little French, and plays her flute—I am speculating here—as a way to keep from having to converse too much. She does say that if she weren't Japanese, she wouldn't learn Japanese. It is too difficult, with too many rules. She is a little anxious because she wants to walk all the way to Santiago, but doesn't think she has enough time on her visa and, if she doesn't make it now, she won't be able, financially, to come back for ten years.

We three leave, and I last see Keiko, playing her flute, walking slowly along a winding French country road. Rémi walks with me as far as the *ferme*, which is my *gite*, then walks on with a big "See you in Saint-Jean-Pied-de-Port." He will be there tomorrow, I on the next day, so we may well overlap. I hope so.

The *gite* is wonderful. It really is a working farm, and the lady there, Mme. Barneix, is renowned for her hospitality. She is tiny, vertically challenged, not lean, and when her face is in repose, it is stern. But it is a mask behind which lives a wonderful sense of humour,

Mme. Barneix and me at the Ferme Bohoteguia, Aroue.

and when she starts to laugh, her face scrunches up like a paper bag. I have a photo of her close up when she can't help smiling.

At dinner, I sit with a dozen French and one Belgian, who has walked from his home. There is a lot of good humour and quite a lot of talk about what the *chemin* means. During the evening, I decide to get out my book and ask if someone can translate a short passage from near the end of the book into French: "I feel different from when I started this in mid-April, more at peace with myself. I know and accept who I am. Is there anything else? I still don't know. Does it matter? I still don't know that, either. The physical *camino* is over, but I think that the real *camino* is inside me, and it has just begun."

Two people at the table take on the task and, when they have agreed and finished, I ask if one of them will read it out to the assembled people. They do so and I get a lot of enthusiastic agreement about what I wrote five years ago after I arrived in Santiago. So it seems to strike a chord in these pilgrims . . . and I like that.

Then it's off to bed in the *dortoir*, because it is going to be a longer walk tomorrow, about twenty-five kilometres.

24 May — Aroue to Ostabat

This morning it's foggy, very foggy, and I leave with the prospect of a longer day ahead. After a while in the fog, I start to think about life and how fog is a good metaphor for the future. I am walking confidently along the *chemin*, taking note of the excellent signage, and I can't see 100 metres in front of me. Of course, the analogy fails when I look behind me, because in life the past is quite clear — just a little hazy because there is so much of it. Here what is behind me is just as foggy as the path ahead. In life, I stride confidently along, thinking how lucky I am, and in fact I have absolutely no idea what is out there.

I understand that at some point, the luck will run out and, at my age, it's likely to be sooner rather than later; but so far, the run has been just fine. Somewhere out in the fog that is the future, there is a precipice waiting for me. It doesn't alarm me, because I do not fear death. It seems to me that death is as natural as birth and as necessary.

Imagine the world if nothing ever died. There would be an awful crowd of old people—can you imagine the bingo halls?—to say nothing of old, toothless crocodiles, old monkeys that keep falling out of trees, birds walking everywhere . . . you get the idea. Would we be wiser? Or just older—a lot older?

And at the end of life, there is often pain. But because I am an optimist—to be a military helicopter pilot, which I was a very long time ago, one has to be an optimist—I think that any associated pain will be manageable. Mostly I am curious. I think that the end of life is the end, full stop. But of course I could be wrong. Perhaps this is only the introduction to an unimaginable future. I guess I will just have to wait and see. Don't get me wrong—I am not in any hurry.

This raises a question for me. Why is it that people who are deeply religious and confidently expect a glorious afterlife are so reluctant to get there?

As I am walking along deep in thought—well, knee-deep in thought—I am brought up short by a stone on the path. My right ankle twists sharply to the right and only the boot keeps my foot from going completely over. I get only a brief shot of the pain that warns of a sprain, and then it's okay again.

My whole trip has almost come to an ignominious end. That would be really annoying, to have the whole adventure shudder to a halt because of a stone in the road. Yet, isn't that what often happens in life? Just when things seem to be going well, there is a stone that twists your ankle and throws all the plans out the window.

The fog lifts and it gets warm, but there is no sign of the promised mountains. I did see them briefly some days ago as I left Aire-sur-l'Adour, but nothing since. After one last climb for the day, I get to the *gite*, the Ferme Gaineko Etxea (it's Basque, and the "tx" combination is pronounced "ch," which makes it "Echa"), which is absolutely nothing like the farm at which I stayed last night. That was a real working farm. This is more like a motel, except the rooms aren't private. It's well-organized, clean, well run, and has a magnificent view to boot.

When we are shown to our shared room, there is a funny moment. Two of us, Jean-Pierre the Belgian and I, are taken to our room. There is a Dutch woman already there, in a partial state of undress. This is hardly unusual on the *chemin*, but when we are asked if everything is okay, we both say that it is, but the Dutch woman says, "*Pas pour moi*"—"Not for me." She gets herself organized and disappears. Then she returns to say that she is changing rooms, to one with a couple of women. This is a first for me on the *chemin*.

I have never seen someone refuse a bed or change rooms because of the sex of the other people in the room. It just is not an issue on the *chemin*. I discover later, talking to her, that this is her first day ever and she did not expect to be alone. An experienced friend had convinced her to come along, then the friend got sick and will join her in a couple of days. I expect that her attitude will soften after a few days, but it is understandable now. She is expecting hotel and getting *gite*.

My roommates are Jean-Pierre and two cyclists, one a Dutch woman, a fit fifty, and the other a young German guy, Dietmar. Everyone is fine with this.

Dinner is served for forty people, many of whom are pilgrims and some of whom are tourists. It actually works. It's likely that the aperitif of Muscadet and the plentiful red wine during dinner helps break the ice. The Basque who runs the *gite* is a short, chunky guy, wearing—of course—a black Basque beret. He is about seventy, with a great voice, which he exercises by singing us Basque songs and getting the crowd to sing along. One of the songs, of which everyone seems to know the words, is sung very enthusiastically to the tune of "She'll Be Coming 'Round the Mountain."

He is a proud Basque, which may be a redundant statement, because all the Basques seem to be proud of their independent heritage. By the time dinner is over and all the red wine has been drunk, we can all sing in Basque, probably separatist anthems. He tells us a little of Basque history and culture, including the fact of the uniqueness of the Basque language. They are keeping the culture and language alive by running free schooling for all.

I go off to bed full of red wine and with Basque songs running around my head.

25 May—Ostabat to Saint-Jean-Pied-de-Port

I leave the Ferme Gaineko Etxea before eight. There is heavy fog below us in the valleys, and the tops of the trees are just above the

Sunrise.

fog, making for a surreal and quite beautiful image. I am heading for Saint-Jean-Pied-de-Port, just about five years and one month later than planned. This was where I intended to start my pilgrimage walk in 2007. It didn't happen because the airline lost my backpack, and I waited in Pamplona for five days until I realized that their promise of, "It will be there in the morning" was nothing more than empty air. By the time I came to this realization, I did not have enough time to get to Saint-Jean-Pied-de-Port and walk back through Pamplona, so I started from where I was, in Pamplona.

This is beginning to feel like closing the circle. I walked from Pamplona to Santiago five years ago, from Le Puy-en-Velay to Saint-Chély-d'Aubrac last year and from Saint-Chély to here this year. From Saint-Jean, Pamplona is only three days away and will complete the more than 1,500 kilometres from Le Puy to Santiago.

After about an hour's solitary walk, a young German cyclist, Dietmar, my roommate from last night, pulls up beside me and starts to walk his bike. We end up walking together all the way into Saint-Jean, another four hours. The walk is mostly level between hills that get higher and higher—but still no mountains. Although we are not very high, the treeline is just below the top of most of the hills. They are green on top, and often I can see cattle grazing in the high pastures. It would be nasty up there in a cold rain or in the wind.

Dietmar wants to talk. He has been riding for three weeks from somewhere north of Bordeaux, and today is his last day. He has a train out of Saint-Jean late this afternoon. He is from Minden and he is pleasantly surprised that I know where Minden is. Not far from where I was stationed in northern Germany, there is a place that is a natural focal point for any invasion force from the east. It is called the Minden Gap. He wants to know if most Canadians know about Minden. I

Pyrénées, early morning.

have to break it to him gently that only Canadian soldiers of a certain age who served in the north of Germany would know Minden.

He is a very young-looking thirty-five. I guessed him at twenty to twenty-six. And his is a depressingly familiar story. He was in architectural school, then dropped out because of family illness. First his mother, then his father got ill and eventually died. By this time, he had a job running a machine making cigarillos. He tells me that it's a good job, although his interests are history and geography. Seems like an awful waste to have someone like this making cigarillos.

He talks about how he sees parallels between the *chemin* and life. I agree completely. Every day on the *chemin* is a miniature slice of life. At one point, he asks me if I would prefer to walk alone. It's a very caring gesture, because sometimes people really do need to walk by themselves. But I don't at the moment and I get a strong sense that he wants to talk. Part of this, I recognize, is that this is his last day and he doesn't want it to end. I know exactly how that feels.

As we walk through one of the tiny villages, I see a man using a scythe to cut the grass around his house. I am so taken with this image that I stop and ask him if I may take a photo. He immediately stands up and holds his scythe to his side, creating an image analogous to Grant Wood's 1930 painting, *American Gothic*. I laugh and ask him if he will continue working, since that is the picture I want. He obliges me and goes

Cutting the lawn.

back to scything the front lawn, which is a little less than knee high, and I thank him and capture the picture.

When we finally arrive at Saint-Jean, I drop my backpack at my *gite* and walk down with him to a crossroads, where we sit and have a beer. He still has to find the station and take his bike there, so we hug each other, and he heads off to the train station. I meet Jean-Marc near the church, and we hug each other. Hard to believe I ever called him "Weird Harold." He seems to be less sad now and quite willing to talk with people.

Saint-Jean-Pied-de-Port ("Saint John foot of the pass") is so named because it is at the entry to the major pass to Spain. It was heavily fortified with a still-standing wall because it stood between the open country to the north and all potential invaders from the south—and there were many. There are dates like 1527 and 1620 on some of the tiny buildings lining the steep main street in the old town inside the wall.

Bridge at Saint-Jean Pied-de-Port.

I go back to my *gite*, *L'Esprit du Chemin*. It is a very different operation from the more commercial *gites*. With the exception of the owners, everyone here is a volunteer from elsewhere. At the moment, there are three: Katherina from Germany, Wilhelmyne from Holland, and Judy Gayford, the president of the Calgary chapter of the Canadian Company of Pilgrims. All three speak excellent English, as does Huberta, the *gite* owner, which makes my life a little easier. Today is Judy's last day as a volunteer here.

I have picked this *gite* on purpose. Five years ago, when I was planning my first trip on the *camino*, intending to walk from Saint-Jean-Pied-de-Port, I booked a bed here in this *gite* for the first day of the trip. Then the airline lost my backpack and everything I had, including where I was staying, the phone number—everything. So I guess the bed went empty.

Anyway, they were very upset and sent an angry email to my address at home, telling me, correctly, that this was not the act of a pilgrim. So, for five years, I have waited to get back here, explain what happened, and offer to pay for the missed night. Huberta tells me that I can put a donation in the box, only if I like, for the missed night. Which is what happens, and all is forgiven.

I ask if I can spend another day here, but they are already fully booked for tomorrow. My name goes in the book, and I can stay if there is a cancellation. At dinner, they have a lovely ceremony. Huberta asks that each of us say who we are, where we are from, and something about our own experience on the *chemin*. We are one from Ireland, one Northern Ireland, two Americans, five French, two Dutch, two German, one Dane about my age, and one Canadian. When it's my turn, I tell my story, then read that little passage from my book and ask another pilgrim to tell it again in French.

Dinner is lovely, all cooked and served by the volunteers, who join us at the table. Later that night, just before we put out the light, I am lying in bed in the room shared by the Irishman and the Dane. The Dane, Erik, mentions having done UN duty in Somalia; I mention having done UN duty in Cyprus. He asks when I was there. I tell him the summer of 1968. He was there at the same time as a platoon leader in the Danish battalion, while I was the deputy commanding officer of the armoured reconnaissance squadron. He remembers — I find this astonishing — that my unit's name was B Squadron of the Fort Garry Horse. So we served together forty-four years ago, we never met, and now we are here sharing a room in a *gite* in Saint-Jean-Pied-de-Port. Seems unlikely, doesn't it?

If I can stay here tomorrow, I will. This is a lovely *gite*, very special. If not, then I have to decide to either go to another *gite*, if I can get a bed, or head out to Roncevalles by one of two routes. Three options, and I don't have to decide until morning.

26 May — Saint-Jean-Pied-de-Port to Orisson

This morning I get up, have breakfast, and ask if there is an opportunity for a bed here this evening. They tell me that they won't know unless someone calls and cancels, and it may not be until late in the day. I decide that this won't work and ask if they can check for me at the refuge at Orisson for a bed. They do this but warn me that it is unlikely there will be one available. There are only eighteen beds there, and it is a holiday weekend—again. But they do call, and there is a bed reserved for me if I can be there by two p.m. Orisson is halfway up the high route, also known as the Napoleonic route.

They also tell me that an American pilgrim died in the hills between here and Roncevalles earlier this week. He got lost on the high route in the fog and probably fell. I don't know what happened to him, but it is instructional. Mother Nature is neither benign nor malign. She's indifferent. If you ignore the warnings of the locals—and they are very quick to warn people if going over the pass is a bad idea—then you are, quite literally, on your own.

Leaving Saint-Jean-Pied-de-Port.

Since I have a bed reserved at Orisson, I am committed to going the higher route. I have discovered that the high route involves a climb of 1,200 metres, and the valley route involves a climb of 800 metres. The high route offers me a much better view and a break at the halfway point, based on height. So that is the route I choose. Out of Saint-Jean, immediately into a climb and ever-increasing vistas. On the distant hills, the herds of cows are just tiny dots. The hills are really high, but even here, no mountains.

The weather is co-operating. It's overcast; warm but not hot, and little wind. Even so, with the constant climb, I am soaked within twenty minutes and sucking back a lot of water. At the five-kilometre mark, there is a little *gite*, where I refill my water bladder, which has just gone dry. The *chemin* S-turns up a hillside, and there are cows on both sides of the *chemin* and lying on the trail itself. Happily, they are as docile as one expects from cows—they are year-old heifers, no bulls, and placidly chew their cuds as I walk by.

Soon after, I come upon an American woman from New Orleans sitting at the side of the path. She has been crying and is quite distraught. She started at Saint-Jean-Pied-de-Port and she had no idea of the physical effort required to climb this steep and unforgiving hill.

En route to Orisson in the Pyrénées.

We talk, and after a few minutes, she gets up, and we walk together very slowly up the road. She urges me repeatedly to go on, but I can't leave her. She is just on the edge of complete breakdown. She tells me that she has never failed before at anything in her life . . . four degrees, children, career . . . but she can't do this.

I urge her on, a step at a time. I tell her that Orisson is only a kilometre away and I am sure that they can order a taxi for her to go to Roncevalles. We walk slowly, very slowly, and talk, stopping often, and she continues to keep moving, occasionally weeping, but mostly under control. At one point, she asks me, "Aren't you tired?" and I realize that I am not. It's a lesson for me that even here, on this steep, long, and unrelenting climb, if I walk slowly enough — which I am doing because I am staying with her — it is an effort that I can readily manage. So the French are right; "*Doucement, doucement.*" Slowly, slowly.

Then we come round a corner and there, a delightful surprise, is Orisson. It is only one building, the *gite*, with, across the road, a terrace overhanging the drop-off. She immediately brightens up. We go inside, I confirm my bed, and ask if, by chance, there is another bed available. There is, so I ask her if she wants a bed or a taxi. She immediately opts for the bed and goes off for a sleep.

The view from here is breathtaking, probably twenty to thirty kilometres. And who is here but Jean-Marc? We are starting to be old friends. We have touched lives a dozen times in the past several weeks and it is, for me, very encouraging to watch him come slowly out of his shell. He tells me that he has changed to better boots. He had a friend from home send him a pair.

At this *gite*, the young and attractive black-haired Pantxika (pronounced Panchika) who runs it (very efficiently, by the way) tells me that there are many Americans on the *chemin* right now, mostly due to the popularity of the movie *The Way*. She also tells me that she is in the movie, in some scene walking behind Martin Sheen. I am going to have to find out exactly which scene. Tonight there are five Americans staying here, out of eighteen beds. That is four more than I met the entire way in Spain five years ago.

After dinner, Pantxika asks us to say who we are and something about our *camino*. People are quite shy, so I stand up and do my by now familiar dog-and-pony show, with the little paragraph about "the real *camino* is inside me," etc.

Some of the people here I already know, like the two young German sisters Victoria, blonde, and Patricia, dark-haired, both little, from near Leipzig, whom I met back at the *gite* on my first day in Saint-Chély-d'Aubrac on a rainy day in April. Some are new, like all the Americans, and Robert from Toronto, who have just started today from Saint-Jean. He is concerned because by mistake he left behind in Paris his month's supply of medication, worth about $1,000, and some electronic bits. He is a big, loose-limbed man, very pleasant. And there is a young, pretty Dutch woman, Natalie, walking with her father. Her English is so good and so accent-less that I take her for an American. This will almost get me in trouble later.

I have met and spent some time in the *gites* with a middle-aged French couple, Fernand and Francine from Alsace, and here they are. Apparently they learn to trust me because after a couple of weeks, they share with me why they are walking the *chemin* for the third time. (This is unusual. Most people do not talk about why they are here walking the *chemin* . . . and it is an unspoken rule that you NEVER ask anyone else why they are walking.) They were happily married, busy with their lives, had two children, active boys thirteen and eight years old. Everything seemed to be just fine in their lives. Then the older boy started to get ill and it took a very long time for the medical community to determine the cause. He had a genetically caused disease for which there was no cure. About a year later the younger boy got sick as well and this time the diagnosis was quick and certain. He had the same genetic disease and his fate was equally certain. They each survived about eighteen months from the initial onset of the disease.

Over the space of less than thirty months, these two unfortunates went from a family with two healthy boys to a family that had buried the next generation—the boys died a few months apart, at sixteen and eleven years of age. The mother was the unwitting carrier of the disease; the husband was not a carrier. Often in situations like this, the dreadful trauma of burying their children tears the family apart, but these people are made of sterner stuff. They decided to walk the *chemin* from their home all the way to Santiago in 2009. Then they walked it again in 2010 for the second lost son. The mother tells me that she walks holding the hands of her boys and she can feel them with her as she walks with her husband.

This year they are walking again, but this time it is for them and for the future. She tells me later that when they arrived in Santiago for the third time, she felt a sense of freedom that she has not felt in years. She feels that her boys are safe and both she and her husband can now move on in their lives. Their experience reminds me of just how lucky most of us are in our daily lives and also reminds me that it is possible to deal with terrible situations. It is how you handle the bad things that come your way that is a real test of one's psychological strength. I have never had to face anything even remotely like this.

Early to bed; it is another twenty kilometres with quite a climb in the morning. The weather looks promising.

27 May—Orisson to Roncevalles

Today, the weather dawns bright and clear. It is quite cool, which is a very good thing, since there is a long climb ahead of me. Although I have done the worst (i.e., steepest) part of the ascent, I still have about twenty kilometres to travel and about 600 metres more to climb before I get to Roncevalles. I have breakfast with the group. The language is mostly English, which is a huge change from the last month. I will talk about the effect on me later—it isn't entirely good.

At breakfast, I see the American woman whom I helped yesterday but I don't know whether she will call for a ride or attempt the next section. From here, it looks difficult, even to me after five weeks of steady walking and hill climbing. All those hills over the last weeks were like hills with training wheels. Yesterday's climb to here was brutal, and I know that today's, while less steep overall, might still have particularly difficult sections. I would give her odds of less

Pyrénées morning.

than one in a hundred of making it from here to Roncevalles on foot. What I do not know at the time is that my small assistance yesterday has helped restore her psychological strength.

So off I go. The part I can see in front of me is a steep climb up and around a corner. When I get there, the landscape opens up and I can see forever. There are huge hills, a few outcroppings of rocks and very few trees, which are stunted. Except for the rocky bits, it is all upland meadow. The slopes to either side are very steep, up to the left, down to the right, and I can see how a disoriented person could get in real trouble here. An inch or two of snow on the road to obscure it and a little fog or blowing snow, and it would be really easy to get turned around and get off-track. But that is not a possibility today. The *chemin* winds off into the distance, always climbing, but not steeply. The weather is comfortable, cool, sunny, no wind.

At some points, it is level or even descends a bit. I could do without the descents because I know I will just have to climb back up around the next bend. The *chemin* here is a road surface, wide enough for the occasional vehicle that labours past.

Off to the sides are pasture lands, with a few scattered concrete block structures that take me a little while to figure out. They are three walls, no roof, about five feet high, in the shape of a shallow, rectangular "U." They all face the same way, so it's easy to figure out where the prevailing wind is. They are shelters for the herders if they get caught up here in bad weather, which is both common and extremely dangerous. You just sit down inside the arms of the U, bundle yourself up in whatever clothing you have, and wait the storm out.

The shelters also work for pilgrims caught out here, if they can figure out what the shelters are. There are multiple warnings for pilgrims about not attempting this option in anything but good weather. I saw several signs in Saint-Jean; and in both the *gîte* and the pilgrim welcome centre in Saint-Jean, we got verbal warnings. One American pilgrim died out here this week (this is life imitating fiction, shades of *The Way*) and I would guess that there are more who go unreported or under-reported. It would not be good for local business, which depends heavily on the pilgrim traffic, to advertise the losses on the mountain.

There are herds of cattle and sheep on the steep hillsides, no fences anywhere. At one point, there is a vehicle stopped, with pilgrims clustered around. When I get there I see why. They are offering drinks, chocolate bars, and cookies, as well as the last opportunity to get a stamp in the pilgrim passport in France. What amazes me most are the prices.

If this were Canada, I would expect to see prices elevated as steeply as the surrounding landscapes. Instead, a chocolate bar is half a Euro, less than I would pay in a store in any town. So the couple operating this little "store" must be pilgrims, too, or at least very sympathetic to pilgrims.

I walk up around a corner, and there are big horses, a small herd of them on both sides of the road. The stallion is over on the right, standing quite still, quite alert and clearly the head of this herd. He is big, brown, with huge, strong legs; and now I know where the expression "hung like a horse" comes from.

There are a dozen mares and two foals, one a colt, and the other, a patchwork of brown and white, staggering along beside its mother, trying to get milk and not quite succeeding. This foal is only a day or two old at the most. Her attempts at walking, legs out to the sides for balance, remind me of my granddaughter Bella when she was trying to figure out how to walk.

I can see ahead a couple of kilometres where tiny figures are slowly making their way up a slope off road to the right to a saddle between two rocky outcroppings, where the figures disappear. This may be the Col d'Elhursato (Elhursato Pass) at 1,152 metres, the second-highest point on this leg of the *chemin*. I get to the point where the *chemin* finally leaves the road and heads off to the right up the hill. The path is good, dry, a few rocks, mostly just hard surface and steep. Slowly, slowly I climb, drinking lots of water and taking frequent rest stops, just noting that each step, no matter how short, is moving me in the right direction.

And the good news is that this IS the first of the two passes, so only one more to go before I reach the steep downhill stretch into Roncevalles. I have an enormous feeling of victory and satisfaction at this point. This has been an arduous, demanding climb . . . and I have made it.

Beyond the pass, the *chemin* continues over rolling ground. At one point, the path climbs up and over a small mass of dried mud and stone. I look uphill to the left and see that there has been a small landslide at this point that accounts for the hummock of extra material on the path. That would have been an interesting moment! There is a steep drop-off to the right. I pass a stone marker that says "Navarre" and I assume that I am now in Spain. There is no other indication of a border that I can make out.

The path continues to climb quite gently until, on a level section in a sun-dappled woods, I pass Roland's Fountain. Roland was Charlemagne's nephew and the officer in charge of Charlemagne's rearguard as they withdrew north over the Pyrénées from Spain in 778. The rearguard was caught in these hills and killed to the last man by the local Basques—a much earlier version of Custer's Last Stand. The Basques were quite properly annoyed because Charlemagne's army had pillaged and torn down the defensive walls of Pamplona, a Basque city, as it moved north.

Several centuries later, the *"Chanson de Roland,"* the "Song of Roland," was written. This song is to the French as the King Arthur story is to the English: the heroic myth of larger-than-life and braver-than-life characters from a time shrouded in history.

I continue walking until I enter a huge beech forest. The path is almost level, but the ground is steeply uphill to the left, steeply downhill to the right; there is a stout wire fence on the right side of the path, so there is little risk of falling far. The path is marked with tall, upright posts on the right, one every fifty metres. They are sequentially numbered starting with "one" and have at eye level a little legend, "SOS 112," with a telephone symbol. It's clear that people get in trouble up here, probably from exhaustion, and this is a very quick way for them to call for help and for the responders to locate them accurately.

In the forest, there is a small memorial to a sixty-four-year-old Japanese pilgrim who died here in 2002. It is just another reminder that we are all here temporarily.

Still climbing very gently in perfect, cool, walking weather, I come to the Col de Lepoeder, at 1,440 metres the high point on this whole section. Almost immediately I come to the steep descent into Roncevalles. The advice we have all been given is to take the road to the right, but instead I take the off-road trail down through the large trees.

It is a steep descent and would be deadly in rain or mud, but I have neither today. It is as steep and difficult as was the descent into Montrisol a year ago, but I am older and wiser. Again, slowly, slowly works. I stop where there is a convenient fallen tree trunk as a seat and have some of the sandwich I had brought from Orisson. I am comfortable and happy, unlike during the descent into Montrisol, when I was furious. It is all about how I choose to view what's happening to me. The two German sisters catch up to me, flashing big smiles, chatting with me as they pass.

This isn't a race, so it doesn't matter that I am likely the slowest person on the path. There are reported to be at least 400 beds at the *gite* in the monastery at Roncevalles, so I am not concerned about finding a place to sleep.

And I finally arrive. Roncevalles is a tiny village of thirty inhabitants, a huge church and twelfth-century Augustinian monastery, a hotel, and two restaurants. The *gite* is inside the monastery structure and is out of bounds to tourists. I am here at one and the *gite* doesn't open until two, so it's stack the backpack and poles against a wall, off with the boots and on with the sandals. And here are the German sisters, Victoria and Patricia, and the very pretty Dutch woman, Natalie. Her father has not yet arrived. I never do figure out who he is.

I get into a little potential trouble when I ask Natalie if she has an adapter for the European power outlet. This is because I still think

The gite *at Roncevalles.*

she's American. I am looking for one to borrow to recharge my camera battery, since I lost mine weeks ago. She says, "No, we all use the same power plug in Europe," and that is when I discover she is Dutch, not American. I apologize for the error, since many Europeans, not to mention most Canadians, do not want to be misidentified as American. She laughs and says that it is not a problem for her. That makes it not a problem for me.

The enclosed courtyard is covered with white stones, easy to walk on but very bright in the sunlight. It is just a little too cool to sit in the shade, so I move to a bench on the sunlit side of the courtyard opposite the *gite* door. The story I heard is that the *gite* is one huge *dortoir* or sleeping room, so imagine my pleasure when I discover that it has all been renovated, with modern facilities and cubicles or "boxes" with two bunks in each. I am assigned bed 121, which is, happily, a lower bunk.

I sit outside and talk with the German sisters, and they want to know how I learned German. I tell them about my military service in Germany and they want to know when that was. When I tell them, they look at each other and laugh and say, "Our mother was ten that year." That puts everything into perspective—my oldest son was ten that year—so I tell them that they could easily be my granddaughters. We decide that they can be honorary granddaughters.

Some of us attend the Mass that is held in the large and very ornate church here in the monastery. Four priests in full regalia conduct the Mass in front of a gilded wall that is storeys high. It is a huge contrast to most of the churches that I have been in over the past few weeks. Those few that are still functioning are simple, bare walls and cold. This church is very wealthy by comparison, and I wonder how they manage—until the collection plates are passed among all the pilgrims, who are mostly quite grateful to be here after their arduous walk today. The mystery is solved—new people and new pockets every day.

Afterwards, Patricia, Victoria, and I have dinner together at one of the restaurants where I had previously made a reservation. I offer to buy dinner, but they will only agree if I buy one and they buy the other, so that's the deal. It turns out that I have to pay for all three in advance, so they don't get to pay. I had been warned that it was necessary to make a reservation. There are about 400 pilgrims here and two small restaurants. Do the math. After dinner, Patricia very shyly tries to give me ten Euros. I tell her, no, just some red wine, which I intend to mean a glass of wine for later. They agree, and then it's off to bed.

It is early to bed again here. The *gite* closes at ten and the lights are off until six a.m. tomorrow.

And, oh yes, I found a friendly American couple from Portland, Oregon, with a power plug adapter that I borrowed and recharged my camera battery, so I am good to go again.

Based on my admittedly very rough calculations, with all the hill-climbing that I have been doing, Pamplona ought to be about the same altitude as Machu Picchu, but it's not. In fact Pamplona at 460 metres is about 100 metres lower than Saint-Chély-d'Aubrac, where I started six weeks ago, so it has been a net *descent* over the 750-kilometre distance. I am amazed, since I can recall every uphill walk with startling vividness while the downhill parts only registered if they were particularly steep or treacherous underfoot. Much like life, I am intensely aware of the difficult parts, while the easy bits fade away or never even register.

28 May — Roncevalles to Zubiri

I am out of Roncevalles very early. The lights come on at six a.m., and there is no breakfast here, so it's up and out. I have twenty-two kilometres to get to Zubiri, from which it is only one more day to Pamplona. It is a little hard to believe.

I have a brief fright just as I get up. I go to the window and look out. It is still dark and it looks in the courtyard as if it had snowed last night. It is quite cool, and the ground is covered in white. It takes a few minutes before I catch on that I am looking at the white stones that cover the inner courtyard. Apparently, Natalie's father makes the same mistake at about the same time. Natalie tells me that he reports snow, but she is sceptical.

The *camino* here to start is wide, level, and paved. Then it runs through a dense forest, and although the sun is up, there is a morning twilight. Quite an eerie effect.

After about an hour, I come across a little roadside café, where I have coffee with Patricia and Billy, the Irish couple from both coasts of Ireland, and Robert from Toronto. He is ecstatic because he has found his missing meds—in his backpack in a seldom-used pocket. The German sisters pass me, and one of them, Patricia, shows me a bottle of red wine that she has in a pocket of her backpack. So that is how they have resolved the red wine issue. We agree to drink it later on.

Later in the day, I walk out of the woods across a road to a vehicle set up in a sunny clearing to service the pilgrims. Again, this is a good stop, and I buy a drink similar to Gatorade. It tastes good, and anything to boost energy is great by this time in the day. I am about to leave when Robert appears. He had been lying down; he fell asleep on the grass and is walking about looking a bit stunned. Because he is wandering and acting a bit bewildered, I ask him if he would like me to walk with him the three kilometres down a winding path in the forest. He says he would, so that's what happens.

We arrive in Zubiri, where I have booked a bed in a *gite* (*albergue* in Spanish), *El Palo de Avellano*, "the hazel staff." Robert comes with me and is able to get a bed there as well. I think he's lucky, because beds are still pretty scarce. The *albergue* is well done and uses pass-cards to access the *dormitorios*. That's a nice touch, because the town, with an industrial centre, is big enough to have people capable of theft. The German sisters are here, as is the couple Marcel and Mireille from Strasbourg and their friends from Colmar. We all sit outside in the back garden in the sun and share the red wine that Patricia has carried all the way from Roncevalles or somewhere en route.

Later we are all in a little bar in the town, having a *demi*. We are sitting indoors at a table with benches. Someone wants to have a picture of the group, so we have to squeeze together in order to all fit in the frame. Patricia, the older and darker of the German sisters, who has been sitting across from me, comes over to my side and leans back against me, her back against my chest, and snuggles in. For some reason, this move wakes up my pheromones. Her innocent move triggers a powerful wave of reaction in me. I have my arm around her waist, my hand resting lightly on her stomach and it would be a matter of a few inches to slide my hand higher. But I don't do it. I just sit there, enjoying her proximity for a couple of minutes until the photo op is finished and she moves back across the table. When I think about it later, two reasons come to mind. One is that this move would likely create disappointment or disgust in her and I would really dislike that. The second is, that if she did accept it, it would create disappointment and self-disgust in me . . . and I would also really dislike that. This is where responsibility trumps nature. On the other hand . . . sisters?

Today I was thinking about my emotional state when I was in the *gite* at Orisson with all the Americans, and the fact that I did not

Patricia.

Victoria.

much like it. What was going on with that? I think it might have been because for five weeks I have usually been the only native English-speaker and therefore something of a rarity; unique, so to speak. And apparently, I don't like being not unique.

But is my uniqueness based on my ability to speak a specific language? Surely not. And the same goes for what I do or did for a living, where I live, my age, sex, religion, and all those other groupings that we humans use to conveniently categorize others. So what makes me unique? What makes me "me" and not anyone else? I thought at first that it must fall somewhere in the relationships that we have with others. But then I recall that hermits, who might have no relationships with others, are still unique. So that's not it.

Perhaps my sense of uniqueness is an illusion, created by the individually focused society in which I live. Perhaps if I lived in a large and densely crowded country like India or China, I might not have this sense of uniqueness. So at the moment I don't have an answer to the question, "What makes me unique?" Perhaps a better question is, "Am I unique? And, if so, how?" And an even more useful question is, "Does it matter that I am or am not unique? Does anything in my life or in my awareness change either way?" Things to ponder.

Later in the *dormitorio*, one guy speaks long and loudly on his cell phone, then talks with his bedmate for another twenty minutes or so. The lights are out and the outside light is fading. The other half-dozen people in the room are all in their beds, either sleeping or trying to sleep, and this rather ignorant guy is either unaware or doesn't care about the rest of us. I am really tempted to say, "*Tais-toi!*" [shut up!] but I don't. Eventually, he quits talking. I think he's Italian.

29 May — Zubiri to Pamplona

I am up for breakfast in this very nice *gite* in good time. It is very strange to be contemplating the fact that this is my last day on the *camino*, that I will today have completed the 1,500-kilometre journey that I embarked upon over five years ago.

Robert tells me at breakfast that he did not sleep well, and that there is a correlation between getting up early [before the lights come on] and the number of noisy plastic bags that one uses in one's backpack. He quietly identifies several women with whom he will not share a room in the future.[31] He was in a different room from me.

The *camino* from here to Pamplona runs along a valley that also carries the main highway and traffic north, so we are never out of earshot of the traffic. A German woman, tall, strong, well built, honey blonde, with a natural smile, dimples, and kind eyes, in her early 40s, catches up to me and walks with me all the way into Pamplona. She takes few photos, but when she does, I recognize the pattern and ask her if she is an architect. She is. Claudia has her own business in a city not far from Frankfurt.

We pass through the tiny village of Burguete on the Irati River, made famous by Hemingway because he liked to come here to fish. He stayed in Burguete in 1924 and 1925 and described it in his novel *The Sun Also Rises*. There is an endangered species of horse named after this village. I did not see any horses here. Of course not — they are endangered, remember?

At one point, we walk in a woods beside and a little above a stream to our right. The path is level and narrow, but firm with a thin layer of decomposing leaves on top of dirt. It is a steep slope, about ten feet down to the water. Some cyclists catch up to us from behind — we passed them while they were adjusting something a couple of hundred metres back — and call out to warn us; I step to the right to keep out of their way. My heel lands on a soft piece of mouldering leaf mass. I lose my balance and just about develop a closer relationship with the stream than I would prefer. I manage to grab a piece of a shrub as I teeter on the edge and it's just enough to keep me from falling down the bank.

We cross over an old bridge and stop in Trinidad, just north of Pamplona, for lunch. There is an old chapel here beside the river, and

---

31   When Carroll and I travel, she loves to use Ziploc bags to keep her stuff organized and she rustles them at me deliberately — but never before dawn.

we go in to see what it's like inside. Nothing special, but as we wander inside the chapel, the door we entered closes behind us and the lights go out. It is black in here. I try the door handle—it is immobile. I try it several times but it is clearly and irrevocably locked. What to do? Then I hear a voice in the dark from a side wall: "The door over here is not locked." There is someone else in here with us and she has found a way out. It is quite a relief after a few uncomfortable moments.

We sit on an old bench in a little plaza overlooking the river and eat lunch. Claudia has brought some old bread, older cheese, and even older sliced meat. I have brought my appetite. We debate the merits of the sliced meat but eat it anyway. It has no ill effects. She notices my Lowa boots and tells me that she trained in a pair of Lowas but they gave the right edge of her right foot grief, so she found another brand and tried those. Finally, her father gave her a pair of his old, well-worn-in boots and suggested that she try those. On her way to the station to begin this trip, she was being driven by her husband and she sat with two pairs of boots in front of her: the new pair and her father's boots. She was still undecided. When she got out of the car, she took her father's boots, which she is wearing now. Her feet have been fine.

At one point in a field as we walk I come across a simple black cross with the inscription:

Fin del Camino.

Fin del Camino
Rosanna di Verona
2006

It is a memorial to another pilgrim, this one a woman from Verona, Italy, who died here on her *camino* six years ago.

For most of the distance, our path is on the east side of the valley, running parallel to the highway, and quite flat. Then we cross the highway and do a series of these annoying little hills that the folks in France like to use as the *chemin*. As we walk, we talk about all sorts of things. She tells me that she has stayed the past few nights in *dortoirs* and has not slept well. She thinks that she will find a better place to sleep tonight. It occurs to me that I may have a solution for her problem. I tell her that I have a room reserved in a good hotel in Pamplona. If she would like to share, I am sure that we can get a room with two beds rather than one. She considers this for a bit, then says that this will be okay with her.

We enter the suburbs of Pamplona and walk through unusually well-marked streets to head toward the centre of the city. I have reserved a room at the Hotel Maisonnave, which is where I stayed in 2007, before embarking on the *camino* to Santiago.

When we cross the last bridge just below the high fortified wall, Claudia turns to me and says, "Well, you are here. How does it feel to be finished?"

And the answer, after some moments of thought, is simply: "Quiet satisfaction," and it is quite true. It is the 29th of May and I have walked about 750 kilometres since the 22nd of April, about six weeks. I have been wondering for some time how I would feel—whether I would have the feeling of anti-climax that I had in Santiago five years ago. Happily, I don't.

We walk to the front steps of the Hotel Maissonave, where I started in April of 2007, and now, only now, do I feel completed. The journey is finished and the circle is truly closed. Claudia takes a picture of me with the hotel sign, I check in and determine that we can have a room with two

In front of the Hotel Maisonnave.

beds. When we get into the room, it's fine at first, although the two beds are pushed together. I am okay with this; she is less comfortable, but I figure that we can pull them apart. No big deal. I take my boots off and lie down on top of one of the beds. Then we see that the shower enclosure is a clear glass panel, no kind of visual isolation. She sees this, hesitates, then turns to me and says that she will have to find another place to stay. She can't do this. I am not sure what it is that she can't do, but she is set on leaving, so I do not try to argue with her. I tell her that I understand, and I do kind of understand, but it doesn't feel good to me. She does not want to be here and that is her decision. She leaves and goes off to find an *albergue*.

I send a message home to Carroll and to the Hospice at May Court that I am in Pamplona and the walk is over. And I think: *Not bad for an old guy.*

After showering and changing into clean (cleaner) clothes, I go to the train station (by taxi), get my ticket for Barcelona, visit the cathedral to get my pilgrim passport stamped, and head off to the Plaza del Castillo, where I make one tour of the Plaza and see no one I know. Claudia sends me a text message apologizing for her behaviour and asking me to call her on her cell phone. I am a bit peeved so I don't call.

I find a strategically located bar and sit there nursing a beer. Someone comes up behind me and covers my eyes. It is Mireille from Strasbourg. She and Marcel join me, then Robert from Toronto shows up and he joins us. We all enjoy basking in the sun, drinking a beer—somehow they keep coming—until six, when Marcel and Mireille go off on some errand. We agree to meet here and figure out where we will go for dinner. At seven-thirty, when they return, I haven't moved; I've just been sitting here nursing a beer or two and contemplating the world. So we decide to eat right here.

There is a little boy here on the edge of the plaza somewhere between three and four years old, black hair, black eyes, round face, wearing a red, short-sleeved T-shirt and red shorts, playing here just beyond our table. He has a rubbery thing that looks like a bright-red sea urchin and he is kicking it happily back and forth in an open space. He waits for people to walk by and then gives it another good kick. I think that there might be a soccer gene, and if there is, this little boy has it.

Dinner is about what you might expect in a tourist-trap restaurant but it is flavoured with bad jokes in several languages. Mireille and I speak French and English, Marcel speaks only French, and Robert is about 15 percent fluent in French . . . but it works. After dinner, I spot Claudia walking in the Plaza and I run to catch up to her. I realize that I should have returned her call. Failing to do so was just pettiness on my part—I was punishing her. She is a good person; she was just upset at the moment for whatever reason. She is very happy to see me and happy to join us.

Robert has to be in his *albergue* by ten—he missed the curfew in Roncevalles and almost got to spend the night outside, so he has been sensitized. Mireille and Marcel say goodbye and promise to be in Ottawa in September. I have to have the Thatcher *gite* stamp ready by then for their pilgrim passports. It is to include an upside-down turtle and a snail. I think there's a message for me there.

Marcel, Mireille, Claudia, me, and Robert in Pamplona.

Claudia and I sit for another hour and talk about her life and my life. I tell her that I think she is a good person, and she seems comforted by this. Eventually, it starts to get chilly, and even the Spaniards are starting to leave the Plaza. I really don't want this evening to end. So it is goodbye to Claudia with a big hug and a promise to keep in touch; then back to my hotel for a well-earned sleep.

30 May—A Last Day in Pamplona

I arrived here yesterday and will leave tomorrow for Barcelona, where I will meet Carroll on 2 June. Today, the only thing planned is a dinner at the Iruña Restaurant with the two German girls, Patricia and Victoria. They stopped yesterday somewhere short of Pamplona and are coming in today from the north, so we arranged to have dinner together. The Iruña is where I ate one night in 2007 while waiting for my errant backpack before leaving by foot for Santiago. I remembered its name and its location in the Plaza del Castillo. The Iruña is also a place that Hemingway made famous in *A Sun Also Rises*, written mostly here in 1926. Hemingway features on every menu at the Iruña, so they are doing him a reciprocal favour.

It's early afternoon. I am sitting at a strategically placed table in a café at the corner of the Plaza del Castillo. I think that anyone I know will have already passed through Pamplona and will be on his or her way. I order a beer and am sipping on it when I spot two guys I know walking through the plaza. I know their faces but cannot for the life of me remember who they are or where we met. I catch their eye and they turn and walk in with cries of, "Guy, Guy!" So they know who I am. Advantage: theirs. We greet each other and then I try to figure out who they are. It takes a while as they give me increasingly obvious clues—it's like a TV game show—and then I have it.

They are two of the three brothers from Campuac back in late April. The third brother, my namesake Guy, arrived by car with all three wives, and in the morning we all walked off on the *chemin* for a couple of days. They are Pierre and Jacques, the two brothers who are walking all the way to Santiago. Why are they so late to be here? They ought to be at least 100 kilometres farther along the *camino* by now. It turns out that one of them has developed a sore shin that requires a day off every few days to recuperate, but he is determined to walk all the way, so here they are. They enjoy a beer with me then leave to walk on for a few more kilometres today to a place called Cizor Menor, five kilometres beyond Pamplona.

I go back to my hotel for a siesta—I am in Spain, after all—then at around six-thirty I walk back to the Plaza to meet the German granddaughters. As I walk across the Plaza, I meet the Dutch woman who had so much trouble with privacy a few days ago, along with her friend, who has now joined her. When I see them both together, I realize that they are a gay couple. She seems more relaxed here. I hope that her privacy issues will diminish as she travels the *camino*. The *gites* (*albergues* in Spain) don't pay a lot of attention to personal privacy.

As soon as I sit down in front of the Iruña, Patricia and Victoria appear, looking radiant in their skirts and their youth. I ask the girls whether they always get along—they are, after all, siblings and close in age. Victoria says that they do almost all of the time. She also says that Patricia is the "deep" one of the two, and the only time she gets annoyed with Patricia is when she is practising scales on the piano, for hours at a time. Patricia protests that that is the only way to get her hands to "remember" the notes. I asked if they have boyfriends at home, and they both respond no. I think that the guys in Leipzig are missing out on something really good. These two are lovely young women, warm and attractive.

We order paella for three and cannot eat more than about half of it. It is a bit of a trick, since there are whole shrimp in the shell and big pieces of chicken in the paella and we are issued nothing but a fork each, plus one big spoon in the paella. So it is very Mediterranean to pick pieces out of the paella with our fingers, dismembering the shrimp from its shell and using only the right hand of course in the paella. I do hope we all remembered how to clean ourselves using only the left hand.

With my "granddaughters" in Pamplona.

After dinner, we head off just outside the Plaza for ice cream. The ladies insist that, since I bought dinner, at my request as an honorary grandfather, they buy the ice cream. I acquiesce, and we all get a variation on chocolate. Mine is chocolate with orange, always a favourite with me. We sit together on a bench and eat our ice cream as I wonder if I will ever see these fine young people again. We exchange offers of a pilgrim welcome if they get to Ottawa or I get to Leipzig. I do hope that it happens, although the odds seem remote.

Eventually it starts to get quite chilly, and we reluctantly—at least for me—say goodbye and head off to our various beds. In the morning, I leave for Barcelona, where I will meet Carroll in a couple of days. I am reluctant to have this journey end, although it must end, as all journeys do, even this magic one we call life. This physical journey is over but the other one, the one inside of me, is well and strong and will help guide my life.

My life's journey continues . . .

LESSONS REMEMBERED

> *"The course of a life seems random, but all lives are shaken into a pattern that makes sense only in retrospect."*
>
> Paul Theroux, *The Lower River*

Note for readers: If you read my previous book, *A Journey of Days*, about walking on the Camino de Santiago in Spain, then you will recognize many of these lessons from that book. Most of those lessons are repeated here, but there are many new lessons as well.

So what have I remembered on this journey across France and Spain? The first lesson is the realization that, five years ago, when I wrote rather smugly in *A Journey of Days* that "*There are no new lessons learned, just the same old lessons relearned,*" I assumed that the lessons I noted then were all the lessons there were for me to relearn. It occurs to me that, reflecting back on my recent journey on the Chemin de Saint-Jacques, the lessons I observed are mostly, but not always, the same lessons that I had learned in my rather long lifetime and had sometimes forgotten . . . or cheerfully ignored. I do not actually need to have walked on the *chemin* to make this observation, although it came more easily there because I had fewer distractions and lots of time to think. The lessons that follow are in an order that makes sense to me, but feel free to read them in any order that makes sense for you . . . or just sample them randomly.

There are always new lessons to be learned

No matter your age or experience, there are always opportunities for new lessons. What I have learned on this journey is that I will keep on learning new lessons or relearning old lessons as long as I draw breath. So I AM both older and wiser now than I was five years ago.

Planning and preparation are useful, but flexibility is essential

This lesson was brought home when I took the wrong trail out of Estaing and ended up meeting and being welcomed by Daniel and Arlette and their two grandchildren, Victor and Cassandre. I was so far off the planned route that my guidebook was useless. I spent three wonderful days getting to know a family who live their beliefs openly and happily, no proselytizing at all. They were happy and thoughtful people in spite of the truly wretched weather and trail conditions. And in three days, I was back where I needed to be, but with new friends.

Walking with people creates a sense of family

The strong sense of family that Karsten, Marina, Paula, and I had five years ago walking across Spain was not a one-off event. Being here with like-minded people in a remote wilderness environment with a common goal promotes a rapid sense of interdependence. I have heard this referred to by my daughter-in-law Laura (TJ) Sharp as "trail magic." I am beginning to understand it a little better.

There is no such thing as bad weather, only bad clothing

I found that the weather was a major factor on the *chemin* in the early weeks and then periodically thereafter. It was cold and blustery, rained for two weeks, and had rained for two weeks before I started, so the path was often muddy, sometimes actually a full-blown stream of running water. The only time I got in trouble, though, was the day when I walked in a cold rain without the rain pants and failed to find the Abbaye Sauvelade. By the time I arrived, I was hypothermic and it was self-inflicted. The lesson was learned—again. But as a Canadian living in Ottawa, one can't really hide from the weather except by hibernating all winter.

The body is marvellously resilient

However, I have to treat it like the fine tool that it is. I trained only a couple of months to walk the *chemin*, walking about eighteen kilometres with my loaded pack and my boots every third day and resting in between. I knew that the first week of walking the *chemin* would be the real training for the long walk, and it was. My body was ready for it, in most ways. What I found, at the end of each day's walk, was that I was physically tired. Thirty minutes' sleep provided enough recovery time to allow me to enjoy the rest of the day. The overnight sleep provided time to allow the body's mechanisms to rewind, purge the accumulated poisons, and let me wake up refreshed in the morning. The rest days were exceptionally good at allowing a deeper recovery. I planned for six rest days and took only two, but I often walked quite short days, only ten to twelve kilometres. These short-distance days were so effective that I did not need more rest days.

You don't have to walk fast to walk far

The Chinese saying, "A journey of a thousand miles begins with the first step," is exactly right. When I trained for the *camino* five years ago, I was able to walk about six kilometres each hour. When I started the *camino*, I planned on being able to keep up that pace. Of course, I could not. This year, I have trained and walked more slowly, because the end result is the same. I am not in any kind of race, and walking more slowly gives me more time to enjoy the countryside, which is often quite spectacular. I have been in rural France and, at the end, rural Spain, and found them to be quite unlike the tourist impressions of either country. The pace each day depends on many variables, among them weather, ascent or descent, road surface, personal health, state of the feet, joints, and muscles. In life, I procrastinate and often I delay starting something because I think that it is going to take a long time to finish it. Of course, logically, if anything is going to take a long time to finish, that is the best reason for starting as soon as possible.

I am stronger than I think, physically and mentally

The act of walking over 800 kilometres was a challenge for me in both dimensions, but not an insurmountable one. I was pretty confident when I first embarked on it that I would be able to complete the plan, but soon learned that I was wrong about that. The second year, I was less confident, but the dreadful weather and the frequent hills combined to, remarkably, boost my confidence. By the time I hit the Pyrénées, I was sure that I could handle them—and I did. I was even able to help someone else who was having a real problem make it up that first day's climb.

I need to be able to withstand setback and failure

In 2011 I intended to walk from Le Puy-en-Velay to Pamplona, about 875 kilometres. I walked (and rode) only about 130 kilometres before deciding to pack it in and go home. My reason was valid. I thought that I was experiencing potentially serious cardiovascular problems, and the remote Aubrac plateau was a very bad place to have medical difficulties. There was often no cell phone coverage, and I believed that a minor heart problem there could turn very nasty. I have passed several tasteful little memorials to other pilgrims who died here and didn't expect to. Of course you know that the medical community in Ottawa tested me thoroughly and found no underlying cardiac problem. It turns out that what I had—and have—is diabetes, controllable with diet and a little pill every morning. There is a big advantage to me this year in knowing that I do not have any cardiovascular problems. As I walked with some difficulty up the long hills in France, my heart was racing like a trip-hammer. Knowing that there was little chance of a heart attack, quaintly known as a "cardiovascular event," made the climbs just tiring, not frightening. All I needed to do was go slowly, as the French say, "*doucement, doucement.*" Softly, softly. It's good advice for life in general.

There is a big difference between having a failure and being a failure

We all experience failures in our lives, but that doesn't make us a failure. "The essence of a resilient personality is knowing that deep in the bones."[32] Having a failure is a temporary condition, a setback, if you like, while being a failure is a statement of a life condition. Another lesson, specific to this journey, is how to deal with the loss of a dream when the plan simply does not work. I had a failure last year, but I am not a failure because of it. Success is how I handle the disappointment of the failure. My physical failure in the first week demonstrated to me that there was a new lesson to be learned here, that how one deals with failure is more important than the failure itself. I plan to learn from it and apply what I learn to the rest of my experiences.

---

32 Thanks to Karen McCann, Seville-based author of *Dancing in the Fountain*, for this observation.

There is no such thing as too much reassurance
In Spain, the yellow arrows mark one unique path and they point one way: toward Santiago. In France, the GRs (*Grandes Randonées*—major hiking paths) are all marked with a small white and red rectangle. They are two way and sometimes intersect. They are well-marked by thousands of anonymous volunteers, to whom I am very grateful. Wayfinding is not quite as easy as it was in Spain, because the signage is two way, but I still love to see the red and white markers. Their presence is very reassuring. I think about how important external confirmation is for me and for other people, even if—and perhaps especially if—we seem to be very confident of our direction. This theme occurs over and over again on the *chemin*. I shall have to remember this when I deal with people in the future.

Psychological is to physical as ten is to one
There is no question in my mind that a certain amount of physical strength is required to walk the *chemin*, but not as much as most people believe. What is required, however, is a lot of psychological strength. Where I saw this principle in action was going over the Pyrénées, where I assisted a woman who had reached the end of her capabilities. She walked slowly with me as far as Orisson, then went to bed and slept. She had intended to get a taxi from there to take her to Roncevalles, but when I saw her late the next evening in Roncevalles, she had just arrived on foot over a very difficult and challenging part of the *chemin* over the Pyrénées. Her psychological strength had overcome her lack of physical preparedness. She was exhausted, but she had prevailed and subsequently went on to complete her journey. The message for me? My mind wants to protect me from any possible harm, so it seeks to minimize any threat to myself. I must not let my mind "protect" me when there is something that I want or need to do. Self-talk can hurt me if it's negative . . . support me if it's positive. There IS power in positive thinking.

Obstacles are about as big as I let them be
The first year that I attempted this walk, I was overwhelmed by my own physical condition and abandoned the walk after a week. The second year, when my diabetes had been discovered and treated, my physical condition was just another factor, like weather, condition of the path, weight of the pack, and age that I had to manage as I walked.

I found the hill climbing to be sometimes difficult but never beyond my capability, as long as I walked "*doucement, doucement.*" By the time I got to the Pyrénées, which I had been dreading for five years, it was just another couple of challenging days. I was confident in my ability to complete the walk — and I did.

Wear boots that fit

When I walked 700 kilometres across Spain five years ago, I lost three toenails. They turned black and came off, painlessly, over a period of a couple of weeks. I was wearing boots that I thought fit me and could not understand why my toenails had decided to leave me. This year, when I walked the same distance across France, I wore exactly the same boot, from the same manufacturer, but one full size larger. I had no problems with my feet, I lost no toenails and I had no blisters. The message for me was that I had to pay closer attention to the size of my footwear, even though I thought I was wearing the right size.

Then I thought about the closet full of clothing that I have had for a number of years, but generally don't wear because it's a little too small for me. When I do wear it, it's not comfortable, and it doesn't look particularly good. So thinking about my boots, I think it's time that I cleared out my closet of the clothing that I have kept, hoping that I will lose enough weight to be able to wear it again. Since I haven't managed to do that over the past twenty years, it seems unlikely that I'll manage to do this in the next six months. The broader message is that I should take a look at everything in my life and see if it still fits. This includes old ideas and all the other stuff in my life. What I have to do with all of this is wear boots that fit.

I have to walk my own *chemin*

I have discovered that I must walk at my own pace, stopping when and where I want for rest or for food or drink. While I often walk with someone else for a while, if our paces differ, I either go ahead or fall behind. Here is a powerful analogy to life for me. Each of us has a path that we follow and that we may choose to share with someone else, often a spouse or close friends. Some of us who are extremely lucky find, as I have found, a spouse who shares my need for family and connections, shares my sense of humour, shares my political views — mostly — and who both shares and understands my need for solitude, since she has the same need. We don't agree on everything—we watch completely different TV shows, for example, but we agree to disagree when necessary. Thus I am able to walk my own path while concurrently walking with someone else.

Spirituality is all around me

It is in my fellow pilgrims, as well as in the people working in the *gites* by conviction and often as volunteers, and, by extension, also in me. Their spirit of caring, warmth, concern—yes, even love—has been all around me since I started the walk.

I am in a world of people who are friendly with each other; where even strangers ask about your well-being . . . and are genuinely interested in the answer; share without being asked when a need is evident; a world where help is offered freely whenever help is needed. This is the world of the *chemin* and the world of the *camino*. The spirit of the people on it makes the *chemin*.

The *chemin* that I am on at this moment is just a microcosm of what the world could be like if people would give up their lust for power, for advantage over one another. I like this world of caring and respect and love a lot and my lesson is to try to figure out how to extend this bit of world into the wider one. I think that I need to start by being open to the possibilities of spirituality around me.

Life is all about relationships

This is one of the most powerful lessons that I relearned on the *chemin*. For some people, life is about power or money, but not for me. I thrive, I expand, I positively bask in relationships. They are so powerful for me that in 2011, I abandoned my stated aim, which was to walk across France at my own pace, and adopted the pace of a small group of people with whom I wanted to keep up. This year, I walked more slowly and did not walk so far each day. As a result, people who were also walking usually were ahead of me in a day or two, and I seldom saw them again. But I made close contact with some of my fellow pilgrims and also with a number of the people who ran the *gites*. I remain in contact via email with many of them. We share a little piece of history, and it creates a close bond between us.

The life of a hermit, while attractive in many ways, is not for me. I am happy alone, seldom lonely—except for one evening in Cahors—but I have a deep-seated need for approval. I crave the applause of the audience. I also realize, once again, how much I depend on and value the relationship between Carroll and me. I never doubt her commitment to our lifelong relationship, and that stability has been, and remains, a major part of my life.

Pheromones help create the physical attraction; responsibility is what you do with it

The prime directive of every species is continuing the species. Pheromones play a major part in that exercise. Evidently pheromones are going to be around all of my life. All my life, this is a lesson that I have had to remember frequently. I sometimes misread things like a long, thoughtful glance or a friendly touch on the arm or a full-on hug as something a little more meaningful than intended . . . I think. Even now, I am still powerfully attracted to some women. Apparently, some women are still powerfully attracted to me, although I think now it's mostly the grandfather thing. However, I have already done all I plan to do to support the continuation of the human species — four children, two grandchildren. And casual sex without love is a fool's game, "*chagrin d'amour*," as Edith Piaf used to sing. Not that I could not be an old fool, but I *choose* not to be one now, sometimes with some real regret. I have met on this journey a lot of really warm and attractive women of all ages.

Keeping in touch with others via social media keeps me out of touch with myself

The use of social media tools has transformed lives, including mine. As a rule, the increase in communications is a good thing. I am more in touch with our family and with distant friends than was possible before cell phones, free world-wide calling, and the acceleration of the Internet. I have "friends" on Facebook and "friends" on LinkedIn that I would never have had even ten years ago. The transformation, however, goes both ways. I really don't care about what celebrities are wearing, who is marrying / sleeping with / breaking up with whom, or how they look in bikinis. Okay, I'm lying, I like looking at them in bikinis, but I don't much care who they are. The real downside is that I seem to have less time when I can be alone. And I have found again, here on this long walk, that being alone for me is an excellent opportunity to think about what is important for me and to think about people, events, and places in my history that are unfinished business. It is when I am alone that I can seek out the internal concerns that I have and try to determine how best to put them to rest. I need to be "out of touch" for a little while to be able to do this. That means unclipping the cell phone and turning off the laptop and the iPad. And I can always let the landline telephone go to the answering machine. If it is critically and urgently important, they'll call back.

Being an adult is also learning to live with the results of all your mistakes

We all make mistakes. It's part of being human and it's a great way to learn how to do things better the next time. But mistakes have consequences. One of the frequent consequences is a sense of guilt about something, a commission or an omission of a deed that you did in the past and now fervently wish that you had not done or failed to do. One of the powerful tools of the Catholic Church is that of confession, in which you tell your sins in confidence to a priest, who is bound not to repeat them, and you, after some imposed penance, can walk away confident that your sins have been forgiven. Those of us who do not have this option sometimes, in the hope of expiation, tell our past sins to an understanding bartender or to a friend or spouse. The problem with telling a friend or your spouse is that you have just put the burden on him or her. You walk away and they get to carry your guilt around with them. So what I have to do is carry my own past sins with me and learn to forgive myself as best I can.

Do not judge others— and do not be too hard on yourself

I have spent my whole life judging others and have found most of them wanting—that is, insufficiently like me. What I have learned, again, is that different is not bad, it is just different. I travelled for a period with a man whom I first dubbed "Weird Harold." When I learned about the terrible tragedies in his life, I was truly ashamed of my first impression and my quick judgment of him. If we were to know all the background of anyone else, we could probably understand his or her behaviour, even if we strongly disagree with it. Judging at first sight was a common and valuable human trait when we lived in tribes and could never trust the motives of a stranger from an adjacent tribe. It still has its place, but can cause me to make decisions about others that prevent me from learning from them. I have always been a quick learner, although I have not always successfully retained what I have learned. Hence the life lessons *remembered* or *relearned*.

You of course know the old Native saying, "Before you criticize someone, you should walk a mile in their moccasins." That way, when you criticize them, you're a mile away, you have their moccasins, and they are barefoot.

I am not the worst thing that I have ever done

When I called Jean-Marc, a fellow pilgrim, "Weird Harold," I was quickly assigning him to a category of people that I would like to avoid. Categorizing people is convenient mental shorthand for us to decide quickly how to deal with others. It is a life survival skill that has come down from the very distant past, when we had to decide quickly whether the stranger was a threat to the tribe or not, and it still has its place. The problem is that it is not always accurate and can at times be very damaging.

Let me give you a partially hypothetical example. When I was a boy, I stole a candy bar from the corner store. My mother found out about it and made me take it back and apologize to the store owner. Hardly a federal offence, but I could have been labelled a thief. Fortunately, I was not. Later, in my teen years, I stole money from a man who had befriended me and who could not afford it. I was never able to pay him back. This part is true and has always haunted me. I could have gotten caught and imprisoned. I could have been a thief and a "con," and when released, an ex-con. Some people would put me into a box labelled "thief" and "ex-con." For the rest of my life, I could go straight and do great things in business or in art; but for some, I would always be a thief and an ex-con. While accurate, these descriptions are insufficient. They are not complete. Fortunately, they did not happen.

I am not the worst thing that I have ever done. None of us is, not even pedophiles and terrorists and murderers. Pedophiles and terrorists and murderers have done evil things, for which they are rightly punished, but even they are more than just the worst thing that they have done. Which of us would wish to be categorized as the worst thing that we have ever done? Not me. Would you? Christ is reported as saying, "Let him without sin cast the first stone."[33] Consider the permanent categorization of people in the same light. You and I are

---

33 St. John 8:7.

not known as the worst thing that we have ever done. My lesson is that I must remember to give the same leeway to others.

Mother Nature is indifferent — neither benign nor malignant

Of all the species that have ever lived on earth, about 99.9 percent are extinct. That's species, not individuals. That would seem to be a little malignant, but it's not. It is just the way the world works. Species form, grow, live, adapt — or not — and finally leave the scene to make room for newcomers. A few species — sharks, gingko trees, ferns, and cockroaches, as examples — have had a much longer successful run, but even the dinosaurs disappeared after a long and successful period on earth. What makes you think that the human species is any different? You would think that we would know better as thinking organisms; but we live in the biosphere, a really thin skin of habitable land, water, and air at the surface of this planet — and we are messing it up, the land, the water, and the air. Mother Nature is indifferent to species and to individuals, as the American pilgrim who perished in the Pyrénées just a couple of days before I walked over them discovered. He elected to walk over the high route in spite of poor weather conditions and got lost in the dense fog and perished. The lesson for me: Pay attention to my environment, local and global. It is up to me whether I survive the day or not.

Life is a privilege, not a right

Sometimes I act as if life is a right that I have. If it were true, then I would have the right to choose not to die — and no one has that right. Teenagers complain that they didn't ask to be born. While true, it's pointless, because *no one* asks to be born. Once born, we require the care of parents or guardians for years to ensure that we survive the trials of childhood. For most of history, half of all children died before the age of five. We happen to be living in a period of history and in a part of the world where the historical, horrifying loss rate of young children has been relieved through modern medicine and adequate nutrition.

The loss of a child now is a huge shock. The average age of mortality, at least in the developed countries, has never been higher than right now. But our living conditions and our lives are not something that we should be taking for granted. One super-volcano or one well-placed meteor, or a nuclear exchange, or an aggressive biological organism could change all this in an instant. So I need always to remember to be grateful for the family and friends that I have; for my health; and for the fact that I live in one of the world's most peaceful and abundant democracies. This life is a privilege and I must never forget that.

The universe will unfold

It just will not unfold exactly as I expect . . . or perhaps even remotely as I envisage. I try not to have expectations about the future, but I think that having expectations is part of the human condition. For example, I wake up each morning expecting that I will live through the day. I go to sleep each night expecting that I will wake the next morning. I trust that the universe will continue to operate as it has so far in my life. So far, it's worked perfectly, but one day it won't. And when it doesn't, the universe will continue to unfold without me. That is natural, and I am okay with it. Not just yet, however. There is too much I want to experience yet.

My meaning in life is what I decide is important for me

Like many others, I have struggled in my life with life's purpose. Am I here for some purpose? If so, how do I determine what that purpose is? I read a powerful book about this, Viktor Frankl's *Man's Search for Meaning*, and think about it often. He convinced me that the meaning in my life is simply what I choose it to be. Some may choose meaning described for them by others, but as a humanist, I cannot do that. I must seek my own meaning. And I am content in the meaning of my life. What I have chosen to do in my life does allow me to make a positive difference in the life of others—family, friends, and strangers—and that gives my life meaning.

The ultimate freedom that I have is being able to decide how I will handle whatever comes at me

This is another of Viktor Frankl's revelations from his experience in the extermination camps. He realized that he had no control over his situation, his clothing, his work, his accommodation, or his mistreatment by the guards and capos. He did not even have control over whether he lived or died. At any time he could be murdered or selected for the gas chambers. And he came to understand that while he had no control over what actually happened, he had total control over how he could react to whatever happened. As he pointed out, this is the one freedom that cannot be taken away from a person, not by others, not by events. So I can, on my much smaller and less horrifying scale, decide that I can walk in truly dreadful weather on truly dreadful muddy paths and up and down big hills cheerfully, since I am here, and cheerfully is how I decide to handle these conditions. And I think that I will be able to handle whatever life throws at me if I remember that I can choose how I react.

It is more about the journey, not so much the destination

It seems to me that I have always known this, but it became abundantly clear on the *chemin*. The way itself is the reason to be on it. When I got within a day of Saint-Jean-Pied-de-Port, at the northern edge of the Pyrénées, it was an unwelcome reminder that the journey was finite and was, in fact, coming to its end. The analogy to life is clear. I remain unconvinced that there is a destination after the end of life, so, for me, the journey is the only part that makes sense. So far, my life experience has failed to convince me that there is anything after this life. If your experience and belief are different, I applaud you.

If I really have a dream —make sure to do it while I can

A wish without a date to start is only a dream. I walked the *camino* in Spain five years ago. Last year, I intended to walk the *chemin* in France, but only got partway. At that time, I thought that I would not be back, but here I am again. It feels like an enormous victory to have completed what I set out to do. Even sitting in the airport in Ottawa, on my way, I wondered if this was a smart move or just plain stubbornness, unwilling to admit that I had bitten off more than I could chew. My method of commitment, I can see in retrospect, is that I tell everyone what I am going to do . . . and then am too embarrassed by the possibility of failure to not do it.

When I decide to convert a dream into an action, I pick a date that is not too far in the future to start. If the date feels really easy, then I bring it closer in time . . . a lot closer. When it starts to feel quite uncomfortable, then I know that I have a good starting date. Then I work backward from the start date to figure out what I have to do to make it real.

Now is the only real time there is, so experience it

While I was writing this section of the book, we received some very bad news. A friend had been killed in a bizarre accident in Houston, Texas. Shari Epstein, forty-nine, the mother of two young children, was out for her morning constitutional walk when two cars collided near her and one of them, out of control, hit and killed her. Until recently, she had been the director of research at the International Facility Management Association, which was how we knew her. The message for me is that, as Shari did, we must live and enjoy every day to its full extent because every day is a gift—it's our present. Don't take life for granted.

The only real now that I have is the one I am experiencing in this moment. The past is history and cannot be changed, only remembered. The future is an infinite set of possibilities that might or might not be realized. So it becomes important that we are mindful of now and experience the only moment in which we exist. I must remember to use all my senses—vision to see butterflies and flowers and sunsets; hearing to capture birdsong and the laughter of children; touch to feel silk and skin and the soft fur of cats and dogs, and the feel of a small child asleep on your chest; taste for ice cream and single malt Scotch (not together); and smell to experience apple pie and cinnamon and pine woods. The Romans had it right—*Carpe diem*.

What can you do with these lessons?

First of all, understand that these are only *my* lessons, the lessons that I remembered or relearned. They may or may not correspond to your experience. If you find, however, that a particular lesson strikes a chord in you, that one of the lessons resonates for you, think about how your life might be different if you applied the lesson to yourself. If you like what you imagine, figure out how to make it work for you. I hope that my experiences and my story and my lessons will inspire you to follow your dream and to live more of your life in the moment.

WHATEVER HAPPENED TO . . .?

Of the people I walked with in 2011, I have stayed in touch with three: Karsten, Francine, and Max. The Parisiennes Sylvie, Felicia, and Jocelyn I have lost touch with; and Max I did not hear from for eighteen months after we parted in Paris at the Metro.

After I left them, Karsten and Francine walked on for a few days then went back to their homes. Later that year, Francine came back to the *chemin* and walked the rest of the way to Saint-Jean-Pied-de-Port. This year, she returned and walked on from Saint-Jean-Pied-de-Port.

What about Max? He has completed his undergraduate degree in psychology, except for his thesis (as of February 2013), and plans to walk some more of the Chemin de Saint-Jacques.

Just after I arrived in Pamplona this year, Karsten also came back and walked from Conques to Saint-Jean-Pied-de-Port, just missing Francine there by a few days. Now he is back in Berlin, teaching. As for Francine, after walking from Saint-Jean-Pied-de-Port to Santiago, she is back in Besançon.

I have been in touch several times with Daniel and Arlette from Paris, who helped me so much when I got off on the wrong path after Estaing. He even sent me a YouTube video about the *chemin* as experienced by Cassandre and Victor. I put the video address on my blog in early February 2013. The children, Cassandre and Victor, continue to do well in school. I received an email from Cassandre in which she tells me that she is in Grade 6, she has a sister and a dog, and that she will be twelve in mid-April. All four of them, grandparents and grandchildren, are returning to walk another part of the *chemin*, from Conques to Moissac, in May 2013. Then Daniel and Arlette are going to act as *hospitaliers* (hosts) for pilgrims in the convent at Saint-Côme-d'Olt from late May to early June.

I have an ongoing correspondence with Anita Dann, the friendly and warm host from the *gîte* in Montréal-du-Gers. You may recall I stayed over there for two nights to sustain myself. First I got her recipe for the vegetable soup that she served us there. Over the winter, she spent two months on the Mediterranean coast of Spain. And she has organized the only *hospitalier* training in France in 2013, to be held at her *gite* in March and taught by Hervé, who was there while I was.

We had a visit here in Ottawa on 17 September, 2012, from Marcel and Mireille Nuss from Strasbourg. In Sauvelade, I invited them to join me here for a pilgrim welcome, which they accepted. They did tell me later in our pilgrimage that I had to have a *gite* stamp ready for their pilgrim passports, so I had one made courtesy of my daughter-in-law, TJ Sharp,[34] from the Atlanta area, who drew the wonderful turtle-themed stamp for me. Our *gite* is named *Gite la Tortue à l'Envers*—the Overturned Turtle. You will note that the turtle has a beard and a Tilley hat. It's me after the Lauzerte bench incident, when I fell backwards off the bench and could not get up.

You will remember that on 4 May in the *gite* at Lascabanes I met Brigitte, the nurse from Holland, and Henri-Pierre from Toulouse, with their story of romance on the *chemin*. I had not heard anything from or about them for almost a year, but then in March 2013 I got a message from Henri-Pierre telling me that they had walked some 500 kilometres together over the past summer, and that he is often in Holland. I am just delighted that this fairy-tale story is working out.

The last time I saw Jean-Marc, the man who had tragically lost his entire family, was in Orisson on the way up the Pyrénées. I found out later from fellow pilgrims that he completed his journey to Santiago, where he seemed to be in reasonably good spirits. I hope that his demons can be laid to rest there.

So what's new at the "Par'chemin . . ."? Vincent and Sylvie (the wonderful and loving *hospitalier* and *hospitalière* at the *gite* in Espalais on 8 May) started the winter in November last year by walking the *camino* again, each walking alone on their separate ways. She walked

---

34 See more of her work at ***http://www.Sharpshooterstudio.net***.

on the Camino Frances from Léon to Santiago and on to Fistera and Muxia, while he, seeking solitude, walked from his home to Saint-Jean-Pied-de-Port, then to Handaye, and on to Laredo, a day or two before Santander on the Camino del Norte. He found the solitude he was looking for on his wet and windy way. They have also added an organic vegetable garden. That is the biggest new project for the year. And they've embarked on building their own greenhouse from mainly salvaged windows. So if all goes well, they'll soon be ready to deliver "from organic seed to fraternal dish."

Pierre and Marie, the charming and warm couple with whom I walked from 8 to 11 May, are heading back to continue their *chemin* from Condom (where I last saw them) to Saint-Jean-Pied-de-Port . . . and they plan to sleep their first night in Condom in the same *gite*—"Le Champ d'Etoile"—where I slept last year. He is still married, but the final divorce judgment is the same day they plan to go on the *chemin* again, which will leave him free to marry Marie. Their children are after them to marry and merge the families. Apparently the kids are tightly connected on Facebook and other networks and don't need any urging from their parents. They don't yet live together but they have found a house in Illfurth. Marie loves the kitchen, so I think it's a done deal. Pierre says that he doesn't "know to how to change her mind . . . And what women want . . . (even in France it's still the same) but I love her and I follow our way." I just received an email with a video attachment of Pierre singing "Proud Mary" from Creedence Clearwater Revival. He tells me that I am stuck to this song forever!

I last saw young Rémi from Cahors on the day I walked from Navarrenx to the Ferme Bohoteguia at Aroue. I do not know his last name or email, so I think it unlikely that I will ever see him again. But I remember him almost every day, walking with his grandparents' photographs all the way to Santiago.

I have heard from Mark Dejongh, whom I first met on 25 April in Sauvelade and encountered again at Espalais on 8 May. I did not see him after that, but he recently told me that he walked all the way from his home in Antwerp to Santiago, a distance of 2,350 kilometres that took him 112 days. He is happily back home with his children and grandchildren, loved his pilgrimage, but does not think that he will walk this length of pilgrimage again.

Back home in Ottawa, I received a message from the woman

from New Orleans, whom I assisted the first day in the Pyrénées: "I was that woman you helped the first day of my climb, Mary Ann from New Orleans. I did not think I could make it . . . and neither did you. I did. I am now back home in the U.S. and I can say humbly that I made it and I will never be the same for doing so. You were one of the many 'angels' my Heavenly Father sent me on my journey. Thank you for giving me hope when I thought I had lost it."

Victoria and Patricia, the German sisters and my "granddaughters," returned home to Leipzig from Pamplona but they didn't stay there long. Patricia moved to Nuremburg, where she is actively engaged in helping people with mental and physical handicaps reintegrate into the working community. She sent me a lovely story about language: "By the way, writing in English isn´t so easy. Mostly I'm thinking in French. So now my way of writing is: creating ideas in German, then making French sentences and after that I´m thinking about how to express myself in English :)"

Victoria, the younger sister, has moved to Landau, about 600 kilometres from her home, also for work. (Landau is just a little north of Lahr in Germany, where I flew many years ago.) In August, she started a two-year internship to become a teacher in the German system. I know from the husband of my niece who lives in Germany that teacher training throughout Germany is rigorous, so Victoria will be working hard and she knows it: "I've never imagined that working life is so stressful . . . But I know that the beginning of professional life isn't easy and it will become better after the two years."

I got an unexpected chatty email from Keiko, who is back in Japan. When I last saw her, she was doubtful about her financial ability to make it to the end, but she did! She arrived in Santiago on her thirty-first birthday and was there on 25 July, the feast day of Saint James. She says, "It was one of the happiest days of my life."

Robert from Toronto continued on from Pamplona and walked all the way to Santiago. Along with Carroll, my wife, I had dinner with him and his partner Franc back in Toronto late in 2012. Robert, who quit his job in order to walk the *camino*, went back to school, taking Events Planning, and has started a catering business, Camino Events: "Of course! I just thought why not call it after the thing that inspired me."

From Natalie, the young Dutch woman walking with her father: "For me the *camino* offered a change to step out of the daily life situation, look at it from a distance and find myself again . . . connecting with nature and like-minded souls was very good. When I got back I could reconnect with my partner again from a loving place. Also I was able to change my perspective on the reorganization, feeling blessed to still have a job instead of feeling the loss of colleagues and friends at work. Last but not least, I was so caught up in physical, material, mental things, my well-doing, that I almost forgot about my well-being."

From Claudia, whom I met on the last day's walk into Pamplona: "Everyone has his own reason to come here and it is unbelievable that people who do not really know each other are speaking about their lives . . . I'll never forget my first *camino* and especially the Day-Walk with you, Guy." She plans to walk more of the *camino*.

A last observation: Many of the people who run the *gites* in France are incredibly dedicated to providing their services to pilgrims. Many of them are pilgrims themselves, and many may be religious, but it does not show up in their conversations—no proselytizing, only their warm and loving care of the pilgrims who pass through their doors.

ABOUT THE AUTHOR

Guy Thatcher served in the Canadian regular armed forces from 1955 to 1980. He then pursued a second career for a further twenty-five years as a management consultant. He holds a degree in Computing and Information Science from Queen's University in Kingston, Ontario, is a Fellow of the International Facility Management Association, and is a lifetime Certified Management Consultant.

He is married to Carroll Thatcher, with whom he has four grown children and two grandchildren. Since 1991, he has been a home support volunteer for Ottawa's Hospice at May Court. He walks, travels, gardens, reads voraciously—biography, history, science, and science fiction—and plays a truly dreadful game of golf.

He is the author of *A Journey of Days*, about his walk across Spain on the Camino de Santiago.

Guy lives in Ottawa, Canada. You can visit his website at **http://www.guythatcher.com** or contact him at **journeyofdays@yahoo.ca**.

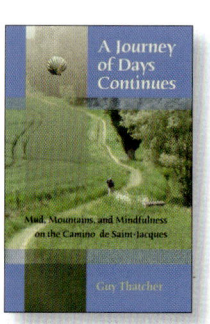

TO ORDER MORE COPIES:

GENERAL STORE PUBLISHING HOUSE INC.

499 O'Brien Road, Renfrew, Ontario, Canada K7V 3Z3
Tel 1.800.465.6072 • Fax 1.613.432.3634

www.gsph.com